PRAISE FOR
VOICES OF LOVE
FROM THE LIGHT

Throughout history, great souls have dedicated their lives to help guide humanity to its divine destiny, serving as lighthouses of truth and emissaries of love, guided themselves by great masters. They are called by various names: *mystic, sage, teacher, adept,* or *initiate,* and Philip Burley is one of them. In this new book, through his remarkable gift as a spiritual medium, Philip welcomes us to a conclave of enlightened masters that we, too, may awaken.

—*Michael J. Tamura, spiritual teacher, clairvoyant visionary,
and award-winning author of* You Are the Answer

Many have been able to access messages from the inner dimensions, but few have refined the art of mediumship to the level that Philip Burley has. His pure motivation is the probable reason that our most beloved leaders and teachers in the spirit world have chosen him to be their messenger. This book is a gift to humanity.

—*Julia Ingram, MA, New York Times bestselling co-author of*
The Messengers: A True Story of Angelic Presence *and*
The Return to the Age of Miracles

I experienced profound peace and joy after reading this remarkable book. You'll pick it up again and again—to be reminded of the magnificent Universe in which we live.

—*Anita Bergen, editor and bestselling author of*
Life and Other Options

Philip Burley has done a phenomenal job of channeling messages from some of my favorite teachers in the spirit world. Only Mr. Burley could have brought through such extraordinary content. This is an amazing book!

—*Joyce Keller, medium, television and radio host, and bestselling author of* 7 Steps to Heaven *and* Calling All Angels

Readers will discover answers to questions such as: "What is life all about?" "What happens to our departed loved ones?" "Is there a spirit world?" The messages in this book have the power to influence our world toward a more loving and peaceful existence. With great clarity, they expand our understanding of our purpose on earth and in the afterlife. I find new pearls of wisdom every time I read it.

—*Suzanne Nault, MPs PCC, psychologist, speaker, and co-author of the #1 international bestseller,* The Expert Success Solution

This book will take you on an empowering, enlightening, and spiritually satisfying journey that answers many of your spiritual questions and leaves you feeling comforted about your place in the universe. Be prepared to be hungry for more from each master who has chosen to speak through Philip.

—*Susan Apollon, psychologist, educator, and award-winning author of* Touched by the Extraordinary

Without a shadow of doubt, I believe that the veil between heaven and earth has been pierced. Beautiful words, thoughts, energy, and blessings will flow to each person who takes the time to read this book. It is a gift to be in the presence of the great masters and leaders who speak in each chapter. You will feel as though you've met them in person . . . because you have!

—*Regina Bowden, PhD, management consultant, president, Transformation Inc., co-author of* Aligning for Change: Collaborative Strategic Planning

While reading this incredible book, it was no surprise to me that my respect for the work of Dr. Dolores Proiette and Philip Burley was greatly reinforced. The book will provide great support for both seasoned spiritualists and those just beginning to dip their toes into spiritual teachings. I will be recommending it to friends, family, and colleagues.

—*Kiersten Hathcock, founder, The Little Light Project, Inc.*

This book will inspire all who hunger for the highest levels of truth to go inside and experience God as Love. Once we have that experience, we know we are never alone in growing and learning—on earth or in the afterlife.

—*Diane Zantop, MA, Certified Integrative Yoga Therapist, spiritual mentor, and Reiki healer*

Philip Burley is dedicated to truth in his work and in his service to humanity. His clear intention provides a laser focus for each of us to become Self-aware and to accept the quickening within us that true spiritual work affords. Philip's new book is an instrument pointing to the actual felt knowing of the truth of being.

—*Rev. Bruce Kellogg, Ordained Unity Minister*

As you read this spiritual classic, you will experience an energetic transmission of healing and the transcendent Divine. It is a book to be savored sentence by sentence, word by word, and insight by insight. Its panoramic look into the workings and wisdom of the world of Spirit is evergreen material that will benefit readers for years to come. It will be cherished by many.

—*Yanni Maniates, MS, CMI, bestselling author of* Magical Keys to Self-Mastery: Creating Miracles in Your Life

From gifted spiritual channel, Philip Burley, and professional hypnotist, Dolores Proiette, comes a masterpiece filled with great truth and wisdom. It will inspire and comfort all who read it.

—*Dean Shrock, PhD, bestselling author of* Why Love Heals

I was thrilled to sense the love and enthusiasm the masters felt as they shared their truth with humanity. Their words remind us that we are far more capable than we know and can make more of a difference than we think. The book provides fascinating glimpses of life in the spirit world and the ways we are always attended by spirit beings who love and guide us.

—*Mary Bell Nyman, founder, Psychic Horizons Center,*
Boulder, Colorado

Have you ever wished you could sit down and talk with inspired leaders and enlightened masters of days gone by? In this unique offering, you can listen in on conversations with many masters, ranging from Harriet Tubman to Jesus, who bettered the course of innumerable lives. Well worth the read, the discourses presented in this book are a delicious gift to the soul.

—*Rev. Master Samanthia I Am,*
Ordained Interfaith Minister, author, and spiritual counselor

This book is a gem filled with the teachings of twenty spiritual leaders, each of whom offers something special and unique. It opens doors to a whole range of knowledge and experience, helping us to understand that we can explore areas within ourselves that will expand our awareness beyond our bodies and small minds. Thanks to Philip and Dolores for making available such valuable material.

—*Dr. Hal Stone, psychotherapist, teacher, and co-author of*
Embracing Our Selves

Voices *of* Love *from the* Light

From Mastery Press by Philip Burley

On Wings of Love

Your Walk With The Masters

Confronting Depression to Stop Suicide

Caring for a Loved One with Dementia

The Power of Self Awareness

Heart's Healing

The Spirit World, Where Love Reigns Supreme

The Hum of Heaven

The Wisdom of Saint Germain

The Gift of Mediumship

A Legacy of Love, Volume One: The Return to Mount Shasta and Beyond

To Master Self is to Master Life

Also from Mastery Press

Love Knows No End, by Diane Macci

A Wanderer in the Spirit World, by Franchezzo
As transcribed by A. Farnese

The Blue Island: Beyond Titanic—Voyage into Spirit, by William T. Stead
As Channeled through Pardoe Woodman

From Dandelion Books by Dolores Proiette, DCH, PhD

Unveil the Past, Heal the Future through Hypnotherapy

Voices *of* Love *from the* Light

Conversations with 20 Great Souls in the Afterlife

Jesus • Buddha • Abraham Lincoln • Albert Einstein Yogananda • Harriet Tubman • Edgar Cayce Eleanor Roosevelt • Saint Germain…

Philip Burley
with Dolores Proiette

Nothing in this book is intended to represent or suggest an endorsement of the author, the professional hypnotist, the publisher, or any of the content of the book by the deceased persons included in the book or by any of their family members, associates, or organizations. My intent in channeling the transformative words in the book is to uplift, inspire, and enlighten the reader. These accounts have been carefully collected from different sources through trance channeling and are provided here as I was able to channel them, with minimal editing. As some channeling is limited or influenced by my ability to connect with, and receive from, the source being channeled, no representation is made as to the factual accuracy, completeness, or objective reality of any channeled statements, but only that the channeling experience itself was and is as represented by the medium and observed by the hypnotist. If there are any apparent inaccuracies, they are the result of my trance channeling with the original sources, and they are included to maintain the authenticity of my experience.

TABLE OF CONTENTS

EDITOR'S NOTE

—Anne Edwards

If you could attend a meeting where Jesus, Buddha, Albert Einstein, Harriet Tubman, Eleanor Roosevelt, and Abraham Lincoln were discussing spiritual truth and the world situation, would you go? If each were to turn and speak directly to you, would you listen? Would it help you to know that such great souls keep a loving watch over the earth, and they are always active on our behalf? This book ushers you into a sphere where the door between this world and the afterlife swings wide open, and we discover that great leaders from another dimension are eager to speak to us. Trance Medium Philip Burley and Hypnotist Dolores Proiette have given them the means to do so!

I met Philip long before he became a professional medium, and our families have been friends for years, but after they moved several states away, we didn't see them often. In the early 1990s, a close friend who was seriously ill with breast cancer asked me to attend a meditation circle that Philip had traveled to conduct near our Northern Virginia home. While I was eager to see Philip and his wife, Vivien, and I wanted to support my ill friend, I was less interested in the subject of the meeting and had no idea what to expect.

As the program began, Philip gave brief spiritual readings to some of those gathered before turning to my companion. I was surprised to hear him announce the presence of someone she and I had both known—a dear friend who had died a few years earlier. As I listened, her characteristically direct but compassionate manner was unmistakable, and her penetrating words affected me deeply. That the personality of someone I had known came through Philip so clearly got my attention! Within a few weeks I traveled from Virginia to Pennsylvania, where Philip and Vivien lived, to receive my first spiritual reading. While I had long doubted the accuracy of messages from mediums, I didn't want to approach the experience with a defensive attitude, and it helped that Philip was an old friend whose sincerity I trusted. I arrived at his office determined to be open minded.

As my reading progressed, I found the content of the messages meaningful, but I was most affected by the extraordinary energy of healing and love that transcended the words being spoken. After the reading, without any effort on my part, I realized my spiritual journey had taken a significant turn. I found that all I had to do to experience God's presence was to be very still. It seemed clear to me that my new level of awareness was not induced by Philip himself but by his facilitation of direct contact with my guides and loved ones in the spirit world. I realized God's grace was ever available, no matter where life was taking me.

I continued to receive occasional spiritual readings from Philip over the next decade or so, usually by telephone, since we were not geographically close. But when I retired, my husband and I moved from Virginia to the Phoenix area, partly because we had family and friends nearby, including Philip and Vivien. When Philip learned I was a former English teacher with years of writing experience related to another career, he offered me the job of editing this book and several others, and I was more than happy to accept.

Do I believe that beings from the spirit world have spoken through Philip for the chapters in this book? Do I think channeling is real? Yes, to both questions, for a number of reasons:

1. I have known Philip for decades and trust his honesty.

2. As I edited the manuscript, I detected the unique personality of each speaker. Eleanor Roosevelt was ebullient and encouraging, Buddha was reflective, and George Washington was straightforward and to the point.

3. Even from the most skeptical point of view, it seems incredible to think Philip could script, memorize, and recite with fluidity such a large volume of content in the presence of Dolores Proiette, the professional hypnotherapist with whom he collaborated.

4. Philip's ability to provide profound spiritual messages is based on talent and training, but even more on his decades of devoted study, meditation, prayer, and service. His work includes numerous books and thousands of readings, workshops, classes, and presentations, plus eight years of leading a national prayer project for America and the world. This book reflects the authenticity and authority of his lifelong spiritual endeavors.

As you read, you may find yourself thinking that the beings who speak through Philip express themselves in an informal, ordinary way. More than one of them said they are not on some remote plane far above us. What they have experienced within themselves can be experienced by any human being who follows the spiritual practices they describe. The reality they speak of already exists within and around each one of us.

Whatever you decide to believe about channeling, truth is truth; so you can evaluate what is said simply on its merits. In the face of extreme polarizations occurring among many people on earth today, this book offers the vision of a world where differences contribute to the best solution to problems rather than to conflict. And it provides simple, effective guidance to help our human family attain greater spiritual awareness, one person at a time.

—*Anne Edwards*

INTRODUCTION

—*Philip Burley*

I have worked as a professional medium for more than three decades, and I am releasing the contents of this book because I am confident that what is written on these pages is real, just as the voice of spirit has been real throughout my life. Since childhood, from the early morning hours to the middle of the night, and sometimes in the midst of day, I have heard and seen the very real beings who populate a world far vaster than ours—the spirit world. I didn't choose to have such encounters; they just happened, perhaps because of the makeup of my being or even because of destiny. But, for whatever reason, I see and hear beings in the spirit world, and I know each of us is a spirit who came from the Spirit of God. When we leave the physical body, we will exist in a spiritual body, able to move freely into the spirit world to live among other spirit beings. Depending on our level of development, we will be able to communicate directly or indirectly with loved ones still in their physical bodies.

I have channeled the spiritual master, Saint Germain, throughout my career, so I know firsthand that a spirit can speak directly through a willing and practiced individual with mediumistic abilities. After so many years, I can now go into a self-induced trance almost instantaneously, and Saint Germain is able to easily take over my vocal cords and speak freely to individuals and audiences. I am always looking for ways to expand my abilities as a medium and channel, and long before this book was conceived, I became interested in the work of Edgar Cayce, a medium who channeled healing messages and other information from the spirit world while under hypnosis. As an admirer of Cayce's work, I wanted to see if entering a deeper trance state under hypnosis would enhance my ability to channel Saint Germain and other masters. But it was not something I was willing to undertake lightly. Before I attempted to follow Cayce's example, I wanted to find a uniquely competent hypnotist with a high level of sensitivity, skill, and credibility. I had been praying for more than a decade to meet such a person when I met Dr. Dolores Proiette.

My "chance" encounter with Dr. Proiette was *no* accident. Almost as soon as we met, I knew she was the person who could skillfully and safely guide me into a deep state of hypnosis. As a summa cum laude graduate with a doctoral degree in Clinical Hypnotherapy who also holds a master's degree in Education and a PhD in Philosophy, Dolores brings to her practice of hypnosis extraordinary skills and a high level of professionalism. Though she is a person of great faith who has experienced the manifestation of spirit in her own life, she approached this project by taking the position of a researcher who wanted to learn the truth about channeling. Over many months, Dolores and I met in the small office where she had her hypnosis practice. Before each session, we reviewed questions for the individual who would be coming through to speak, and I said a prayer to prepare the spiritual environment, as I do before any channeling or spiritual reading. Here is a representative prayer from the transcript of the session with Buddha:

> *Heavenly Father . . . In every moment, our strength comes from you, and it is so in this hour. Our success in this endeavor depends on your intercessory intelligence, guidance, power, and presence. Anoint Dolores in her part of this work and me in mine, so that enlightened beings of spirit can come close enough to speak in their own words and in their own reality, not ours. We are not seeking to write a book that reflects our attitudes, philosophy, or way of life; we are not even looking to prove the value of hypnosis or the authenticity of channeling. We are seeking truth of the highest caliber that will bring a broader, deeper understanding to people on earth. We are grateful to you and to those in the spirit world who work with us on this project and in our lives, and we thank you for this opportunity. We pray this prayer in divine love, amen.*

As each session began, Dolores sat patiently beside me to guide me into a state of hypnosis so that spirit could enter my aura and use my vocal cords to speak. Because "I" was not present, I trusted Dolores completely to guide the interaction. She recorded not only the channeling but her own observations that I kept my eyes closed as the words of each speaker flowed through me without pause. She saw my demeanor and vocabulary change and experienced transformations in the energy around us as each master came through. She also meticulously transcribed each session. Having Dolores present to consistently facilitate, witness, record, and transcribe everything that happened was invaluable. This book is a compilation of the transcripts of all the hypnosis sessions I had with Dolores, plus a final message dictated to me by the Master Jesus.

My editor, Anne Edwards, was able to take the dialog between the hypnotist, Dolores, and the channeling spirit and turn it into accessible prose without losing the meaning, tenor, or spirit of the communication. There was an extraordinary need to maintain the accuracy of the content and the unique expressive style of each speaker. I have reviewed the book many times, sometimes rechecking the original transcripts, and these needs have been met. Readers will be pulled deeply into each chapter as spirit speaks to humanity on earth, and the careful, thoughtful editing of the messages plays no little part in bringing about this outcome.

Some may question the phenomenon of channeling, but as several speakers in the book convey, we all experience it to varying degrees. For a spirit to completely take over someone's vocal cords to speak or someone's hand to write is unusual. And it requires intent and practice. But many of us think, speak, or write words that are *inspired*, and this is no less a form of channeling. How do we think our lives are infused with "bright ideas" or progressive inventions? Yes, we have our own creative thoughts, but ideas are also placed within our minds by guides, teachers, and loved ones in the spirit world. Spirit channels information through the mind's eye or the mind's ear while we are conducting routine activities, considering a problem, sitting in meditation, or even while dreaming. This is the ultimate meaning of the word inspiration.

Spirit prompts, warns, comforts, and guides us throughout our lives, and we can become more aware of this through the liberal use of our *imagination*. Albert Einstein remarked on the importance of imagination in his work; and Pythagoras, the father of geometry, said his insight into mathematical science came not through logic but through a vision in which he saw images that revealed to him the truth of geometry. A child afraid of the dark is a victim of imaginings not based in fact, and anyone, including a medium, can be misled by undisciplined imagination. It is important to exercise judgment. But after decades of work, I know the *proper* use of imagination is the path, the key, and the door to communicating with the spirit world.

To accurately turn the key, one does not conjure up images, words, or ideas but simply observes and conveys what arises. Our first impulse may be to dismiss what we receive as "just" our imagination, but paying attention often yields very positive results. Those who dare, in faith, to venture in this direction, guided by sound principles and common sense, can step surely into the world of beings who have left the physical plane but remain very much alive in the spirit world.

The door of spiritual sensitivity opens onto a world of magnificent existence with vistas that are not approximated on earth. The gift of mediumship has allowed me to peer into the homes and lives of many souls on the other side as they convey to their loved ones on earth just what their life in the spirit world is like. It has also afforded me a deeper experience of divinity, heightening my awareness and appreciation of the great, eternal, and unconditional love our Creator has for each of us. I know God is real—beyond description and measure, yet deeply personal and available to each of us. Just as I know God and spirit are real, I know they channel inspiration to us by many means, whether or not we are consciously aware of it. Using our own minds, hearts, and discretion, we determine our response to the guidance and love we constantly receive.

Some are bound to wonder about my state of mind and want to know just where I am during a channeling experience. Over many years, I have learned to effortlessly relax into a trance state so Saint Germain can come in to speak through my vocal cords. Other mediums present in the audience on such occasions have clairvoyantly seen me step out of my body and stand beside it while he comes in. More than one has independently seen me surrounded by a deep blue light and Saint Germain by purple light when he is speaking through me. Some have seen "me" walk away and disappear while he is speaking. Following a channeling session, if I am asked what Saint Germain has just said, I really don't know. Rarely, because the words have passed through my being, I have a lingering residual remembrance. In my channeling experiences under hypnosis, I had to listen to the recording or read the transcript to know what each master said.

Neither the hypnosis inductions by Dolores nor the entrances and exits of the masters who spoke for this book were ever exactly the same. For example, Eleanor Roosevelt was present and ready to speak the moment I relaxed enough for her to step in. I literally felt her vibration to the extent that I seemed to *become* her until I vacated my body and she completely took over. Words are inadequate to fully convey such an experience. In other instances, when I heard a spirit begin to speak, I simply faded away and did not know more until the session was coming to an end. I would come back into my body as the visiting spirit was saying closing words and beginning to disconnect from my energy field. Everything was done precisely and with much care on the part of spirit. At no time was I harmed, nor did I have any fear of being harmed.

I pride myself in being balanced in my work as a medium, and I make much use of common sense, for if the phenomena of mediumship and channeling are to be accepted, they must be approached objectively and even scientifically when conditions lend themselves to this. Just as truth is needed to guide love in the right direction, right understanding and conduct help to guide one's interaction with the spirit world. Based on my experiences over many years, I have unwavering conviction about the authenticity of my channeling for this book and about all of my channeling experiences. I am beholden to the power and presence of God and those he has sent for my ability to stay spiritually attuned enough to allow such messages to come through. While I acknowledge there may be some inaccuracies based on my human limitations, I believe my work as a medium is generally sound, grounded, and consistent, and I trust I have done my best.

In reading this record of channeled interviews with enlightened spirits, the serious reader will observe that each personality is uniquely reflected in the words that come through. Those who read with healthy skepticism will discover the inspiring possibility of a world beyond the one we inhabit on this physical plane. In turning the pages of this book, within the conversational exchanges recorded, all will encounter significant truths, delivered in simple, eloquent, and direct ways that deeply affect the mind and heart. May you, dear reader, find yourself touched as deeply as those moved to tears as they read the manuscript prior to this book's release. May your encounter with beings from the highest realms of spirit give you greater understanding and appreciation of your life and the afterlife. And may your reading of this book awaken within you an awareness of just how close and loving are those in the spirit world as they watch over us individually and collectively, seeking to guide the destiny of humankind to the right ends and to God, the Creator of all.

INTRODUCTION

—*Dolores Proiette*

When you feel completely in sync with someone you meet for the first time, is it coincidence? Predestined? Orchestrated by powers existing beyond our five senses? Let me start at the beginning: At a local farmers' market, I was captivated by an exhibit of stones, crystals, and geodes, each with a lovely face molded into the rock. I felt an instant rapport with the artist, Ella, and we exchanged business cards. I was surprised when she called months later to invite me to a party at her home, saying, "I never invite customers to my parties, but I think you're supposed to come!" Ella said my card had fallen to the floor three times that morning from a shelf where it had rested since we met, even though there had been no breeze or anything else to disturb it.

She trusted her intuition and decided I needed to be at her Christmas party. Even though I had to arrive late, I was determined to attend.

When Ella answered her door, she said excitedly, "I know why you're here! There's someone I want you to meet!" She introduced me to a group of people conversing around a firepit in her backyard, and I began talking across the circle with Philip Burley. The woman next to him kindly gave me her seat, and we became totally engrossed in conversation for almost two hours. I learned he was a professional medium and channeler of the spiritual master Saint Germain, and I shared some of my own experiences as a hypnotherapist. At one point Philip calmly said, "Milton Erickson is leaning over you listening, and he says he is very interested in your methods." Erickson, a founding father of modern hypnosis, is someone I greatly admire, and I was deeply affected by Philip's words.

This conversation became the basis for my lasting friendship with Philip and our determination to combine our talents to develop a book. My role would be to put Philip in a hypnotic state and ask specific spiritual entities to come through, and Philip would serve as the channel for their messages. We made a list of those to be channeled that we would modify from time to time. We frequently referred to the list but followed no fixed order in selecting the next master to speak.

Over the years, my work in the field of hypnosis has primarily consisted of helping people get to the cause of mental, physical, or emotional pain and alleviate it, often by reframing how they saw their situation. The experience under hypnosis is part of each one's path, and whatever happens can be therapeutic by opening doors to a reality of which a person has been unaware. It is not my place to negate, criticize, or judge the experiences of my clients, and I work only to help them heal themselves, keeping an open mind to what they bring into each session. I decided to approach the channeling sessions in the same way, allowing the experience to unfold however it might.

Before we formally began sessions for the book, Philip channeled a spiritual master in my office while the tape recorder was running. I did not touch the recorder during the session, but when I listened to the tape later, I could hear none of the channeled information. The words Philip and I exchanged before and after the session were clearly audible, but the channeling itself was missing from the recording. Philip said the energy coming through in channeling is at such a high frequency it cannot be heard on some tape recorders. To ensure that no further information was lost, I activated more than one type of recorder for the subsequent channeling sessions.

In hypnotizing Philip, I followed the same process I use with my clients. During each session, he reclined in my office chair with his eyes closed, and I asked him to imagine himself surrounded by protective golden-white light as I guided him through the stages of relaxation. Following the initial steps, each session was different, as I had no preconceived idea of what images to use to deepen the hypnosis. My objective was to help Philip reach a somnambulistic state so he could become a clear vehicle for a master's energy to come through. One of his guides, Black Hawk, said Philip would be surprised to read some of the information in the transcript of the session, as he would not remember what had been said. Several other entities said that when they spoke, Philip was present only in a passive sense.

Even though I have come to believe in the reality of the spirit world, I am by nature a skeptic, consistent with the old adage, "I'm from Missouri—show me!" In spite of indications that channeling was indeed occurring, I questioned in my mind whether the masters were fully present. Though I was accustomed to not imposing conclusions on my clients' experiences under hypnosis, I found myself seeking validation that the words coming from Philip truly belonged to those asked to come through. My question was to be answered in a number of ways.

Several days prior to a scheduled channeling session, I became aware of statues of Buddha in stores and in the homes of friends. I also began to see his image in my mind. I did not give any of this much thought until the morning of the session when I was again strongly impressed by an image of Buddha. When Philip arrived, before I could tell him about all of this, he told me Buddha had come to him in his morning meditation and asked to speak that day. We laughed as we recognized the strength of the energy coming through to each of us at the same time. This was the first of several occasions when we were both prompted by the master who was to speak next, and it was one of many experiences that helped to validate the process for Philip and me.

Philip said he would also channel St. Paul that morning, so we prepared questions for both masters. I then hypnotized Philip and asked Buddha to come through. Without warning, I was almost overcome by the energy that filled the room. I felt totally surrounded by unconditional love, and I experienced a deepening sense of calmness and peace as the session progressed. After Buddha left, Philip rested for a few moments, still under hypnosis, before I asked St. Paul to speak. The energy in the room changed immediately, and I felt an active, robust presence, entirely different from what I felt when Buddha was speaking. This was the only day Philip channeled two masters in one session, so it gave me a unique opportunity to witness a striking and immediate contrast in the energies, personalities, and expressive styles of the speakers.

I experienced further distinctions among others who came through: Mother Mary came with comforting, compassionate energy, and Albert Einstein with the energy of enthusiasm and excitement. I also recorded my observations as Philip's posture, body language, and demeanor varied, sometimes markedly, with each channeling. I continued to be impressed that the masters spoke fluently, at length, and without hesitation for up to an hour. The cumulative effect of all my observations over many months ultimately removed any lingering doubt about whether or not the channeling was real.

My work with Philip has ushered in a new phase of my professional development by helping me understand and integrate certain patterns I have observed in my hypnotherapy practice. I have learned more about the technical and strategic elements of hypnosis through reading the transcripts of channeling sessions with my spirit guides Milton Erickson and Albert Einstein. Their words contain a wealth of detailed information that has the potential to help professionals in the field of hypnosis to have greater success in their work. In speaking on the subject of hypnosis, each of these masters described in depth how it works, and they gave specific information on how healing takes place at the energetic level.

After months of working with this material, I have also grown personally. I have greater acceptance of whatever life brings, enjoying happy times and learning how I can grow through sorrow or pain. The words of the masters confirmed that many things happen for a reason, even though we may not be aware of what it is. A traumatic event can contribute to our growth and help us to meet our future. I am convinced we all have guides to help us and we are never alone. It is a great comfort to know that many of my past struggles have been part of a foundation for my growth.

As you read this book, ask yourself how the content contributes to your understanding of your own beliefs and values. What feelings do the words bring up for you? What thoughts resonate strongly? What unifying threads seem to run through all of the messages? Do the words seem true to you? Are the ideas logical? Do they have practical applications for your life? I have no wish to change your way of thinking, but I do encourage you to consider new possibilities. As you read the words, let your mind expand; open your heart and see what happens.

I am humbled to be part of this endeavor, honored that I could be the hypnotist to facilitate the channeling for such precious information, and grateful for the joy I have felt in working with Philip on this project. I invite you to travel with us, through reading this book, to meet spiritual luminaries who have much wisdom to share.

—*Dolores Proiette*

Voices of Love
from the Light

There is glory which thou canst not see,
There is a music which thou canst not hear;
But if the spaces of Infinity
Unrolled themselves unto thine eye and ear,
Thou wouldst behold the crystal dome above
Lighted with living splendors and the sound
Of their great voices uttering endless love
Would sink forever thro' the vast profound.

— Frederick Tennyson
"Images of Heaven, Reflections of Glory"

SAINT GERMAIN

The Comte de Saint Germain (Saint Germain) was known as the Wonderman of Europe in the 1700s. People who wrote about him claimed he never aged, spoke several languages, used many names, traveled in time, and worked passionately for peace. He was said to be kind and wise. Saint Germain has been described as an accomplished alchemist, inventor, artist, and musician. Stories surrounding his heritage, birth, and death indicate he was thought to be of royal heritage.

Saint Germain traveled widely in Europe and was at times a confidante of King Louis XV of France and his mistress, Madame de Pompadour. He knew King Louis XVI and Marie Antoinette as well. The philosopher and skeptic Voltaire wrote of him, "Le Comte de Saint Germain is a man who was never born, who will never die, and who knows everything." Many contemporary spiritualists consider Saint Germain to be a master within the highest realms of spirit who continues to work with humanity to bring wisdom, love, and truth.

CONVERSATION ONE

Saint Germain

We celebrate life to the fullest extent possible, and that includes all people. You, each of you, anyone who hears my voice or reads my words, you are the object of God's love, you; you, in your uniqueness. There is only one you. You are the object of God's love, and in that love, there is no time.

—*Saint Germain*

SG: I am here. I have been waiting for Philip to be out of the way. I am smiling as I say that, but I do need to have a clear space, mentally and emotionally. As you were taking him into this state, he was focusing away from this procedure, so we had to work to bring the concentration of his energy back. As he aligned himself mentally with each part of the body that you named, that which you were trying to achieve happened. It is all about the focus of the mind, isn't it? Where thought goes, the heart and everything else go.

The experience of hypnosis is about teaching people to focus. The more people learn to rein in the mind and become focused, the more hypnosis approximates what happens in meditation. With a facilitator or using self hypnosis, anyone who practices enough will learn that meditation and hypnosis are part of one reality. If the mind is focused in that energy, whatever is intended will happen. This could include a change in thinking patterns, eradication of a harmful habit, or formation of a positive habit.

From a spiritual point of view, the coming together of your two souls is valuable because of the combination of your individual energies with the outer reality of your gifts. Each of you is as important as the other. By uniting your minds and hearts in one cause, you create a platform for us to come through in a magnified way, and we are very grateful to have this opportunity.

The need is great. The book you are writing will be one of many, but it is intended to reach certain people. If it can also be brought to a broader readership, we can try to eliminate superstition and fear about both hypnosis and channeling. We can help people realize they are all channels and no one is independent from God, the inner reality of every human being. God is always channeling through, and there is no place he is not pouring himself in. It is as if you are a glove, and God is putting his hand in you. Under circumstances like this, he is pouring himself into your whole being. In a larger and practical sense, you are channeling God.

The science and benefits of channeling apply to many things. In medicine, teaching, law, parenting, or any other field, those who learn how to focus their energies and concentrate their minds are the ones who make the breakthroughs. By focusing enough to bring their minds and bodies into oneness, they are able to channel their own energies and to draw in like-minded spiritual beings who work with them to achieve their goals. It is a win-win situation.

I am here to provide information that will help you to facilitate Philip's channeling and assist with his being open to me; information that will enhance this experience for all of us. This experience, dear one, is a long time coming, and I am sure you feel that within yourself. Isn't that true? You have had the hope and the dream that you would be able to apply your skills as a hypnotherapist and doctor to one or more individuals to facilitate our coming through to lend our help. That is happening now. It is like shuffling through cards in your hand to find the best one to play to win the game, and Philip came up. This will continue, and we are very happy about that.

I know you hear me, but in order to maintain our rapport and keep the circuits flowing between us, I will ask questions now and then. This is not out of curiosity or because I do not understand what is happening, but so I can maintain my focus.

It is your energy that pulls me through. Philip's energy is there in its openness, but he is not really here except to hear things occasionally. I am talking to you, not to him, so *you* are the point of focus by which I can concentrate upon the earth plane and stay here. It always takes someone on your side of the veil to draw us through and help us maintain the focus.

Spirit, such as that in you, is magnetic. When you on earth act as a plus and we act as a minus, or vice versa, depending upon the level and force of the energy coming from each individual, we are able to hold each other in place like two polarized magnets. I am anchored here because of your interest, intent, and focus.

I have been eager to come through directly to speak about the book. More chapters will unfold; and while you want to have an objective approach to this process, people's hearts may not be moved to read the book unless it also inspires them and applies to their every-day lives. I am known for the fluidity and eloquence of my language without intent. That ability comes from my character and nature, but more than that, it is a part of the foundation of my being. I am also practical, because God is practical; and from a practical point of view, we want to look not only at how you are using the process of hypnosis, but at all of life.

Everything exists because of God. When you look at life through the eyes of God, everything has purpose. Many people want to see God as being outside of this world *(chuckle)* because there are things in the world to which they have aversions. Some husbands do not want to be in the delivery room to watch their children being born because not everything about the experience is pleasant for them. People have special names for human waste, and they make jokes and laugh about it. We do too. You might find it interesting that Saint Germain is talking about this, but human waste has purpose. Human and animal waste is used again and again to bring nutrients to the earth. It is rather a miracle that God was so inventive that he created all without wasting anything. What you call waste, God sees as a by-product that can be reused in the cycle of life. How much more practical can you be?

It is the same when leaves fall from the tree to decay. When you are trying to rake leaves in the fall of the year, you may see them as waste, but to us they represent another great miracle of God. A tree re-uses the energy of decaying leaves to feed itself. If that were not so, many of your forests would die. When we understand all of this from God's perspective, we can see God is present both in the miraculous and the practical aspects of life. Some of the practical realities are miraculous in themselves, don't you think? We could give many examples, but you have understood what we are trying to say.

(*Deep breath*) The Master Jesus is here to greet you. There are things he wants to say as this experience goes on, but today he is coming through just to say he is here. He is standing in the space to your right and just to the left above Philip's head but not completely behind him. He is wearing a white robe that is an emanation of his soul. It represents the quality and level of spiritual attainment, or how close one is to God, the source of life. It is run through by threads as you on the earth plane would describe them, but it is made of light. If he wishes to, Jesus can change the appearance of his robe at any time because it is all a projection of his state of mind.

We are all light beings whose central core contains as much spiritual and physical DNA as you could ever want. It manifests as spiritual energy, and though it is invisible to you, it is very visible to us. Both form and essence are included within the DNA, and this duality is necessary. God, being invisible and infinite, had to find a way to understand and see himself. He created form into which he could place himself, watch himself, and work with himself, as a beautiful woman looks in the mirror to fix her hair and put on her lipstick and mascara. God is peering, as it were, into the mirror of life where he can see everything about himself. In this way he even seeks to direct and redirect energies.

There is a measure of limitation in every form. Each is temporary, and each has a higher purpose. Though the form of a stalk of wheat is beautiful, it exists for the higher purpose of providing the seed that can be ground up and turned into bread and other products for human beings. The stalk itself must deteriorate and enrich new soil for other plants. Stones and crystals have forms that appear to have great longevity, but in time, even they deteriorate. As with all forms, they have a higher, deeper purpose, if only a philosophical one. People study them to better understand their own nature. The whole earth plane exists for humanity.

Your scientists understand that the sun is burning out, but God continually replenishes it, and that part scientists do not see. The sun is a form through which God can *shine* his energy upon Planet Earth at a certain distance, so it may flourish, and people may have all they need to live. Looking far out into the universe, your scientists can see stars being born, stars that are dying and stars that have died, in a continual process of creation, maintenance, and deterioration. It is important to understand all of this so one can see the bigger picture of life.

As you know, there is also a limit to the existence of your body. Understanding this, you can truly realize that the greater life is ahead. You should still appreciate every moment on earth and not just look toward making the transition, because that would be like squeezing the juice out of an orange and failing to drink it. You should fully taste and enjoy what is going on in life and, at the same time, realize you are always moving forward. Like everything else, the body must go through the process of creation, maintenance, and deterioration, so it might ultimately fulfill its purpose in releasing your spirit at the end of your physical life. Then you may take your leave of this vibration, this existence on earth, and go into the higher spheres of learning and being. There you will understand much better the laws and the science behind all of this. Am I speaking too much?

Dr. D: *Not at all.*

SG: Well, you know, I could be like a running brook, a roaring river, or an endless ocean of information. I am not speaking simply to hear myself go on, but because this book is to touch the lives of people who have many different mentalities. You and Philip have discussed wanting it to have practical as well as spiritual applications. For this reason, the book will include a variety of information that makes it edifying and stimulating for the purpose of enlightening many kinds of people. Readers will be encouraged to explore the practices of meditation, self hypnosis, and facilitated hypnosis and challenged to think more deeply about themselves, life, and life beyond.

Many things come to light when your spirit is moving forward. People cannot find God when they are stagnant, immobilized, and simply waiting for God to do something. God is a being of action, and you will find him in action. To tap into the personality and the intellect of God, you must be active. If you want to really find God, go out and serve other people. Love someone who is worse off than you. Pick up the phone and speak to someone who is lonely. You may do any one of a number of things to find God, because God is energy that is ever flowing and everywhere.

This does not mean you should never be still and meditate, because that in itself is a form of activity. You are there, in place, and the atoms in your body are swirling and whirling around. You are very active as opposed to being in a totally sleeping state. There is a posturing of the body and the mind as you wait for the presence of God to emerge, and then it can.

Dr. D: *What can you tell us about human suffering?*

SG: People need to understand the root cause behind their suffering and how it is prolonged when it could be more rapidly eliminated. It is prolonged mostly because of the continual recycling of certain experiences in the mind. When people hold onto painful experiences in a subjective way, they are reborn in the mind again and again, and the condition of suffering continues. Why don't things happen more rapidly through the intervention of spirit in human life? Why does it take so long to become? I will touch upon that. Though we may not cover the whole answer in this setting, I will say what I can.

The timetable for the unfolding of events in life is not in human hands. Though some readers may totally disagree with this statement, this is because you are not in touch with the higher dimensions of existence. In my world there is no time. For those in the lower realms of spirit there *is* time, not in the sense that there are watches or clocks, but in the sense that time seems to pass slowly. Why? Beings in these realms are suffering from the idea of things they could or should have done or not done on the earth plane, and there is regret. They may have a sense of guilt and shame for immoral things they have done, particularly if this applies to the way they treated other people. These experiences show forth in a person's consciousness, and that is what creates his or her hell. Because of regret and guilt, time seems interminable.

When you are at a party where there is good food, good company, love, laughter, and pure enjoyment, the night seems to fly by. Being in God's energy creates the reality of no time because you are suspended in joy and peace beyond your comprehension. The glory of God cannot be described in earthly terms within a book.

The glory of God is the great beauty found in his love and the peace that comes from that love. Those who hear or read words from me through this gentleman are often swept up into a sphere of unbelievable peace and love. It is here, now. I bring it in my wake because I come from that source, having dwelt there for longer than I can remember. With it comes a wave of deep compassion that is hard to find elsewhere, compassion that says I *know* you. I know all of your heartaches and problems. I know all of your joys and sorrows. I walk with you every step of the way. I know every word you ever uttered, every feeling you ever felt, every sight you ever saw, and every sound you ever heard. I know you comprehensively. I have deep, deep love for you in the totality of your life, for you are mine. It is *I* who set you forth on this journey into life. It is *I* who am bringing you back. Speaking on behalf of God in this case, in his compassion and presence, I, Saint Germain, am filled with tears at this moment, because it is all so simple and yet so magnificent. This that I speak of, which the written word *cannot* totally convey, is the glory of God.

Yes, there are angels; and yes, when spiritual beings appear to the human sensitive, that person perceives our presence, light and love. We appear glorious against the backdrop of your otherwise drab world and darkened spiritual reality. But we are not different from you. You, too, are made of light. You, too, are enfolded in the deep unending compassion of God. You, too, are being ushered forward, ever forward, toward your divine destiny, into the arms of God. As soon as the soul wakes up to this living light of God, as soon as that light dawns within the psyche of the soul, you can experience yourself nestled in the very sphere of timelessness. This is what creates bliss. This is the source of the bliss that the great ones speak of. It is not foreign to your reality.

When you hold your first child, you experience joy and peace beyond words. A new mother is often speechless, and the only way she can manifest her joy in that moment is through tears. That is bliss. When you walk in the garden or on a mountain, and one single flower in all of its beauty captures your attention, you feel sweetness and joy. That is bliss. All of this is God, all of it. When you are out there in the world at large, buying, selling, eating, and drinking, your attention is away from your own soul, your own spirit. Although these things may be necessary to existence on the earth, as long as they are more important to you than your own spirit, more important than God within you, you shall not realize bliss, and time will drag on.

As Jesus and the great ones have demonstrated, you will find the God presence within by turning inward and systematically, carefully, prayerfully walking that inner path of self to your very essence. It is in that walk, that adventure, that journey, that time disappears. The great ones have described this as being in a sphere of endless love. There is no up; no down, no in, no out; just an endless sphere of love and light, suspended away from time in eternal bliss. That is here, now, for your taking. That is here, now, for your enjoyment, peace, and fulfillment. There is no place to go and nothing to do. Hidden in plain sight is our Creator, in the recesses of your own mind, in all the nooks and crannies of your life experience, ever in the background, the backdrop against which your life unfolds.

As I speak, I am deeply moved, because these higher truths are the reason that I, Saint Germain, come. It is the reason that all the great ones come. We have been to the top of the mountain, and we know of what we speak. We celebrate life to the fullest extent possible, and that includes all people. You, each of you, anyone who hears my voice or reads my words, you are the object of God's love, you; you, in your uniqueness. There is only one you. You are the object of God's love, and in that love, there is no time.

Now I will step back for a moment to allow you to ask anything further.

Dr. D: *How do you in spirit world choose someone on earth with whom to work as a channel?*

SG: The operative word is rapport. Did you ever try to speak to someone who would not talk to you? What happens? Unless you have enough in common, it is hard to have a substantial conversation. You may meet someone at the bus stop on a sunny day and talk about the weather, because you know you have that in common. If you go into other topics, the rapport may not be broad or deep. To have true rapport with someone, especially on higher levels of the soul, you must have something in common relating to why you are doing what you are doing and why you are living.

I work with Philip because we have internal factors in common, and this is true for most spiritual beings in their work with individuals. Philip has a heart like mine. He has had his problems, as I did—as we all do—but he is willing to learn. Most important, he wants to know God and wants to do God's will. From the inception of my existence until this day, that is who I am. I want to know God and do his will, because I have discovered there is only one will, the will of God. Until you know that experientially, until you have knocked your head against the wall of ego long enough, you do not wake up to that fact. There are many who have suffered from their own egos and attachments, but have still sought God over and above all. If we ask them how they acquired a relationship with God to the depth that they did, they will tell us, "I surrendered. I surrendered."

If you truly live your belief, you will outgrow it. Though the child in the first grade may use simple arithmetic all of his life, he grows beyond this understanding when he moves into higher levels of education to learn algebra, geometry, and trigonometry. For us to work with someone as I am doing now, that person must be willing to learn and grow through questioning life. There must also be humility. Unless you search and ask questions, we cannot give you the answers, and you cannot find them. There may be gold, plentifully, bountifully, under your feet, but unless you dig into the soil, you will not find it. These attributes are of vital importance, especially if the soul is to do a higher work. All of these conditions are not necessary in lesser situations, but they are required in working with one who is devoted to God.

All people, all of you, have guides and teachers assigned to you from the spirit world, though many do not know we are there with them. Can you imagine our frustration? The degree to which your guides and teachers can interface with your light, help you, move you forward, warn you, and all of those things, depends upon your degree of receptivity to them. If you increase your awareness, then the rapport will deepen and broaden. There will be consciousness between you and spirit, and we will be able to truly communicate.

As Philip will tell you, Jesus, other spirits, or I often wake him up. Sometimes we come in at night, but mostly in the morning, just before he awakens. Because he is spiritually aware, we can speak and commune with him. Would that we could do this with all people! This is our goal, to be able to communicate with each individual. Until the advent of the day when we can do that, we are patient. We go as fast as we can with each of you.

Timing is important in determining whom we choose. If there is something monumental to be done through a president of the United States, head of another country, or someone in a leadership role on any scale, there is a certain timing in the unfolding of God's will. While there may be two people of a similar nature in a certain place, the one who is closest in time to what we need to do will be chosen. Because Abraham Lincoln lived when he did, he was in perfect timing to become the one to write the Emancipation Proclamation to end slavery. This became the hallmark of his administration and the greatest work he did. Had George Washington not been where he was at the right time, he would not have been the father of your nation. Someone else would have been.

Each child is set on his or her course, and spirit guides are there from the beginning, assigned even before a child is born. Yes, babies have their guides, too, and the angelic world interacts considerably with them. All of you have at least two angelic beings with you from birth, to guide you along the way. Are there those who come spontaneously? They do in some cases, especially if the individual is awakened to spirit world and makes requests. Even then, a spirit guide must have enough in common with someone to work with that person. We must be able to converse, if only through heart and unconscious awareness.

How an individual is "wired" and educated is important, because we borrow from the library of the mind, of life experiences. We could influence William Shakespeare because he had natural eloquence and a facility for language. He also had a big mind and could look at life in a broad way, still seeing the individual aspects quickly and easily. Otherwise, he could not have written the great things he wrote.

Mr. Einstein is with us today, standing behind you, Dolores. He could be used by higher forces, not because he was interested in education, because he was not, but because he had a curious and brilliant mind. More than you may expect, he was highly intuitive and could perceive the reality of energy in a unique way. He could know and understand the higher truths he brought through that changed human history, such as $E = mc^2$.

We have not exhausted this topic, but we want you to have the opportunity, if you desire, to ask more questions.

Dr. D: *Thank you. How does the spirit world interface with the physical world?*

SG: Everything is vibrational. A stone or rock may look inert, but it is not, because it is made of atoms, which are in constant movement, and this creates the vibration. Much is determined by the elements involved and the speed with which the electron goes around the nucleus. The reality relating to vibrations is related to the degree of solidity, pliability, and flexibility of an object. Electronically, your physical bodies vibrate at a lower frequency than ours; so for us to interface, using your word, with the physical world, we must lower our frequency. Through the application of meditation and concentration, you can raise your vibration, raise your frequency, and meet us halfway.

To help train and guide a person and correct his or her course, we work with the spirit out of body at night. Philip often meets me and other master teachers on the other side, and it is the same for you. Those who work with you from the other side usher you through by conversing with you out of the body at night. While it does not happen all the time, it happens often enough, according to the providence of the soul, to make it possible for us to effect a change. It helps us to influence you on a great enough level to bring forth deeper and deeper understanding and awareness.

When leaving the body at night, you may experience something akin to a very rough or very fine vibration, and you do not know what this is. It is the liftoff of the spirit as you are moved in consciousness away from your physical body. Since the spirit vibrates at a higher frequency than the physical body, there is a certain dissonance between the two frequencies as the spirit leaves the body. There are some adjustment factors as the spirit moves away from the lower frequency. Because frequencies can be both electronic and magnetic, the spirit must get out of the magnetic field of the physical body, and we assist with that. It is a matter of focus and concentration. Anyone can leave the body consciously when trained how to rise up into the higher frequency of the spiritual mind, away from the physical mind. You are always there anyway, but it is a matter of where you place your energies and your focus.

In the case of channeling through writing, sometimes we are simply impressing a particular individual from outside. People may experience our thoughts as their own and not even be aware that we are influencing them. Many who write poetry or other literature have not one wit of understanding that we are providing the thought, topic, or expression for their work, but we are there.

From each of you radiates a magnetic field that you call an aura. There are many elements and factors within this auric field that determine how we interact with you, including the frequency or vibration of your own thought. What and how you think are particularly influential, and we attune ourselves to that energy. We come in on that wavelength as we approximate, match and become synchronized with the frequency of your brain waves.

Thought and feeling are two sides of the same coin. Without thought there is no feeling, and all feelings have some thought attached to them. We can come in on your feeling as well as your thought. When you are open to us in a very blissful state, perhaps singing hymns as you center on God, your auric field is open, and we can pour into you that which you may call an anointing. You may say you are experiencing the Holy Spirit. This is true, for we are spirit, and we come for a holy purpose.

We can be conglomerate, coming sometimes in great numbers to overshadow a whole congregation. This was much more possible in the early church than it is now because your culture is becoming exceedingly left brained. Still, there are those who are humble and simple in their thinking; not ignorant or stupid, but innocent and childlike. When they are praising God and singing, we can easily overshadow them. They experience our presence again and again, and they give God the credit. Yes, it is God, because God manifests himself through us. We come in God's name and for his purposes. We are God's agents as we make contact and bring through this kind of influence.

Last night I listened as Philip spoke with a young doctor who was visiting his home. She said that in the beginning there were times when she did not know what she was doing, and it was frightening. Schools do not teach you everything about everything, and you have to learn by experience. Sometimes doctors are influenced by master doctors, including ancient spiritual beings who have all the expertise one could ever want. For example, Hippocrates, the Father of Medicine, is here in the spirit world, and he knows the body completely, including how it functions and how to heal it.

Some doctors may be operating on someone unaware of the need for a certain procedure. We can overshadow them and put a vision in front of their minds. They may experience this as their own imagination, whereas it is a vision we have given them in a time of emergency. If the auric field is open enough, we can actually work through the hands of an individual. If you were to take a poll of doctors worldwide, you would find among them a certain number who have had the experience of actually seeing the hands of a spirit over their hands, guiding them.

The heart is very important in our interfacing with you. When it is open, childlike, and receptive, we can easily enter in. We can often bring about immediate changes, both in awareness and in the emotional field, but you have to want this. We cannot just come in and do anything. No. There is a plan, a design, a road map. We have to be experts in knowing and conforming to what God is trying to do through the soul. We are not allowed to just randomly remove suffering. We know there are higher plans for each individual, and there are things we are not always aware of. There may be things that we are aware of that cause us to know we must exit and do no more, even to relieve suffering, so that a person is able to learn and grow.

As they grow, people may change spirit guides and teachers. When we have done enough with an individual and find no more deep rapport, a spirit guide will come in who will be of greater assistance. The new guide could be a man or woman, depending on the situation. In a broad sense, our interfacing with you on the earth plane relates to the mission of each person. What is the central purpose for which this individual came to earth? That purpose will tell you what kind of spirit is with you. Philip was born to be a medium, a bridge between two worlds. One needs to imagine only slightly to know what kind of beings would be working with him.

If you want to know what kind of beings are with you, ask yourself, "Who am I?" "What is my essential nature?" "What do I think about and love the most?" "How do I spend most of my life?" Then you will know. A spirit who was an interior decorator while on earth is not likely to be working with a doctor.

There are also levels within each individual to consider. A doctor may need one or more doctors from spirit to assist in medical practice, but for the spiritual or philosophical side of life, there may be a master teacher who is not a doctor, but a philosopher, interested in the evolution and growth of the spirit. The same is true for anyone, in any field of work.

One may be assisted by one of the masters in person or an archetype of one of them. For example, Jesus does not come to everyone individually because he can broadcast himself out and appear to be present. The compassion, caring energy, concern, and love are all there because God is pouring out through this archetype, this form, this symbol. During a recent meditation, Philip saw Abraham Lincoln. Though it appeared to truly be Lincoln, it was an image given for higher purposes, to help Philip discern what to do in a certain situation. It was not necessary for Lincoln to come literally, as he did not need to converse with Philip in this case. Lincoln helped to project the emanation and bring it forth, so that Philip could reach the conclusions he derived from this vision.

Dr. D: *Is the trance state for channeling spirit helped more by self hypnosis or through the assistance of a hypnotist?*

SG: A hypnotist can help to objectify the channeling experience and make it happen more easily. The most important thing is that the subject is receptive. The person does not have to be an absolutely perfect subject, but he or she must desire to have this experience. This could be because of curiosity or a wish to remove certain spiritual residue. It is case by case.

If you want to use the science of hypnosis and can afford it, we recommend that you work with a reputable person who can help you. After a period of time of working with a skilled hypnotist, you may want to learn and use self hypnosis. What is ideal is a combination of both, you see. Hypnosis is a means to the ends of achieving higher understanding and eliminating things that cause suffering in the life of the individual.

You know all of this.

Dr. D: *Is there other information you would like to give that I have not asked about?*

SG: No. I think we have covered enough for today.

End of session.

MILTON ERICKSON

Milton Hyland Erickson, MD (December 5, 1901—March 25, 1980) was born in Aurum, Nevada. He was confined to a wheelchair most of his life because of polio. As a psychiatrist, Erickson specialized in family therapy and in medical hypnosis, and his work in the field of clinical hypnosis was substantial and influential. He contributed to the development and application of Neuro-Linguistic Programming (NLP), a therapeutic technique based on the theory that people's perceptions and attitudes can be changed to improve their behavioral and mental health. Erickson was the founding president of the American Society for Clinical Hypnosis and a fellow of the American Psychiatric Association and the American Psychological Association. He died at the age of seventy-eight in Phoenix, Arizona.

CONVERSATION TWO

Milton Erickson

With healing love and compassion, they become the very manifestation of the divine presence and cause transformation. Such healers are the messiahs among you. They may not have a title or crown, but they are so one with God that when they meet another human being, they are love itself. They are healing itself. They are light itself. They are God come to earth.

—Milton Erickson

Comment:

Dr. D: *In the beginning of Milton Erickson's session, I called on Saint Germain to come through Philip because I thought he would be the one conveying the message of each speaker. But after Saint Germain's initial remarks, Milton Erickson spontaneously took over Philip's vocal cords and began to speak directly through Philip. I did the same thing for Albert Einstein in another early session, but he, too, soon began to speak directly through Philip's vocal cords.*

SG: I am here. This is Saint Germain. I was with you over the weekend to radiate the violet light over your husband to help with his healing. You can do that, too, with your own consciousness, by finding a color of violet that vibrates with you, even in your imagination. You can use your own mind to radiate a violet color that is compatible with you or to anyone you wish to heal. If that person is aware of light frequencies and their interplay upon the body electric and the whole system, he or she can sit for a few minutes and visualize that color as well. It will draw me in.

Now, you have questions for me today.

Dr. D: *Yes. Is it time to have Milton Erickson come through?*

SG: Yes. He is here, standing to your right in a glow of white light. He chuckles as he says he has been waiting for this time. You are the first one to approach him in this way, to ask questions and make his answers available to the public. He is more than happy to cooperate. The first thing he wants to say is that he is standing without any assistance and there is no wheelchair within miles. He is in good shape and is quite youthful.

Mr. Erickson radiates his energy into you and assists you in your work. He has been very much working with you, and this experience will enhance that arrangement. This should increase your confidence because you can do more together than you could individually. Since he is a being in spirit, he can help your clients as he interfaces with you in depth. He can work with you to rearrange mental and emotional energies, which can speed the healing process of your clients. Of course, there are certain restrictions. He, you, and all of us must follow spiritual and physical laws, and we can never go against anyone's free will.

Dr. D: *What information does he feel would be valuable to include in our book? What would be valuable for others to know related to hypnosis and channeling?*

SG: He is hearing your question, but I want to confer with him, so give us a span of time to converse. (*Pause*)

Milton Erickson Speaks:

ME: Saint Germain began today by talking about violet light and the realities surrounding light energy. There is a broad array of things we can touch upon, but I would like to begin by talking about light energy.

The energy between the hypnotist and the client radiates from both at varying levels. The spiritual sensitive can see the auric field that radiates out of the core energy, or God presence, in an individual. This energy comes out in waves and levels. Though the ocean is all one, at different levels within it you will find various species of fish, animals and plants. When we are working metaphysically with the energies of the human being, in healing, acupuncture, hypnosis, medicine, or in any way, we are working with various levels of energy.

The cause of human disease originates in the matrix of energy of thought. Where thought has been incorrectly arranged, with fear, misunderstanding, ignorance, or anger, it coalesces into a thought form that can manifest in the body. Cancer, for example, can result from improper diet or other external cause, but if there is no predisposition within the thought energy, or spiritual DNA, then it will not happen. This is why things such as cancer tumors can be eradicated by the mind. They can also be eradicated through the use of machinery or chemicals, but the mind is capable of doing the same thing because it creates. Where the mind creates, it can also destroy or dissipate.

When you are sitting with any client, the more you can find in common with that person, the more rapport you can establish. The more your minds and hearts blend as one on the spiritual level, the more your auric fields become one. When you meet someone with whom you feel oneness, someone who does not feel like a stranger, it is because your energies blend, they do not repel.

When you hypnotize people, you are not only working with their minds, their psychology, but also with their energy, from a holistic standpoint. Clients with whom you have the greatest success are those with whom you have the greatest rapport. It may not be overt common interest, but a rapport that is deep in the soul. You have a common walk upon a common path toward common goals. Philip and you find harmony because you are both interested in the field of spiritual things and in the experience of accessing the human mind through hypnosis. Your rapport with each other makes it easy for you to induct him into a hypnotic state so we can come through.

When there is not enough rapport with a client, you can enhance your own energy field with love and blend it with your client's energy field. This will help us to help them. Love is the key. Love neutralizes negativity, you see. When you are with a client, have deep compassion, as you already do. When you do not find the relationship is going well in trance or in communication during hypnosis, center yourself upon divine love and visualize love pouring in from the universe. It is everywhere, but by visualizing it you can enhance it, establish a deep rapport with your client and be better able to help.

You are a healer, not only through the process of putting a person under hypnosis to work with the subconscious mind, but by radiating the energy of compassion. This greatly influences the flow of love energy from you. When you combine your concern, which we call compassion, with empathy, you feel the person's situation and can enter into a deeper rapport. You become that individual.

When working with channeling, Saint Germain is able to find rapport with Philip on different levels, so they have been able to engage with each other in this way for the past three decades. There is a huge matrix of energy surrounding this work, but there must be compatibility and harmony among all parts for the energy to stay unified. Because you are similarly motivated, you can enter into this energy and this process moves forward smoothly. People on earth may be unaware of these energy fields in the way we are speaking of them, but they are important. In the years to come, as people understand energy fields more and more, they will consciously use them. They are already using them to enhance life, but not to the degree that they could.

Through the research conducted by particular individuals, you on earth know the power of prayer thought. Prayer is the channeling, transforming, and use of energy. The scientific experiments done in proximity or in distance on plants, animals, or human beings, show that thought energy has a great impact at the atomic, molecular, cellular levels on all of life. If this can be done with animals and plants, how much more can it be done with human beings who are the most sensitive and, under the right circumstances, most open to change?

You on earth suffer greatly for lack of knowledge about these things. If you knew more about them, you could speed up the process of healing the mental suffering that becomes lodged, not only in the mind, but in the body electric, the energy field of the emotional body. By using this energy correctly, especially when people are under hypnosis, you can create change and alleviate suffering much more rapidly than you could if you have to wait until they understand everything.

Many things do not need to be understood for a person to be healed. After all, there are things that you use every day that you do not need to understand in order for them to exist. You do not totally understand how the air you breathe in goes into the lungs, into your cells, and so on. You may have read about it, but you do not understand everything; you just breathe without thinking. You do not have to know all of the details in order to breathe.

Everything is energy and is therefore vibratory. In working with individuals using hypnosis, counseling, medicine, or any other healing modality, the more you go toward that level of higher understanding into the world of causation and the world of energy, the more you are going to approximate God. God is all energy, coalesced as consciousness or awareness. When we bring in more of that presence, that higher frequency of energy, we can expedite the healing process. That is what the masters do.

A truly adept spiritual healer is a channel for the speeding up of energies, whether the healer is working with a mass gathering of people or with an individual. People who have cancer or any other impairment in their bodies can sometimes be quickly healed, because we speed up the process. We know that through proper food, rest, and the right state of mind, certain problems of the body can be healed over time. When a truly skilled healer uses the inflow of energy to bring about change, it is not really different from the body healing itself. It is just that the healing is speeded up. This is what you sometimes call a miracle, though it is not really a miracle. We have engaged the energies so completely, comprehensively, and knowledgeably, and on such a high level, that this healing can take place.

I have come back to this point about the radiation of energy because I am trying to build a thesis that will enable your readers to appreciate what happens from our point of view when we are working with individuals. We are working from the higher frequencies of life, the higher levels of existence, but all is one. I wanted to speak on this level to enlighten people and expand their understanding. Now I think I have thoroughly covered this topic.

Dr. D: *How effective is it to use hypnosis to heal groups, and what would be the process?*

ME: It is case by case, as you know from your years of experience helping individuals through hypnosis here in your little office. People have varied responses. Some go deeply and quickly into the state of being hypnotized, some go slowly, and some go not at all. When clients are not receptive, this has to do in part with rapport, as I was explaining earlier.

If individuals in a group are willing, it is possible to put them under hypnosis, but they will be at various levels of trance. Each hypnotist also comes with a level of mastery of the energy used in that process. The more skilled you are, the more effective you will be in helping people in such a setting. The mastery of the energy in any occupation, the mastery of knowledge and action, determines a person's effectiveness in that field. The more you live what you have learned, the more you become it. Then the energy that comes from you *is* that particular occupation or career. A teacher who truly studies and is fascinated by the subject matter taught becomes a walking book of knowledge on that subject. The teacher will radiate that energy. As a hypnotist, working one on one, or working with many, you radiate energy reflecting the degree to which you have studied, learned, and *become* the embodiment of your knowledge.

Hypnosis is more than the process of causing people to go into a deeper state of mind. As a master of this practice, you radiate energy so that a client picks up a frequency from you that both commands attention and brings about a passive state. The energies you radiate, combined with your words, cause the individual to trust you and have faith in you. Then the person can let go and let his or her conscious mind retire into the background. It is the conscious mind, as you well know, that resists, but when there is this combination of factors, especially trust, peace, affection, caring, empathy, and compassion present in the hypnotist, there is greater cooperation. These energies cannot be seen by you or others on the earth plane, but they cause individuals or groups to be cooperative and to go into a passive state.

This is what I want to say, at this point, about working with groups. Have I made myself clear? Would you like any further answer?

Dr. D: *Is it beneficial, then, to do healing with large groups?*

ME: Of course. It is not different from any other healing modality. It is just a different basis upon which the energy is exhibited, radiating out from you. On the earth plane, the effectiveness of one soul in helping another has to do with how much one can become the other individual. Philip is able to know a spirit or someone on earth who comes to him by *becoming* that person. Through having deep empathy or compassion, he can tune into the vibrations or frequencies of the individual, whether it is a client or a spirit embodied before him. It is not different when you are working with hypnosis. When certain trauma comes forth, you may remain objective, but at times you get tears in your eyes and feel a tug at your heart or feel sad. You may have a number of possible emotional responses because you are so much with that person that you are one with that individual.

While hypnosis may be considered a science, science without love or spirituality is rather dead. We on this side know that science is God, and God, in essence, is love. You must mix the two in order to come into full enlightenment. To see the light of God is one thing. Many people talk about seeing the light, seeing colors, getting chills, and so on, but to be truly engaged with God is to be truly engaged in exchanging *love* with God. It is not enough to just feel compassion. One must passionately want to know and be with God, who is all love and all peace. The peace you all long for is nothing more or less than a longing for God. The soul's unconscious longing is always for God. Many people say they want peace in the world. What are they really saying? From our point of view, they are saying they want to be one with God, the source of all peace.

When you are truly adept at doing this kind of work, you can bring this with you in your practice.

Dr. D: *Are there times when clients should not remember what happened when they were under hypnosis so they will not undo the healing work by discounting it?*

ME: There is truth in that. Even when people are awake, they may resist truth because they are not ready to change. Truth always means to "look at me," to look at the truth, examine it, understand it, and apply it. This will result in change, and soul issues relating to karmic realities may prevent that from happening. A person may not yet have enough merit to look at the truth of things and therefore is not yet equipped to change. If it is pushed too hard, any change becomes artificial, and the person will revert back to the old pattern.

As you know, the desire to stop smoking is a typical example of why a person might choose to work with hypnosis, particularly on the external level of the use of hypnosis. Some people are not ready to give up smoking. As a hypnotherapist you may be frustrated when you cannot enable the individual in the subconscious mind to receive the new message of "I do not want to smoke anymore," but it may not yet be time. The karmic record may be such that the balance sheet of debits and credits is not at a point where there is enough credit for the change to happen.

I am answering your question, but I am not saying this to discourage someone who is seeking help. It is most important to make the effort, to try. You can do multiple sessions with an individual, and, through the effort itself, the merit may come forth; but it does not always happen. Not everyone can get rid of certain habits through hypnosis. Why? It is because some problems are very deep within the soul and part of the fabric of the person's emotions. If you find resistance, do not blame yourself.

What else would you like to ask me in this area?

Dr. D: *Sometimes an individual will hold a crystal while being hypnotized. Is that necessary for the flow of energy, or is it helpful mostly for the person's attitude or state of mind?*

ME: It depends on the crystal, and yes, it can help. Crystals are vibratory. They store, send and receive energy. Depending on their color, the stones transmit different frequencies of energy. Rose quartz will bring about a certain response and amethyst another. A diamond, emerald, or other gemstone has a unique frequency. The color of a stone indicates a specific frequency, and a specific frequency indicates a different color. Sunlight is made of frequencies. When you see a rainbow in the sky, it is the frequency of the varying vibrations of sunlight passing through the raindrop that causes the various colors. Colors with various frequencies can appear through the right means such as a crystal. Holding a crystal or placing it on the body can have a dramatic effect on the individual, but this must be done wisely.

This knowledge is in the realm of science and needs to be understood by scientific authorities. This will help individuals to work with those stones or crystals that are most compatible with them for whatever problem they are having. Mental clarity can result from the use of certain stones, and that is literally so. The inducement of greater spiritual vision, which you call clairvoyance, can be enhanced by the use of certain stones, including the placement of those stones on the body. This is a science that is being explored even as we speak, and many people are already practicing it, but I would advise you to practice it with wisdom. If an individual wants to use a crystal, be sure it is not of the wrong frequency, or it could actually block energies.

Dr. D: *Is there anything you have not said related to hypnosis and channeling that would be informative to readers of the book?*

ME: People would be wise to use hypnosis, but their experience will be enhanced if they understand it first so they do not approach it in ignorance or fear. The more you know and understand, the easier it is for you to be receptive and for the hypnotist to help you make desired changes. It is the same for any activity in human life.

Hypnosis is a metaphysical tool in that it deals with the eternal mind. It can transport an individual into the superconscious mind to the plane where I am able to come through to have this experience with you. During hypnosis, changes take place in the subconscious mind, a part of the mind in which things are stored that are not in the forward knowledge of the individual.

People are often not aware of certain ideas, experiences or pictures stored in their subconscious minds, though these experiences interplay greatly with their conscious experiences. For example, if a child has a traumatic experience, the conscious mind may not remember the experience as the person moves forward in life. Deep in the subconscious mind there is the whole element of the reality of the traumatic experience that happened in childhood. Under hypnosis one can look objectively at the experience and come to understand its components, or even subjectively enter into the experience and relive it. It can be revivified. By re-experiencing the trauma of that experience, you can know how it is affecting you today. In this state of mind, you can give inklings to the hypnotist and to self about how to solve the problem. Again, you do not have to understand everything for healing to happen, but getting beyond the fear of all of this is important.

Prayer and meditation have a similar effect. It is the innate nature of human beings to go deeper into themselves, into the state of being removed from the earth plane. Through the right kind of prayer and meditation, one can reprogram oneself. We in the spirit world can come in and help to rearrange energies, bringing forth the subconscious mind so one knows what to pray about. This process can help someone to relive or revivify a memory, including associated feelings, so it can be resolved within that person. The deeper the meditative state, the closer it approximates the state of hypnosis where one is working with higher and deeper energies. This is what hypnosis is about. Others before me delved deeply into this and understood it through practicing it.

This is my opportunity to say to those reading this book, avail yourself of the hypnosis experience as you feel moved to, but remove the ignorance and fear that often surround this process. Study enough to understand hypnosis so that your experience is enhanced.

Dr. D: *Is there any other information you want to give?*

ME: Some people would say, "You know, hypnosis is about allowing someone to go in and fool around with your mind." I would answer this by saying that God does this all the time. He does not play around with your mind, but he is a part of the whole fabric of who you are. Your reality is built upon the God presence and cannot be separated from God. God is there from the inception of you; ever there, guiding quietly, working with the totality of your mind. He is ever guiding individuals to remove the obstacles to spiritual attainment and to heighten their spiritual awareness.

God will allow the bringing forth of trauma so that one may look at the truth of the reality of self in order to resolve such things.

Sometimes resolution occurs in the dream state, sometimes through reflection, sometimes through meditation, and sometimes through prayer. *Sometimes* it happens just by coming upon similar difficult circumstances in your life and reacting in a positive way, erasing the negative effect of the old memory. This happens all the time.

Sometimes people are afraid to speak in front of others because there is a building block of fear about this in their subconscious minds. Then, because they are highly motivated by self, by us, by God, they suddenly stand up and speak. The component of fear in the subconscious mind is transformed so that such a person can move beyond it. This is not different from the dynamics that occur when a hypnotist is working with a client. Isn't that interesting? You can see that hypnosis is not unrelated to your experience. It is just that it came upon the earth to be used as a different approach. It is not different for the evolution of the soul from other approaches and applications. Don't you just love this? We do.

Having studied me, you know how much I loved this work because I understood the mind. I had problems of my own, including a physical impairment. I asked myself the question, "What am I going to do if I cannot use my body like other people?" By asking this, my mind became strong, and my determination became even stronger. My will to order and my will to do were magnified more than in the average individual. I knew what it was to be physically impaired and what it was to suffer, to be different, to be pointed at, and to be mocked. I could appreciate what it means to be incapacitated by something over which one has no control.

Because of my own impairment, I came to have deep compassion for my patients, whatever their state of mind or degree of mental or emotional difficulty. In that compassion, it was the Christ Spirit that came to me, you see. Jesus had this same compassion, for he had suffered so much as a human being, as the son of God, and as one who came to show the way to truth and to God. His suffering made him vulnerable to the suffering of others and open to helping individuals overcome their pain, their fears and their spiritual and physical impairments. It helped me greatly to go through what I went through, because it made me capable of dealing with individuals from whom others would turn away. They did not have a clue as to how to work with some of the individuals I could help. As was said earlier in this session, empathy enables you to enter in and become another person.

I would be remiss not to say this: The most important point in all of this is compassion. Within compassion is empathy, love, caring, and wanting to alleviate the suffering of the person before us, because we *become* that person, and we feel what they are going through, at least in part. Through our hearts, through our sensitivity, we get a glimpse of a person's situation. We want to bring in love through our compassion. We want to bring in an ordered mind and understanding to help the person before us to see their reality, subjectively or objectively, and move beyond it.

The experience of suffering is not given or allowed for the undoing of a person. No, indeed, every experience of suffering is a stairstep toward God, and that is how God uses it. Again, the essential thing in working with someone who is suffering is to have compassion. You can take a course in Reiki or a number of courses in healing, but if the essence of soul is not filled with compassion, empathy, and divine love, you will not be a good agent for the passing on of healing energies. Healing can be done mechanically, but it is not nearly as effective.

One who is truly a healer, as Jesus was, can simply hug an individual and bring about transformation. A true healer does not need the application of thought and the dynamics of the flowing in of energy or of touching here and touching there. With healing love and compassion, such healers become the very manifestation of the divine presence and bring about transformation. They are the messiahs among you. They may not have a title or crown, but they are so one with God that other human beings experience them as love itself, healing itself, and light itself. They are God come to earth.

This ability to heal is available to all people if they will apply themselves in the way that the path toward God tells us to apply ourselves. The pilgrim always starts out on the path, the pilgrim's way, wanting to know the *very* truth of things, with a heart full of longing. But even more than wanting to know the truth of things, the pilgrim wants to be embraced by God, to experience love at such a high level that lasting peace fills the whole being. If you stand in the presence of Jesus, in spirit *or* on earth, you will find he is peace itself, whose center is divine love. This is true of all of the great masters.

Now, have we answered enough questions? Has it not been a delightful hour?

Dr. D: *Yes, it has.*

ME: I am as human as you are. I am so pleased that providence allowed for this time together. You can read my books, the books on what I did and how I did it, but to truly know me is to know *why* I did the things I did. It was because I loved. I came into that place of being because I wanted to love, and because I loved. My own difficulties, my own questionings about life, about self, and about my suffering made it possible for me to become a true friend to individuals I worked with. While I wrote about the science of hypnosis, what I said this morning is the true motive behind my work.

Now I am going to go with Saint Germain. He will remain, but I am going to remove myself. I have been coming through the wavelength of Saint Germain, and that is why the voice is not altered. God bless you. If you have need of me in the future, please call me in.

Dr. D: *Thank you so much. God bless you. And thank you, Saint Germain, for helping Milton Erickson to come through.*

SG: You are very welcome. It is an experience of enlightenment for me because I am learning as I listen. We can look at truth and see different things from different angles. While I know in essence the things Milton Erickson said because I have worked with the mind for eons of time, the language he uses, the inferences, the examples, all of these are fascinating to me, and I am learning too.

Dr. D: *Is Philip in or out of his body when you come through as you are doing now?*

SG: For the most part, Philip is out of his body. He moves in and out, but he is always connected by the silver cord because he must come back into the body. It is not his time to break away from this form. He is nearby, but as he told you before this session started, he does not remember much about what comes through. When he reads the material it will be enlightening and meaningful to him, too. It is a great convenience for us to be able to come in and use Philip's faculties in this way.

Dr. D: *Can any harm come to Philip's body or spirit during channeling?*

SG: No, not in Philip's case. There is residual energy gathered at the solar plexus that needs to be dissipated, and we seek to do that. He also does this through rest, meditation, and prayer. If you understand that the energy content reflects the high realm energies of those who come, you would not even ask such a question.

Individuals who, for example, practice the Ouija Board in some kind of playful setting like children sometimes do, can draw lower entities. Such entities do not care at all about the welfare of those using the Ouija Board. They may be demonic, wanting to hurt an individual out of jealousy or any one of a number of motives. In Philip's case, no harm can come to him. One reason he was chosen for this work is that he is not highly ego oriented, and this protects him from negative energies. He has been working with us for years, even in the foundation of his life, carrying out his role in spite of his own frailties and failings on the earthly level. He is, therefore, very able to be protected by us.

There are many agents, including this wonderful Black Hawk who is a major contributor to Philip's protection, who are always out and about in the space around him. They keep any entity of a lesser nature from touching in with him or entering into his energies. Because of all of this, the likelihood of anything happening is improbable. When he is awake he may be more vulnerable and less protected by us because in that state he can make his own choices, and in this passive state we are making the choices for him. There are agents here who know how to protect, who stand guard when Philip is in this state.

Dr. D: *When others are channeling, what can they do or say to protect themselves from negative energies?*

SG: Do not approach this carelessly. Do not just read a book and try to do it. We do not say that books should not be read, but this is not a game. You can objectify the experience by channeling through writing, and that is the primary way we worked with Philip in the beginning. By doing this, you are not opening your energies in a passive state but in an active state. You are engaged in writing what you feel, hear, see, and think as we overshadow you and inspire your written words. I have done that through Philip; but when I speak directly through him, I actually take over his vocal cords as I am doing right now.

Read what you are drawn to read. If you want to channel, then sit with a good teacher to become grounded. When I say good, I mean one who has a record, not just in writing a book, but a record with other students. I would suggest you ask the teacher for references. What other students have you worked with? May I talk to them? Ask these questions because, you see, you are asking for a change in your life. Once you enter into this experience, you cannot be the same. Because you are seeking to combine your energies with our energies, it is necessary to have the highest spirit world that you can have with you. It is important to know what makes that possible.

What makes for a high spiritual life? What makes for a high frequency in the human energy field or in the human heart? Ask this important question: Who am I, and why do I want to do this? Is it because I want to flatter myself? Is it because I want to impress others? Is it because I want to be used to help other people? A great deal depends upon your motive. There is nothing wrong with channeling by writing in your journal or diary in order to help yourself. That is an opportunity for us to give answers to questions as spirit guides overshadow you. Indeed, as I have said, it is a very good beginning.

The greatest harm that comes to individuals through these experiences is mental disturbance or confusion. If you are afraid of having done wrong or of being invaded or overshadowed in a negative way, you can help to bring this about through those fears. You attract to you what you are.

Anyone can do this work, at least to some extent. In the place from which I come, the purpose is to excel at going toward a higher and higher quality of understanding or truth. With each step, one should move closer and closer to God within and God in the universe.

Dr. D: *What is the process for channeling through writing? Could it include self hypnosis to take the person down to a level where they could channel in this way?*

SG: That might be the preferred approach if you are trying to go deep, but whenever you are focusing the mind you are already beginning to enter into a trance or hypnotic state. Much depends on the degree of your interest in what you are doing. If you are reading a good book and focusing upon it, you are not necessarily channeling, but you may be getting inspiration, some of which is from your own mind and some of which is from us. A book can be so engaging that things can go on around you and you will not even notice. The television can be on, the children can be yelling, a car can go by, but it does not register except in the subconscious mind. It is not necessary to be in a complete hypnotic state or even to use hypnosis, though you may.

In the journaling state you are already sitting there, focused. You have a topic in mind, or spirit places one in your mind, and you write on it. The energy that flows out of your own mind, especially in the case of inspired writing, is often guided by us as it flows through you. Poetry, fiction, nonfiction, all of these, can be called channeled material. If it is not from your mind, it is from the mind of someone in the spirit world who impresses you.

Journaling is a good beginning. It is concrete, and you can see progression if you apply yourself. When we first began working with him, Philip wrote once a week for two hours on Sunday mornings.

I was there, and we wrote a book together that helped to make the public aware of this work. It also enhanced Philip's appreciation of this whole process of mediumship and channeling.

Dr. D: *Is it necessary or advantageous to call in the guides, masters, and angels when someone conducts hypnosis or does self hypnosis or channeling?*

SG: Before they begin such an experience, most people pray. Prayer is the gesture that draws us toward you, depending upon what you pray for. If you are a target of God's efforts to expand you, then automatically we will be there whether you ask for us or not. When you ask for us, the rapport is enhanced. It is deepened and broadened so we can enter in more fully.

Each person's guides and teachers are there from birth. It is not as if you are ever truly alone. You are being constantly ushered down your spiritual path toward the next goal, the next goal, and the next goal. It is the nature of love to want to make oneness with another individual, and that affects us as souls in spirit. Love makes us want to find rapport with individuals and aid them as best we can. Most of all, we want to help them help themselves.

I am going to leave Philip now. This has been a meaningful and engaging time, a very deep experience. I appreciate the fact that Milton Erickson came today and could impart information that will greatly enhance your book and benefit those who read it. That is the most important thing. God bless you. This is Saint Germain.

End of session.

KWAN YIN

Kwan Yin is venerated in Buddhist Chinese legend as the goddess of mercy, and many see her as the Eastern counterpart of Mother Mary. In one of the older stories about her, Kwan Yin was the youngest daughter of a king who wanted her to marry someone who could advance his own wealth and power. Instead, Kwan Yin became a nun, hoping to alleviate the suffering of others, but the king influenced the convent to make her life very difficult so she would agree to the marriage. When the king became seriously ill, he was told he could be cured only by medicine made from the eye and arm of one without anger. When Kwan Yin heard this, she gladly gave her arms and eyes to heal her father and was reunited with her family.

CONVERSATION THREE

Kwan Yin

. . . use all of your energy to make the best of life. That is why you are here. Those who have grasped the understanding of this truth are the ones who are elevated in the spirit world. There is no magic. There is no mystery. It is like turning the light on inside the darkened room. When you take your suffering and use that as a stepping stone toward higher understanding, then you turn on the light in yourself, and it can never be put out.

—*Kwan Yin*

KY: I am here. I did not need Philip to be more relaxed, because I began to establish my rapport with him earlier this morning. Over the last few days I have been visiting him. This is not a small occasion for me.

There are many who sit at my feet and look up to me, but very few understand me. There are countless statues of me around the world. Few understand that I am not a statue! I am alive. I do not always sit in a meditative state, and I am very busy if I want to be. I do not feel the weight of the world on my shoulders as some may think, though I do hear and feel the cry of individuals and the cry of people everywhere.

There is no pressure in my world to be or do anything except to be happy. If there is anything I would like to get across and drive home in this privileged opportunity to speak, it would be this: *Be happy.* The essence of God is joy, laughter, and love. Even my own people, meaning we Orientals, are sometimes too serious. We should take an example from the animal kingdom. There is a liveliness and playfulness about animals, even as they grow older. They are not self conscious and do not take themselves too seriously.

Stories abound surrounding me, but I am human, just like you. When I was on earth, I had to walk my single, solitary path. As many know, I was blinded in an effort to save my father. They put out my eyes in exchange for his life, and that is the basis for my being thought of as an elevated soul. Do not think I was untroubled by the act in which my sight was removed from me. I went through months of depression. How could I not? I loved my father beyond measure. I came into the earth plane with that quality, and I still carry it. Still, as a human being, I had to go through my own experience, my own dark night of the soul, that period of time when I was lost in fear, nothing made sense, and I did not know where to turn. My inner awareness of my own spirituality, coupled with some of the ethics and mores of my time, steered me in the direction of caring for others as I cared for my father.

I would do a great disservice to humanity to allow myths surrounding me to be perpetuated when I have this chance to speak.

I want you to know I am as human as you are. I have longed to say this for many years, but this is my first opportunity. I am not saying this to bring your idea of me down, but to draw you closer to me. I would not lessen your appreciation of me as one who can help you, any one of you, but I would also draw your attention to your own divinity.

You do not have to suffer as I did in order to know God is real—as love, as light, as healing power, as the force behind all forces—and God is dwelling in you. This realization is the source of peace and happiness. It is not discovered through intellectual knowledge but through experience. You may not be happy now, and there may be things happening in your life that rob you of your aliveness of spirit, but you are not going to help yourself by dwelling on those things or reliving your sadness.

Begin to act as if you are happy. If you need to, put on the costume of the clown of happiness and begin to laugh even when you do not feel like it. Smile. Lift your head up and smile at those who pass by, whether they smile or not. Be filled with that kind of energy. You will find that if you start acting as if you are happy, the happiness that you are, buried deep beneath your seriousness, will start emerging.

The energy that you are is drawn out of you by your actions, not just thinking and feeling. So *act* as if you are happy. If you desire, sit down before you start your day and meditate on being happy. See yourself laughing, smiling, and not taking life too seriously. Live out this reality. You will bring forth a nature that is already in you, but hidden.

This world can do things to you. I could have become a bitter person, but I chose not to do that. I chose virtue over vice and the positive over the negative. If that is what brought me to where I am today, to be able to speak to you and to stand as a representative of God, then it has all been worth it.

I greet all of those who know of me, who have their statues of me, who have experienced me, who turn to me. I am here for you as an elder sister. Whatever you would like to say to me, I am open, willing, and ready.

Dr. D: *Can you tell us why human beings go through what you called the dark night of the soul? All people seem to go through some form of this struggle. Is this for inner growth?*

KY: I can easily address that question. Where there is no resistance, there is no strengthening. Where there is no struggle, there is no deepening. With struggle, you ask the questions that would not be asked otherwise. Why am I struggling? What is it I am doing to draw this to me, those things that cause me to struggle? I am tired of struggling, so how can I overcome my struggles?

If these deeper questions of life were never asked, the inner recesses of your soul would never be touched. God is within. You are encased in a body that is attached to the earth plane in its need for oxygen, light, and foods that come from the earth. Some of you are attached to the animal meats you eat. For the real you, the eternal you, these things are secondary. The primary purpose for the eternal you is to awaken to your real self, to your own spirituality, to God within you.

By design, life is such that it will cause each of you, to varying degrees, to learn to go inside and ask questions that will enable you to awaken to God within. That is God's plan. The great souls among you are held up because of their virtues, because of how they confronted suffering and how they overcame. All of them had their share of confrontation and suffering. So it was for me, and so it is for you.

You will solve your problem of suffering when you start searching for why you are suffering. It is not accidental, and it is not all because of bad reasons. After all, the diamond has done nothing wrong by being uncut, by being in the rough. By polishing the stone and cutting its many facets, the potential within is released, and an ordinary, actually crude-looking piece of stone is turned into something of great beauty.

You came to the earth plane to be in a body and to get fully involved in your earth experience, but God would not have you stop there. He also seeks to bring out your great beauty; your eternal, majestic self. That is what this life is about. I happen to be one who did not understand what was happening to me, but I did ask the right questions. Life was a good teacher. I listened, I watched, I obeyed, I followed, I became.

Dr. D: *People often compare you to Mother Mary, as if you were the Mary of the Far East. Have you and Mother Mary met in the spirit world? What do you both think of the comparison?*

KY: From my point of view, it is a good question. I do not know how Mary feels. She is not here at this moment, though she knew of my coming here today. How could I not know her? Those who have attained the higher levels of spirituality all meet in convocation.

I am not only appreciated in the Oriental world, I have come to be appreciated in the Western world. Why? It is because I am a universal master. We are all one family, and the differences in colors, languages, foods, customs, culture, or the slant of the eye have nothing to do with mastery. I have risen above my connection to a particular region of the earth, and I seek to dwell in the region of the hearts of all people. This is also true for Mary, beloved Jesus, and all who understand what life is truly about.

As I said, Mary and I have met in convocation, and we have also come together at the calling of our names and the burning of candles before our statues. We do not think upon it, though I do not say that to make light of people's needs or their worship. Mary and I both feel that many of you do not understand us, and this is by virtue of the fact that you do not understand yourselves. We are honored by the fact that you look up to us as elders and that we can set an example, but we would want each of you to awaken to the fact that God is as much in you as in us.

We want you to awaken to your own inner greatness and beauty and learn to worship it in the sense of appreciating and utilizing it to the best advantage for self and the world. We have done that inadvertently. God in his great wisdom has been orchestrating what we have been doing for all these years. In the end, neither of us takes credit. Instead, we give credit to the God force of love and wisdom that abounds in all human beings and throughout creation.

Mary would say, as I am saying, that we are honored to serve. As human beings, yes, each of us has a mother's heart. In that way we are similar. Because we minister to people from different cultures, we have had to adapt to appreciate the differences in thinking and approaches to spirituality in the two hemispheres. People associate us in their minds because of our common trait, a mother's heart.

Dr. D: *People call upon you in prayer to help them. Would you please share your thinking about this?*

KY: Yes, I will. It is important for people to know we accept the heart that is offered up in honor of us; but what the earth needs now is to come out of these times to a higher level and to be closer to the greater truth of things. It is okay to burn candles before statues of saints or other individuals. In that way, you have our allegiance, and we come in great numbers to help. So many of your problems would be solved, and your worship of us would be unnecessary, if you understood that you obtain what you need in this life through your own realization of God within. God is within you as a center of divine wisdom, divine love, and the power to do all things.

The more you attune yourself to this reality, this vibration, the magnificent energy of God's presence within, the more you will become a master. That is who we are to varying degrees. We know the truth and have no need to look up to someone else. We look within ourselves and look up to God within us. We know our center of worship is within ourselves. Our worship is to recognize the innate God presence in each of us and to know there are no exceptions to this fact.

The more you know yourself and worship God within you as the living temple, the closer you come to the kind of freedom, happiness and peace you are yearning for.

Dr. D: *Could you expand on who or what God is to you?*

KY: I will begin with where God is. I like the idea that you look up to me because you find God within me. I know this may be a stimulus for you to find God within yourself, because I am not different from you. The essence of God and of human nature is love. The fact that you reach out to others and others reach out to you demonstrates the need to love and be loved. God is love, and God is the limitless creation. God exists both as the material creation and as the energy that is provided for material things to exist or to be. This is God.

This entire universe, in its endless and ever-expanding reality, simply reflects to human beings, as they become wiser, that they have unlimited potential to expand. They have unlimited potential to broaden love, to encompass all people, and to incorporate, through life experience, the great wisdom that God *is*. One can apply this understanding and this knowing to all of life.

It is true to say God is everything, but it is truer to say God is love and that he loves you as himself. Where God is present with the holy person, one can feel it. There is an element of solemnity, a great indescribable beauty, and the manifestation of an unchanging inner peace. One knows God is here, now, and God can be known by one's waking up to this fact through one's own experience.

Dr. D: *Many people look up to Buddha, Confucius, Lao Tzu, and other masters of the Far East. Do you as masters ever gather? If so, what do you talk about, and what do you do?*

KY: This question has been partially answered by what I said regarding Mary and myself. Yes, we do get together. On the earth, those who are leaders and those who are responsible, whether it be in your city, state, or at a larger level, gather at times because of a desire to be stronger together and to work together. Not everything can be done by one person. A true leader encourages people around him or her to assume greater individual responsibility. So it is with us in the spirit world.

We all feel responsible because we were born that way, and because responsibility is something that dawns upon us when so many people turn to us for help. We cannot help feeling responsible. I have shed many tears for others, mostly because they are suffering needlessly in their ignorance. As many have said, it is not what happens to us, but how we respond that matters. Sometimes people respond in a way that increases and expands their suffering. But their suffering could be relieved if they could redirect that energy toward a higher purpose.

We get together regularly because the earth and its people are being guided systematically by us. Nothing happens that we are not aware of. We can see far in advance what is coming. We know the will of God regarding what you have to go through to cleanse this earth. We get together for those purposes also. We pray and send out our mental energy together. We vibrate together in one accord during these gatherings in order to protect and raise the energy of the earth.

Dr. D: *What do you think about the work we are doing to put this information from the great masters into a book for others to read?*

KY: You have no choice but to do it, not because it is a command that has come upon the two of you, but because the wave of God's love for humanity is manifesting in a singular way for those prepared to receive it. More and more people are aware of the spirit world, but they have yet to interact with us at such a level and to such a degree that they become elevated. Once you *can* interact with us at this level and to this degree, you will be able to better your lot, utilize the union of spirit and earth for the common good of man's elevation, and grow closer and closer to your real self and to God within.

This is a good time to say one of the things I wanted to say: Many do not know about our presence in their lives, and with good reason, because they are centered upon the materiality of this world. It is also true that we are not easily detected by most people. Right now, in this room, there are currents of air moving, comprised of molecules and atoms. Are you aware of any of this? No, because the movement is so subtle that it is impossible through the human senses to be aware. If a breeze begins to blow, then you can feel the movement of molecules and atoms in the atmosphere.

So subtle is our presence that I came into this room silently to your earthly ears and stood here as you and Philip spoke. I could hear the sound of my spiritual gown as the rustling or movement of spiritual cloth, but you could not hear it. That is how subtle spirit is, and why we go undetected. This is also why we can move peacefully among you and work without having to become involved by getting caught up in your lives.

To worship any of us is like worshiping your neighbor. You can do that. You can honor God within your neighbors. You can go next door and burn candles in front of their door. When they come out, you can bow to them. It is all appropriate. In the Orient, we bow to each other for that reason, recognizing God within each person. True worship, however, is to love others as you love yourself. This does not mean to give platitudes or speak sweet words, but to take action to help others in any way you can to meet their needs. For some, this may mean simply giving a warm hello. For others, this may mean helping with one of their children who is ill or making phone calls for them.

To worship is an act of movement. Rather than to worship me, Buddha, or Jesus, look up to us as examples to emulate, but go out and serve the world as we did. Go out and take care of the hungry and the poor. Go out. Be active in making this a better physical world. Therein lies the source of spiritual elevation and unending peace.

I wanted to say these things because they are paramount in my heart. I serve those in the Orient primarily, and as I look upon my own people, so many are crying out. So many are lonely, so many are filled with fear, and so many have little or no provisions for food or shelter. Let those of you who have all you need help those of you who do not. My message is as old as the earth, but it is what I would pass on to have you do the right thing, the thing of virtue and value.

Dr. D: *Are there misconceptions people have about you that you would like to correct?*

KY: There are those who think they know me who may be taken aback by my words. They may think I would not say this or that, but they only have their stories and myths about me. If there is anything I want to make clear during this time that I am with you, it is that I am as human as you are. I rose up from where I was by virtue of overcoming my suffering with positive action, putting it behind me, and utilizing it as a gift.

When you are blind, you may not see all the colors of the world, all the movement of people, and all the beauty of the earth, but your ears and your heart become sensitized to the point that you almost do not need eyes. Inflections in the voice tell you what the person looks like. You can sense whether they have an angelic or beastly quality, or one of all shades in between. You can tell whether it is a sunny day by the warmth of the sun on your skin or whether it is raining by the moisture in the air. You can hear the subtle sounds that you cannot hear when your eyes are overshadowing your ears, and you are seeing more than you are hearing.

In the end, I did not suffer. I found that life was great and that I had gifts beyond the average person. I discovered this because I had to be innovative to make it in the world. Take your own life, whatever it is you are suffering from, whatever needs you have, and do as I did.

You will honor me most if you honor yourself most. You will make me happiest if you will make yourself happiest. You can do this by taking all that you are, both the good and the bad, with your strengths and weaknesses, and use all of your energy to make the best of life. That is why you are here. Those who have grasped the understanding of this truth are the ones who are elevated in the spirit world. There is no magic. There is no mystery. It is like turning the light on inside the darkened room. When you take your suffering and use that as a stepping stone toward higher understanding, then you turn on the light in yourself, and it can never be put out.

Dr. D: *We have thought the information in this book may inspire and educate those who are interested in the fields of channeling or hypnosis. Do you have information that would further benefit people with such interests?*

KY: There are people in whom the truth exists who will read this book. Because of that, they will recognize the truth in this book. We masters will amplify the contents of this book in that we will be drawn to those who are in earnest when they read it. We will help them to expand their earnestness and their appreciation of the words. We will cause them to look up to a higher place. We will help them to find their higher selves and learn anew to live within the light of self, in the presence of God within. We will assist them to rise above this earth as they are intended to do, reflecting the purpose for which they came to earth.

There are people waiting for this book. Will it be the salvation of this world? No. There are many books to read; but this one is a cornerstone laid in a foundation for other things to come on the earth to expand humanity's awareness of these truths. Go forth with courage and know the hand of God is upon your work. Call upon us anytime. We are here for one purpose and that is to serve.

Dr. D: *Is there any other information you would like to share at this time?*

KY: I think I have covered everything I personally wanted to cover. I do not have anything to add except to express my gratitude that you have set aside this time and provided this environment, and that each of you has the training needed for this task. I thank you for making it possible for me to be here and serve Mother Earth and its inhabitants in this way.

This is Kwan Yin. God bless you.

Dr. D: *God bless you and thank you.*

End of session.

Comments:

PB: I was in a cosmic, universal place after she left.

Dr. D: *When we first started, after you did the initial prayer, I said to you, "She is here." I felt as though she wanted to come through right away.*

PB: She would have, but I felt we should continue with our practice of doing the hypnosis to create more energy.

Dr. D: *I took you down rapidly, in a very brief span of time. Before I even had you down as far as I wanted, Kwan Yin just said, "I am here." She comes with a very serene, loving, healing energy.*

BUDDHA

Buddha is thought to have lived circa 500 to 400 BC. He was born Prince Siddhartha in modern day Nepal, with Gautama as his family name. He married early and had a son, expecting to follow his father as king. But his travels caused him to observe old age, illness, and death, and he left his family to search for a way to alleviate human suffering.

After listening to many teachers and following various practices, Siddhartha became determined to sit under the Bodhi tree until he learned the truth. He experienced enlightenment at the age of thirty-five and became the Buddha. He discovered that neither self-indulgence nor self-deprivation was the answer and began to teach the Middle Way. His Buddhist principles drew many students, and today Buddhism is one of the world's most influential teachings.

CONVERSATION FOUR

Buddha

Your goal is to arrive at divine love—all pervasive, never ending, compassionate, understanding, and unconditional love. Most of you do not have this kind of love for yourselves. In your own mind, you sometimes speak cruelly to yourselves, criticizing and finding fault. Thus you bring yourselves down from your highest of states. You keep negativity alive because you fail to realize by experience that you are light.

—Buddha

B: I am here. I radiate a golden light that signifies my presence, and I bring with me a host of spiritual beings who celebrate my re-entrance into human flesh through this medium. Whatever beliefs, ideas, or concepts you may have about me, I come this hour as my own unique self. I do not come to project glory, but as a human being who walked the earth as you do; one who sought the source of my soul and how to realize that source. We are all but waves upon the mighty ocean of God's love, individual manifestations of God's radiant light and all-encompassing love.

There is truth to the story of my moment of enlightenment under the Bodhi tree, but it did not happen exactly as it has been written. The words I used to explain my experience have been changed in part, as happens to most teachings over time. I never sought to create a universal religion, but simply sought the source of my life. People asked me questions and found meaning in my words both when I was young and as I grew older. Some wrote down my words and others memorized them, and so my words became a teaching.

All awakening is within. It is a process, though there can come a moment of greatest illumination in which you understand life, including its source, its purpose, and its outcome, in a flash of insight. I did have such a moment, but it was part of a progressive realization. When you turn the light on in a room, you first notice the light. With full illumination you begin to notice all the other things in the room; and as you wander about a well-lit house, you can see all of it. In the bright light of the day, you can also see the house from the outside. My illumination was progressive in that way, first seeing one segment and then another. Were I to teach today, I might use a different vocabulary to explain where we come from, why we are here, and where we are going.

I am grateful for the opportunity to walk through this passageway of mediumship. This setting is advantageous because of the environment you have prepared and the intelligence you lend by contributing your subjective and objective observations. They will help readers to gain perspective about their own situation and experience. As they step back to look at everything, they will be able to go deeper and higher within themselves.

To search outside for illumination is to look in the wrong direction. Within the self, at the center of life, in that kernel of truth, in that pinpoint of light, is all illumination. It is within your own inner perception that all the answers for *your* life exist. Understanding of your individual existence, its source, and its beginning, is inside. Within the pinpoint of light that burst forth in my own consciousness, I saw life as it is, life as it could be, and life that I wanted more than anything from that time forward.

I was burdened by suffering because I was a very open person who deeply felt the suffering of others. I sought to understand the origins of suffering and felt driven to eliminate my own suffering and that of humanity. This was the impetus behind my efforts to help people and to teach and share what I learned. As I said, I never thought I would become the founder of a religion, but the tradition of teacher and student was already present when I came into the world. In this tradition, students show obedience by sitting at the feet of their teacher, so it followed naturally that I would be honored as a source of truth.

I never had an eye toward establishing any kind of religion because I knew then, as many of you know now, that love is the true religion. I could see there would be a better world if people cared for all beings everywhere, human beings and animals alike, and treated them with kindness and love as anyone would want to be treated. The so-called

Buddha nature that came into existence was one of wishing well and dispersing care and love to all of God's creation, including self.

I have made my entrance here today through Philip, and I thank you for making this doorway possible. Now, if you would like to ask me questions, please feel free to ask Buddha.

Dr. D: *Thank you. Many followers of Buddha do not believe in God, yet you have referred to God by name. Can you explain?*

B: Because of the process I went through, I sought to teach individual initiative, individual responsibility, and the Buddha nature, meaning to care for all beings with compassion and kindness. These teachings do not refer to a Creator, but they infer that the source of life is love. What are kindness and caring for others but attributes of love? In this way I indirectly taught of a source, though I did not label it so. I could see within myself the illumination that I spoke of earlier, and I knew this light was in every person. Rather than to transfer responsibility to a higher source outside of self, I sought to enable all of us to look within and receive understanding from the source within.

Consider the ear. When sound waves pass through the human ear and register as vibrations within the sensing mechanisms in a person's brain, hearing occurs. In the same way, truth is understood from within. You may search for truth through books, in sermons, or in talks given by wise individuals, but truth registers as truth only within self. It is within yourself that you come to say, "Yes, this is truth." You recognize truth within the seat of your own intelligence, derived from the presence of God within yourself.

Within the instrumentality of self, through what you on earth call your heart, you know when someone loves you. There is a registering mechanism that exists within the organism of each person. The energy of love comes through the auric field into the heart center or heart chakra. For this love to have direction and meaning, it must also be understood by the mind.

All is within. I knew this when I was on earth, and I have come to know it more fully with the passage of time. While I have gained higher understanding, what I thought then, I essentially think and know now. I did not intend to eliminate or deny God, but to enable people to go within and find what I found within myself.

In the teachings of Christianity and other religions, it may be said the source is God. We in the spirit world know there is a source, a singular source, by which all truth is dispensed and from which all truth comes. We know the foundation of that source is love, and we feel it intimately. The inner illumination I sought to teach is a manifestation of that love.

Dr. D: *If you could speak to the millions who embrace Buddhism, what would you say?*

B: Much of what I have already said today could help to move followers of Buddha into a less abstract existence. There is a tendency for some, though not all, to be too passive. I would not eliminate the practice of meditation or inner searching to find peace within, but you are in the physical world where change is possible; and while it is beautiful to wish happiness for all beings everywhere, it is through your daily actions you can help to change the world.

I would still teach people to take individual responsibility and to not worship *me*. The many statues of me that are placed around the world help individuals to solidify the idea of a higher being, so I would not remove those images. But I would caution people to find Buddha within; to find God within. The Buddha whom people finally imagined is superhuman, and I am not that; I am one of you. As you aspire toward the ideal, know that you are aspiring not toward Buddha, but the Buddha nature, which is the nature of God.

God is the one who is all encompassing, who wishes good for *all* beings everywhere and whose love is all pervasive, limitless, heavenly, and unconditional. When you look at me, Jesus, Mohammed, or any of the so-called masters, we are but symbols or archetypes of hope to inspire you to *become*. In the end, form fades, and the true student who searches for higher and higher truth will find what I found: illumination within, divine love within, and therefore God within.

Dr. D: *Do you have any advice or comments about this hypnosis/channeling experiment?*

B: I am more than pleased and happy with what you are doing. It is the right thing to do and in keeping with the whole movement on your earth plane toward finding God within. As you can well imagine, sense, and ultimately know, it is not within your province alone to have thought of this or to have made it happen. It is the willing spirit of God, mobilized by our presence, which motivated you to think of carrying out this esteemed activity: *channeling married to hypnosis.*

Because I am a benefactor of your work, I appreciate the way you have opened the door for us. You may have the idea that we are fully awakened and extremely astute. No, we know what we know, and we are learning too. The only way we would feel comfortable being called masters is to say that yes, we have mastered this and this, but we would master more things throughout eternity. We do not say that we have arrived, because we know there are realms upon realms of learning, and there is higher and higher truth. Even when one goes into the highest stages of contemplation in the spirit world, there are dimensions that transcend still higher, the highest of which is the love of God.

We appreciate the opportunity to come back to the earth plane in this way and convey our humanness, our reality. We are not comfortable with pretending, so we are contented to come before you as we are. Some of you will be disappointed that we are not more aloof and that we do not speak in grander language. But think of it; does grander language or being more aloof make one spiritually more evolved? Not at all. What makes anyone spiritually more evolved is to attain higher and higher degrees of love, by which we can love more people as we love ourselves. That is who God is, and there are no exceptions to God's love. *None.*

It brings tears to my eyes to speak in this way because, dearest ones, it is not your goal to read more and more books or to spend hours away from the world in meditation. All of those things are good and well, and they help you to progress; but your goal is to arrive at divine love—all pervasive, never ending, compassionate, understanding, and unconditional. Most of you do not have this kind of love for yourselves. In your own mind, you sometimes speak cruelly to yourselves, criticizing and finding fault. Thus you bring yourselves down from your highest of states. You keep negativity alive because you fail to realize by experience that you are light.

You are simply manifesting on the earth plane in a chosen character to play a role, and at the center of this manifestation is divine intelligence. Once you realize that, you no longer need to continue to manifest your presence here on earth. Your opportunity to play out this character called *you*, by whatever name you are called, is transitory. It is a chance to awaken to higher and higher levels of self. When you see all people as yourself, and you treat every person—stranger or friend—with compassion, tenderness, kindness, care, and love, you have reached the Buddha state, the Christ state, the God state.

I did not come down from the mountaintop only to be with you. I am concerned about *all* the people who call upon me. I am particularly active with those who are most sincere in searching for God within. Even so, I do not bring the illumination; *you* do. It is a dynamic within you, resulting from earnestness and a singular drive toward human freedom. It is found only in God within you.

Dr. D: *When you were on earth, you left your wife and son to seek the path of enlightenment. In light of what you know now, do you have any regrets about this?*

B: Well, dear friends, we all exist on different levels, in different dimensions. That was my earthly dimension. As a human being, of course I have had regret, because my relationship with my wife was the seat of love for me. My wife became resentful toward me, and as a human being, she was correct in her feeling. My son later understood. We were all just playing roles on the stage of life. I better understood my inner voice some time after my moment of enlightenment, and even more after I came to the spirit world. But if I had not listened to my inner voice and followed it while I was on earth, my name would not have become associated with peace or with the kind of receptivity that is filled with compassion and love for all beings.

True, some things in my teachings have been distorted or omitted; but after my passing, they have remained influential and have had a monumental effect upon the consciousness of millions of people. Even though there are things within my teachings that I would change, they have given individuals an opportunity to come to the awareness of true self, real self. Today, my wife knows that. We can converse and smile, and we love each other very deeply. My experience is not so different from that of many who were called out for a special work, including Jesus, the Christ.

You are *all* called out for a special work to carry out your mission, and sometimes that takes you away from others, even if only into the meditation room where you isolate yourself for an hour or more. Some of you meditate overnight, many nights a week. Neither you nor I can cause or enable another to awaken. It is the individual's path, and it is the right of the individual to walk that path, even to be misunderstood. From the viewpoint of the earthly plane, yes, I have had regret, but not in terms of my universal mission, and that is what I came into the world to realize. I followed my path, not perfectly, but to the best of my ability, and my teaching helped more than it hindered humanity.

Dr. D: *You mentioned that there are changes you would make in your teachings. Can you tell us more about that?*

B: I have already referred to the fact that there is a tendency among those who follow Buddhism to be passive in situations where they could be more active. For example, if one experiences truly righteous indignation, I would not act out of hate, but I would act. I would not be tolerant of anything and everything. The human body receives food in a passive way. Your mouth, your esophagus, stomach, and all the organs are waiting passively, receptive to the food that comes to them; but your body revolts against those things that are not compatible with it. In the case of disease or foods that do not agree with you, your body seeks to get rid of those things as swiftly as possible. In the case of poison, for example, the body reacts strongly.

While we favor love, compassion, and care for all beings including self, there are times when it is correct to be upset, to take a stand and oppose those currents, situations, or human beings who disrupt peace. As to this, I would not change my teachings entirely, but I would augment them as I am doing now. I am not advocating that anyone should be caught up in irrational rage or anger or strike another person out of such negative motives. Do not be carried away by negative energy, but do not be a doormat in every kind of negative situation that crosses your path. It is all right to assert yourself against what is wrong, within certain parameters.

Soon after my experience of awakening, I began to teach the path of the Middle Way—a balanced approach to living, rather than the practice of extreme self-indulgence or self-denial. But this ideal is not always realistic in a world where others know nothing of it or know of it but do not practice it. Even if everyone tried to live this way, differences of opinion would lead to sometimes conflicting ways of thinking and doing. Tolerance of difference is definitely needed in a world of diverse beliefs and practices, but not to the extent that it allows the level of destruction, for example, that could have taken place if no one stood against it during the last World War.

I am sure readers will understand clearly what I am saying. Again, I do not advocate violence; but I do not, today, advocate passivity when destructive force rears its head in the world. As the light that you are comes forth, what is important is that you know in your growing intelligence and self-mastery what to do when, and you are not afraid to speak up for your rights as a human being. It all starts with right understanding. That wisdom will give you the ability to discern when to act and when to be passive.

Dr. D: *Can you describe what you are doing in the spirit world?*

B: What *don't* I do? *(Laughter)* There are many Buddhists here, so I move among them and seek to enlighten them. I try to help them to see the reality that God is within them, and they need not have someone outside of them to be an authority over them. Indeed, that can hold people back.

I also participate in universal conferences with many esteemed colleagues in the spirit world. They are really friends, but they hold positions because of their missions on earth. We converse on a regular basis and gather to send emanations to the earth plane; to envelop it in the energy of divine love. We are instruments of divine love and peace, and we are able to channel that love. When we focus on that point of God's presence within, the energy emanates out to everything, including your earth. In convocation we do that for days and weeks, in earthly time, especially when there are disruptions of the most destructive kind on the earth.

Being lords of karma, and understanding the human suffering it has caused, we also know when to give and when to withhold this protection. It is all coordinated by divine understanding within. Even without words, we know what to do and what not to do.

Like everyone, I have my personal life, though not often. On earth I spent much time in nature, as many readers know, and I still enjoy that. I love to garden. There are different animals within my space such as deer, which I particularly love. They are great symbols of perfection, beauty, gentleness, and kindness; yet they are frisky, both as babies and as they get older. They leap and bound around. To me they represent divine spirit. I travel when I can, because in doing so I learn more about God and myself from the people I meet and the things that I see and experience.

The source of life is in the spirit world, and all things began here. As individuals in the spirit world are inclined to do, I partake of all that is here as fully as possible. I celebrate the gift of this world of spirit—the gift of life.

Dr. D: *Is there anything I have not asked that you would like to share?*

B: Of course, as one given this opportunity, I would like to stay, to bask in the energy that is provided through this setting, but I think I have said everything I want to say at this time. I do not want to over-extend my stay with you, and I am given understanding as to what is and is not appropriate to say.

To all those who would read and follow my words, I bow low to you for your effort to become all you can become in this lifetime. I would encourage you to transcend image and seek essence in order to find God within. You will find God in all the great masters because God is their central concern. God is the central message they would pass on to all of those who would do things in their names.

This is Buddha. May all beings everywhere be happy.

End of session.

Comment:

Dr. D: *When Buddha began speaking, the energy in the room became serene, peaceful, and filled with love. I wanted to go into a deep meditative* state; into the blissfulness of the energy surrounding me. This lasted during the entire session. Philip's body never moved or flinched. His mouth was his sole movement the entire time.

Prior to the session, Philip and I prepared questions for the channeling of two masters. After Buddha left, I asked the next master to come in. The energy in the room immediately changed. It was powerful, yet calm, and did not affect me in the same way as the energy of Buddha had. Philip's words flowed more rapidly, and his head moved from time to time as spirit spoke through him.

ARCHANGEL MICHAEL

Archangel Michael is often represented as holding a sword, emphasizing his role as protector. In the Bible, he came to the aid of the prophet Daniel (Daniel 10:13), contended with the devil for the body of Moses (Jude 1:9), and slew the dragon in a war in heaven (Revelations 12:7). Another prominent angel in the Bible is Gabriel, who appeared to Zechariah to tell him that his wife Elizabeth would have a son John (Luke 1:19) and announced to Mary that she would be the mother of Jesus (Luke 1:26). Many unnamed angels are associated with the roles of messengers of God and guardians of human beings. They frequently appear in various religious traditions and in contemporary spiritual writings.

CONVERSATION FIVE

Archangel Michael

This world is more magnificent than you or most people can perceive. When you are in love with God, and when God is at the core of why you exist, then you can see this world as God does. The world is magnificent not just in its outer beauty, but in the opportunity to awaken, to grow, to become—to discover God in this lifetime.

—*Archangel Michael*

AM: I am here. This is Archangel Michael. We had to wait for Philip's guides and others to adjust his vibration. It was beyond our ability to touch in with him until they slowed the rate of movement of the electrical force inside his body. The crystal he is holding is working well this morning, and that helped with the adjustment. I am standing outside of Philip, funneling information through a little differently than I would if I were human. It is not necessary for me to make changes in Philip's voice, because what you are looking for is the truth.

It is a great joy for me that you and Philip independently picked up my signal that I wished to speak today. We wanted to give you this experience to validate for you that all of this is happening in divine order.

I know you have prepared questions, and I am here to answer them. I want to add certain things to your book for the sake of those who read it.

Dr. D: *What is the information you want to give us?*

AM: I want you to understand that I work with both of you, so you can relate to me on a personal level and feel protected. Philip often sees me when he is doing readings, especially for those who already know me and relate to me as an angelic force or guide in their lives. When Philip is working, I come in on the left side in front of him. Though I cannot explain all of this to you now, there are realities in the spirit world that cause us to conform in certain ways. There is a consistency in what we do because we are principled and work according to spiritual law.

You on earth often think of those in the spirit world with reverence, tending to be in awe of us, but that is not necessary. Those who are masters are masters of love. There are times when this love may appear to be cold, because justice must be exhibited, but we do not want anyone to be afraid of us. Everything we do is always for the higher good of an individual. If we allow suffering to come to someone, it is for a higher purpose. Going through self confrontation can be a purifying experience that helps you to see yourself as you are and know what attributes of your life you need to keep or discard. Because there are things in each of you that need to change, there are experiences you have to go through to learn certain lessons, and we guide you on your way.

We come to you individually only for the purpose of loving you so that you will love yourself. We come to help you to forgive yourself for your deficiencies and to understand that you are valuable to God. We come for the sole purpose of leading you on your path back to God, and we have no other desire.

There is much speculation and talk about angels in New Age literature, and we want to clarify certain things so human beings will have a more accurate understanding of the angelic world. We want you to know who we are, why we are here, and what we do.

Angels and spirit guides will fit into your existing belief system in order to lead you, because some things can be understood only after the mind has grown through life experiences. When telling little children about the procreative process, instead of giving all of the details, you say what is appropriate for each child's ability to understand. Similarly, when you on earth have a definite belief about something, we allow that belief to take you through various levels of realization until one day you are ready to understand more.

For example, some of you believe that people who die become angels, but that is incorrect. You may argue this point, and spirit will cooperate with the way you believe, but it is an error to think human beings become angels. The angelic world is a world of protection and love, and it is different from the human spirit world. Angels work closely with human beings, and each of you has two angels assigned to you from the time you are born. They are with you at all times, guiding and protecting you. They are hidden, unobtrusive, and quiet because that is the nature of angels. As they work with each one of you, they represent the quiet voice, the quiet force, of God.

Like best friends, angels parent you, passionately care about you, and watch over you. If it were not for the angelic world, many children would perish before they reached the age of two or three, in spite of all human effort. We are always there protecting, but it could lead to confusion if we were apparent to you. Our purpose is to guide and help without credit and without your even knowing we are there. Today, there are angels around this room, standing for righteousness, purity, and unconditional love. They are here to protect and guide while Philip is in this trance state.

Unlike human beings, angels do not take a physical body, though we can appear to have one. We can solidify before an individual, as happened when the angel Gabriel came to the Mother Mary. Such an appearance occurs according to principles relating to frequencies or vibrations. When frequencies reach a certain level, we can come in on that wave length. When your spiritual senses open up to a certain degree, at that moment we can appear to you in a dream or a vision.

Angels were created first, before the rest of the universe and before human beings, to assist God and to be extensions of the heart of God. We are spiritual beings in the angelic world, but we move in the human world. We have our place in the hierarchy close to God, based on vibration or frequency. We are in a vast, vast place of beauty, because our surroundings reflect who we are, our qualities of character, and our innate nature of beauty and love.

We do not really need a place to live in, such as a house, though we do have gathering places. Though it is hard to explain, you might think of us as gathering in a place like the countryside. Such things are unimportant to us because we know they are just reflections of the manifestation of the soul or spirit. I will not go into all of that now, but I do want to tell you that we were there from the beginning of creation.

Angels were created out of the energy of God, who gave birth to angels and human beings for different purposes. Angels are servants of God and human beings, and human beings are the children of God, higher and closer to God than angels are. An angel is like a nanny, housekeeper, or gardener who has lived in a home for many years and is loved by the parents and children. A nanny carries out the parents' direction or desire, but does not replace the parents. The servant can be like a member of the family, but the role is different. In a similar way, we are here to serve. Though we are servants, we are not subservient. We have dignity just as you do. This is not proud dignity, but based on our position with God. We are instruments or extensions of God for the purpose of bringing higher levels of love and truth to humanity.

We were born out of God as human beings were. Countless numbers of us were created by God, so there are hosts of angels. As individuals, we have individual roles, whether it is Gabriel or I or any of the angels in the hierarchy. Our different manifestations of beauty represent the quality of our character and the level of our responsibility. Many people see me with a sword. Do I always have a sword in my hand? No. It is a symbol; but it is also part of my vesture, among the things that represent who I am. I help to cut away falsehood and protect against lesser energies. I am a force for righteousness or goodness, and I stand directly against evil forces. My energy is of such a nature and magnitude that no one can pass within my energy field if I do not allow it.

When he was on earth, Jesus said he could call upon legions of angels. At any time, Jesus could have called on us to stave off the dreadful things that happened to him, including the persecution and trials that he went through. What does this mean? A human being has the power to call on us and use us as a force for goodness, individually and collectively. We exist for such purposes.

I know you want to know how old I am. As a projection of God, as an angelic being in this position, you might as well say I have lived forever according to your earthly understanding. I always was. How do we convey this? Do we use your definition of years? We do not think about these things. They are not important because, for us, there is no time. There is just being.

We are fortunate to be able to bring much information though this medium because he is an open channel.

Dr. D: *Can you explain more about the difference between the angelic world and the human world? Sometimes men or women do appear in spirit as angels.*

AM: The difference between angels and human beings is in the role and position of each. I have said angels were created as servants of God and human beings as children of God, direct heirs to God. In your language and thinking, the word *servant* denotes someone lesser in status, but that is not the case. It is just a different role. Does the mother do everything the father does and vice versa? No. Human beings do not do what angels do and angels do not do what human beings do. We have separate roles, but we work in harmony.

Before human beings were created, God and the angelic world together had only one focus as the rest of the universe came into existence, and that was man and woman. Before a baby is born, the nursery is prepared. The colors of the room and the baby clothes are selected and the bed, bathing table and other items are purchased and placed in the nursery. When parents are preparing the nursery, they have only one thing in mind, the baby. Like a mother and father expecting a baby, God was in great anticipation, but it was more than that. You cannot even begin to understand the force of God's love for you, individually and collectively. Our role was to help prepare the environment, the atmosphere, the cosmic nursery for human beings. That includes the stars, the moon, and the sun. We helped to bring it all into existence.

You asked why a human being may appear in spirit as an angel. As I said earlier, spirit will cooperate with the way you believe. If people believe strongly that human beings become angels in the spirit world, they may perceive them that way in spirit. Your guides and teachers will fit into your belief system in order to lead you. They will meet you where you are.

Even if human beings do appear in that form, however, they retain their human reality and do not become angels. From our perspective, the shape of the face, the body, the voice, the eyes, the hair, are all outer manifestations of inner reality. A person's appearance may be symbolic of that individual's purpose or character. When a human being appears to another as an angel, it may represent that individual's fundamental nature. It could mean that the one appearing is like a guardian or has exhibited unconditional love like those in the angelic world. It could be that the person serves, takes care of, and protects.

Everything in existence has a philosophical and spiritual basis in God. For example, the diamond is used in its physicality. It is the hardest gem there is, to the extent you can use it to cut other stones, even other diamonds. From a philosophical or spiritual point of view, the characteristics of a diamond can symbolize the highest, most beautiful truth. The highest truth can cut through any falsehood. Even the essence of God could be symbolized by the characteristics of a diamond: multifaceted, impenetrable, unchanging, most beautiful, something to be desired, and something of greatest value.

Dr. D: *You said we may call upon the angels. Is there a correct or incorrect way to do this?*

AM: With regard to how human beings treat angels, how angels treat human beings, and how we all treat each other, there should be respect and love at all times. Without respect there is no love, and the way to treat angels is to love them. By God's standard, the way to treat anyone is to love that individual.

To call on me you can just think my name, "Archangel Michael," and when such a call is wrapped in love, it is easier for me to respond. Isn't the same thing true for you? When a directive or request is given with love, it is always easier for us to unite with your vibration. It would be unbecoming to human beings for you to make demands of us, although there may be a desperate moment when you say, "Archangel Michael, please come! I need you now!" If you have a strong need for me and just say, "Michael!" I will respond. We see far in advance things that are coming, so we are already there. There is not really a need for you to do anything. We are there.

Dr. D: *You mentioned lower forces. What is a way for us to protect ourselves from lower forces or lower energies?*

AM: As I said, no one can get past me. I, Archangel Michael, have a force and quality of character such that I am all light, and darkness cannot penetrate where there is light. Low entities are afraid of this light and are pushed away by it. The energy around them is greatly affected, and they become very uncomfortable. My light creates a kind of dissonance around them, and they cannot be near it.

The base that you provide will determine what you draw to you, so our advice to you is this: Instead of being concerned about lower entities, think about the quality of your own character, and live in love for other people. When you love others and see them as yourself, you will not do anything to them that you would not want done to you. If you live this way, you provide the kind of energy field within and around you through which nothing lower can come. When two incompatible frequencies meet, there is a dissonance. In some instances, there is what you on earth would call a kind of squelching sound. That happens when the two forces repel each other.

In scripture, the phrase "Pray without ceasing" means to stay in love. Look at everything, *especially* self, through the eyes of love. Without becoming too philosophical, I can tell you that the source of all problems is separation from love. When an individual is overshadowed and filled by the love of God, that person feels reborn. That is why many Christians cry when they have a conversion experience. They have allowed in that moment, by whatever means, for the very presence of God to emanate from within them, and in that moment they are spiritually healed.

When you live in unconditional love, loving everyone, there is no need to be concerned about lower entities. Yes, they will come. They will tempt you and try to thwart your forward movement, but when your love is great, they cannot stay around. Instead of worrying about *them*, worry about *you*. In fact, don't worry at all! Rather, find the way to release God within you. Find the reality of God within you.

Because I am an angel, my role, outer form, and energy are different from yours, but the source is still God. It is all God. I know this better than you do because I have never taken an earthly body. I am pure energy, never touched by one speck of darkness. I am light itself because I am truth and love. When you feel me near you, I do not have to do or say anything; I am just there. If you are sensitive, you are overcome and moved to tears, to joy, to ecstasy. That is the nature of my energy.

I am not drawn to or interested in the material world. I do not represent anything but love, and I am interested only in taking care of you and all of God's children. I do not care about any of the myths or made-up stories about me or any of the angels. I care about one thing, and that is to love you to such an extent that you will find God. My goal is no different than that of Saint Germain, Jesus, Buddha, or any other enlightened being. It is to show you the path inside of yourself. This is not my direct responsibility, but I work in cooperation with the masters.

I handle the force of angels to surround and protect the earth plane with the force of goodness. Yes, my sword is real, and I often wear it at my side, though this image of me is a metaphor more than anything else. The beautiful turquoise jewelry you are wearing today, Dolores, is connected in the minds of many with Native Americans. On an inner plane it has a deeper meaning, because to Native Americans turquoise has a specific value. My sword, too, has value because of its deeper philosophical meaning. I am here to separate truth from falsehood, to protect humanity from ignorance, and to work to guarantee that there is no invasion of humanity by lower forces.

There have been those on earth who thought they were all-powerful. They exerted domination in their area and sought to do so in the world. They were allowed to do this for the greater purpose of teaching humanity right from wrong and demonstrating what works and what does not work. Ultimately, they were held back and brought down. They could only go to a certain level of destruction before they destroyed themselves, and this has happened to every one of them throughout human history. We stand against them and help to bring them down, not by might, but by right.

Dr. D: *Are you the projection of an image of the Archangel Michael or the real thing?*

AM: Am I the real thing? *(Laughter)* What do you think? Let me put it this way: The image of an announcer is broadcast from a television studio to millions of homes. Is the image you see on your television the same as the person who is in the studio being projected? To some, I am like the announcer in the television studio, and you are there in my presence. To others, I am the broadcast image that appears to you. Is there really any difference? No. The purpose is the same, so it doesn't matter whether or not I am literally with you. Believe me, when I send my image to protect you, it protects.

What you have to understand is that we are multidimensional, so I could personally and literally appear to every individual on the face of the earth. There is no limit to the number of dimensions I can enter into. Is this necessary? Not for practical purposes, because sometimes all a person needs is the image of me. It is the same for any leader of the angelic hierarchy or for Jesus, Buddha, Saint Germain, or any of the masters. It is the truth that matters. So yes, there are images, and there is "the real thing," but they are one and the same. They are both projections from the soul energy of the individual.

Today I am here in reality, not as an image or symbol. I personally came separately to you and Philip to say I wanted to speak next. When Philip asked you if you had thoughts about who should come in today, you said Archangel Michael might be the one. He told you that when he was driving over I came to him and said I would like to speak today. Why did this happen? It is because all of this is being orchestrated by God. I came to each of you in the way I did to validate that my coming through is no accident. I am here. I have come as I am, sent by God.

Philip told you that when he started this work of mediumship, an angel came to him in a dream, saying he was sent from God to tell him about his mission. I was that angel, though Philip did not recognize me at that time. It was not necessary for me to say, "Oh, hi, I'm Archangel Michael." We did not want to distract him from the message about his mission by telling him who I was. It was not important. We tell you such things when the time is right, just as you tell your children things when the time is right. Today the time is right.

I am here in reality, dear one. I am here in reality. Were the forces different, I would solidify and materialize in this room so you could see me, but your faith is such that we do not need to do that.

Dr. D: *What message would you like to give mankind?*

AM: God loves you. We come in service, in the name of love, to bring you to that reality within yourself. You are the temple of God. As many of the masters who have come through this gentleman will say, again and again, we seek to bring you to *yourself*, to an understanding of yourself. When you discover self, you will discover God. When you discover God, you will discover your eternal self. You on earth call it your higher self, but I would say it is your eternal self. This body is not your eternal self. The body caused you to be different than you really are at the center of self. Some of you have been so separated from that center that you have not even known about it.

A man who is unaware of a great inheritance from a distant relative may go about living life as usual, working at a job, or even living in poverty while his inheritance sits in a bank. If he only knew there is a treasure waiting for him! Once he understands he has this inheritance and receives it, his whole life is transformed. Once you know you are from God, that you and God are one and the same, you will perceive your inheritance of being a direct descendant of God, a part of God. You will know there is no separation, and you will never be the same.

Dr. D: *Do you have any advice for readers of this book?*

AM: Believe, and this will lead you to the truth. When we say "believe," we know you cannot see what you do not see, but hold promise in your mind. That which you believe, if it is authentic, will appear. If God is real, and you believe in God, eventually you will have an experience that will cause you not to just believe, but to know. So believe. Keep believing.

There is enough historical or testimonial information worldwide about Jesus and other great beings in the human or angelic world, for you to believe there is truth to our existence. Believe that, and your own experience will lead you to the validation of our existence. My words today should bring comfort as well as clarity.

This world is more magnificent than you or most people can perceive. When you are in love with God, and when God is at the core of why you are, then you can see this world as God does. The world is magnificent not just in its outer beauty, but in the opportunity to awaken, to grow, to become—to discover God in this lifetime.

Dr. D: *Is there any other information you would like to bring?*

AM: It would be impossible for this book to represent all of the truth. No book in the world is big enough to do that. It is to represent the theme you are focused on, which is how hypnosis and channeling can be used to help human beings go to higher levels of understanding, including a greater awareness of God within. All people will not become channels for public purposes, but they can use hypnosis and meditation to go more deeply into themselves. They can use it to bypass the physicality of self and reach a place within where they will discover many wonderful, higher things.

This book will demonstrate to readers that channeling exists. It will show how hypnosis can help to modify the individual to such an extent and in such a way that we can step through the energies and make our presence known.

Dr. D: *Thank you for bringing such wonderful calmness to this room.*

AM: You would not detect that if you did not also have it within you.

I do want to clarify things so the reader will understand. There is much fear regarding God and the protective nature of the angelic world. Sometimes we angels are portrayed as fierce fighters, but we laugh at this. If you have divine love in your being, you do not have to fight or do anything else. You can just be. I am sure you understand what I am saying.

For all of those who celebrate the angelic world, we are there for you. That is our sole reason for existence. Our motivation is always to love you as we would want to be loved. This is Archangel Michael.

End of session.

Comment:

Dr. D: *As I was preparing for this session, Archangel Michael came into my thoughts. Was he to speak next? As it turned out, Philip and I postponed getting together until the following day, with no discussion of who was to speak. When Philip arrived the next morning, he said Archangel Michael had spoken to him on the drive over. Philip brought with him a large, beautifully faceted, double terminated crystal he had been impressed to hold during the hypnosis session.*

MOTHER MARY

Mother Mary is revered by Catholic and Eastern Orthodox Churches as the Mother of God. Many see her as a feminine representation of God or as a universal and compassionate mother figure. According to the New Testament, the angel Gabriel told Mary she would conceive a son who would be the Messiah (Luke 1:26). Her betrothed, Joseph, was encouraged in a dream to marry her though she was carrying a child who was not his (Matthew 1:20-21).

The Mother Mary appears in a number of Bible stories: She went with Joseph to Bethlehem to enroll in the census and there gave birth to Jesus in a stable because no rooms were available (Luke 2:7). Following the birth of Jesus, a period of time in Egypt, and a return to Nazareth after the death of King Herod, Mary appears in the story of Jesus' separation from his parents at the age of twelve, after a Passover celebration in Jerusalem (Luke 2:49). She appears again at the wedding in Cana when Jesus worked his first public miracle by turning water into wine (John 2:1-11). In the story of the crucifixion, Mary stands near John, the beloved disciple (John 19:26). The last New Testament reference to Mary lists her among those gathered in the Upper Room after Jesus' ascension (Acts 1:14).

CONVERSATION SIX

Mother Mary

Oh, that all would come to understand that there is one God and that you are all children of God, with infinite variety and possibilities. If only you would all celebrate each other's differences—that the white would celebrate the color of the black, the yellow would celebrate the color of the red, and the red would celebrate the color of the white. Fighting would cease because you would see each one as your brother or sister. You would understand that the language, religion, or appearance may be different, but it is all one heart. Dear family of man, what you long for in your soul of souls, I long for, and many, many countless numbers of other souls long for. There is no difference in the heart, among all men and women. Pray for that peace. Live for that peace. Be that peace.

—Mother Mary

MM: I am here. I am so pleased that I could come through so quickly. Though you cannot see it, Philip's body is vibrating with my presence. This is obvious to us on this side. He is a good channel to come through, without too many fixed ideas about how this should happen. I want to thank you for making it possible for me to come.

We could never cover all I would like to say, but you have questions for me, and I very much want to answer them for you, so let's begin.

Dr. D: *Thank you. How do you feel about so many people calling on your name?*

MM: I might just turn that around and ask you how *you* would feel, if you got one phone call after another. I am greatly humbled that the Father decided to use me for the purpose of bringing a special son to earth, but sometimes I get 10,000 phone calls at one time. It is bigger than I am, so I am not the only one handling all the calls. By "calls" I mean the routine prayers and rosaries, as well as those sudden prayers people say when they are in an accident or in harm's way. A team of individuals responds to anyone who needs help, but especially to Catholics and those who call my name. I will not say it is a burden, though I do take it very seriously. I only wish I had more completely lived up to the faith people have in me. There are also many here in the spirit world who believed in me, but labels are not very important on this side.

Wherever we turn on the earth there are needs, especially in your day, and countless numbers of us respond. I do not need to personally answer each need. I do have concern and feel the pull, from what you on the earth would call a metaphysical point of view, but I do not always have to feel the weight of each need. As you could imagine, if I took on all the problems and answered all the prayers of *all* the people, it would be an impossible job. Though the word "conglomerate" may not be a very heavenly word from the point of view of some, there is a conglomerate of spiritual beings who work together to cover all of the earth's prayers and needs.

On the spiritual plane, we who have been given a certain level of fame on earth have adjustments to make like everyone. I do not consider it a burden to be called upon. It is a privilege, but I am not the only one responding to those who call on my name. I do not make a personal appearance to every individual or in all of the experiences of me that people have. When there are so many people calling upon one name, there are helpers assigned to us to respond to all of those in need. Today I am not appearing as an archetype or image. I am real. I am the Mother Mary, the mother of Jesus, but that is not the case in every instance.

Dr. D: *What were your true feelings when Archangel Gabriel came to you to tell you that you would be the mother of Jesus?*

MM: How shall I say it? You can read what it says in the Bible, but the words in the Bible give a simplistic presentation of events. I had been in contemplation for some time. I was a praying individual and sensed that something was going to happen. You may call it intuition, precognition, or whatever you might want to say. I had a dream I did not understand where I saw that God was going to use me in some way. I was young, you know; a teenager. Even though I was already devout and prepared in many ways, what happened still came as a surprise to me.

I was initially in awe of Gabriel, standing before me in this brilliant display of himself. He was not trying to impress me, but his light against the backdrop of the darker reality of earth was so brilliant that I could only feel awe. It was not a dream, but as it was happening, that is how it felt.

After Gabriel appeared, it took me a while to grasp what he had said to me and the meaning of his words. It was through talking about my experience with others, those whom I could trust, that helped me to more or less figure out what was going to happen. Today, you have the whole story of that experience in your book called the Bible, but I did not have that background. I knew some of the scriptures of my time, but I was not a learned person. I understood more as time unfolded, but even then not as much as people may think, because scripture was not available to just anyone. I understood more specifically what Gabriel's message was all about, though I must say again, not completely, and not to the degree that God may have wanted me to understand.

Other information about this experience may come to light as you ask me more questions.

Dr. D: *What can you tell us about the various spiritual manifestations and images of you that have appeared over many years?*

MM: There is a cry from earth. Believers create a magnetic field. There may be someone who is deeply longing to see God and to know God. Someone may be crying to be free from suffering. There is a general cry from earth during wars. There may be so much suffering that God wants to comfort the people and give them some provisions, some answers, so they are not just in the dark. For all of these reasons, I have personally appeared, by direction of the Father, especially among the Catholics and particularly during Mass.

These days, though I still do come personally, there are times when pure spirit manifests using my image, and I am not there at all. In either case, my appearance helps those who believe to increase their faith. You see, when faith is great, our help can slip in more easily because childlike faith opens the heart and mind. Each situation is considered in determining whether or not I personally become manifest to an individual or make any kind of pronouncement. The most important thing is not who appears, but what is said. Is it the truth? If it is the truth, then you should live it.

Dr. D: *Many children now coming into the world appear to have special gifts. What can you tell us about this?*

MM: There have always been children with gifts. It is true that the Father has been pouring out a spirit upon all people these days. Prophecies in all religions are being realized. Conflicts in the world, including the things that are happening in the Middle East, are scriptural in basis. Sacred writings prophesy about these kinds of complications and conflicts in the world, saying there will be wars and rumors of wars, earthquakes, floods and those kinds of events. We are in a day where such occurrences seem prolific.

The children of this age are prepared to handle all of this and to be more perceptive in understanding these events. Through your modern means of communication, children today know much more about world events than I could know as a child. Today you have instant communication through telephone, television, the computer, and the Internet. How shall I say it? Children today have far more opportunity to perceive the phenomena of life in the world. This alone provides for their intelligence to be more stimulated and developed. Many children know much about many things.

Regardless of their knowledge, there are still soul growth issues. For one to be spiritually aware or to be more sensitive is not enough. All children must have structure and discipline, especially those who are talented and spiritually awakened. If they do not have structure, they can become as much a victim as a victor in their openness. Do you understand what I am saying? Some children have the potential to open up spiritually and perceive the spirit world. They know about spiritual reality and can speak of it with intelligence and at length, for they have had spiritual experiences. My advice is this: Pay attention to *all* the children of the world, for they are the hope of the future.

Dr. D: *Can you speak about your life with Jesus?*

MM: Yes, though I will not go into great length. Though it was 2,000 years ago, he is still in existence, and so am I. We meet from time to time, and we have the ability to communicate by thought if need be.

Jesus was a boy like any boy, and I would not color the story to make it historically inaccurate. He was serious minded, as you could imagine, but this was not because he knew what was coming. Some may say that, but it was his nature to be serious. He was highly curious about everything. When he was a child, I favored him greatly among my children because he was so loving.

Even as a very young child, he was concerned about making sure others had enough. I would see him help other children, often forgetting himself. When anyone, particularly some other child, was suffering from an infirmity, a cut on the hand, or anything else, he would be the first one to help. He let me know he could *feel* the pain of others, though he and I did not speak about it. That happened at a very young age. He taught *me*. In saying that, I do not want to state anything out of proportion to how life really was. Jesus was a child. He was *my* child. Even though I had been told what he would become, in the midst of our work-a-day existence, I forgot that. From time to time I would remember and be in awe of it, but for the most part, life was busy. There were other children, and there was daily existence. We were eking out a living so we could have food on the table.

Dr. D: *What is your relationship to Jesus now?*

MM: As I said, he and I communicate telepathically, as you would say. Sometimes we are in convocations where master teachers gather. Once you come to this plane, you see that everyone is either your brother or your sister. You are in relationships as a part of the *family of humanity*, not just your own family. Because Jesus is the individual that he is and was, in terms of being Savior, there is a great reality around him that I could not begin to share with you on the earth plane. His influence and his caring are so overwhelming I cannot even identify with him as having come from me. I guess that is how many mothers feel about their children when they succeed in life. All of us have a sense of inadequacy, sometimes bordering on inferiority, but he did not have that. I was very proud of him. I am proud of him now.

The work in Jesus' name is carried on not only by him, even as the work of Buddha, Moses, Zoroaster, Confucius, and others is carried on not only by these entities. They may lead the work and be concerned and involved in some way, but there are other spiritual beings aligned with those understandings and belief systems who minister to individuals, families, and all people on earth.

Dr. D: *In addition to the appearance of the angel Gabriel, did you have other spiritual experiences?*

MM: Yes, I did, and this is alluded to in scripture. Through dreams, I could sense when there were dangers. I sometimes had a sense that Jesus needed to be protected or that authority figures were near, putting him at risk. I would sometimes know these things ahead of time, especially in the trying times we lived through. Having been given the gift of Jesus, I was also given the gift of perception, and I was always attuned to anything surrounding him. I also had perception regarding his ministry and the things he would do. As a simple person, I could not grasp it all, but I knew God loved him, and I knew I did. I knew he would be a person of influence because, even when he was a child, I saw how people held to his words. They marveled at his beauty, meaning the strength and clarity of his spirit.

Would you like more?

Dr. D: *Would you like to share information about any specific spiritual experiences?*

MM: Because of my perception, I felt heartache for my people. I saw the suffering that would be coming upon them and upon my son, and I cried myself to sleep many nights. Even though I was a praying person, I was limited, like every human being, and God did not show me everything. I had to have faith in the face of uncertainty.

Dr. D: *You appeared to three children in Fatima, Portugal, and gave them a message. What was the message, and why was it given?*

MM: I will not go into the details of it, but it was essentially a warning to the world to come to God. I warned that the world had to stop warring and start loving. I said that certain things would happen if people did not change, and those things have happened. When we come to earth and give these pronouncements, it is not to have you stand in awe, but so you may examine your own life. We penetrate into human consciousness by creating something of a mass manifestation of nature. Not everyone who participated in the event at Fatima was changed, but there were enough to make it worthwhile. Similarly, all of those who read this book will not be changed, but some will be.

Many things contribute to the unfolding of an individual's life. A particular experience may have enough of an impact in the moment to radically turn a life around 180 degrees. This is what we might call a conversion experience. Many Christians are touched by what they call the Holy Spirit. In that moment, God has allowed them to be on a level where they are spiritually clear, seeing beyond the spiritual fog of this world. They can look into a much greater dimension of existence. With that dawning within their minds, they are radically changed.

Would you repeat your question? *(Question repeated.)* I knew what your question was, but I needed to hear it spoken again, for my own reasoning on this side, to decide if there was more I wanted to say. Like you on earth, I do not always remember where we started as we are talking, because so much is in my mind. I am not anxious, but I do want to get through everything from the Father that I feel is important.

Dr. D: *You often appear to ask people to pray for the world. How effective are these prayers?*

MM: If they were not effective, we would not ask, because we do not ask anything that is not possible. The spirit world is a world of use, and we want to be used to meet the needs of earth. As the human heart and mind turn, the energy of the earth changes. Energy is more real to us than it is to you, and we can see it at the atomic level and beyond. When we ask for prayer, if it is from one or many individuals, we are asking for it in order to change the energy around the world. When numbers of people are praying, which happens, there can be a significant, considerable impact upon the psyche of many at one time.

We sometimes ask people to pray because we want *them* to be changed. Some of those reading this book have a mission in life, and they are being particularly influenced by what we have to say here. That is part of our intention as well.

Dr. D: *Would you please share your thoughts and aspirations for mankind?*

MM: *(Deep sigh)* Across the world is a deep, deep hunger for peace. We know that better from our side than you do on your side. There is a cry from within the hearts of many for there to be a time when they can cease worrying or having fear. With your world today there is much fear and insecurity, most of which is created by your leaders. When I say "your leaders," I mean world leaders who have their own personal and national agendas.

Oh, that all would come to understand that there is one God, and that you are *all* the children of God, with infinite variety and possibilities. If only you would all celebrate each other's differences—that the white would celebrate the color of the black, the yellow would celebrate the color of the red, and the red would celebrate the color of the white. Fighting would cease because you would see each one as your brother or sister. You would understand that the language, religion, or appearance may be different, but it is all one heart. Dear family of man, what you long for in your soul of souls, I long for, and many, many countless numbers of other souls long for. There is no difference in the heart, among all men and women. Pray for that peace. Live for that peace. *Be* that peace.

Dr. D: *Is there anything else that you would like to say that I have not asked?*

MM: I think I have no more to say.

Dr. D: *Thank you so much for being here and taking this time.*

MM: It is my privilege to be a servant and a mother image to those who find meaning in my manifestation. God bless you. This is Mary.

End of session.

ST. PAUL

St. Paul the Apostle (AD 10—67) was called the Apostle of the
Gentiles because of his extensive outreach beyond his own Jewish culture. The New Testament relates that Paul had a life-changing vision
of Jesus while traveling to Damascus. He then became a passionate
missionary, promoting the teachings of Jesus through his letters and
travels. Paul's letters were directed to newly established Christian
groups in many parts of the world in which he lived. Among his most
beloved writings are the poetic verses on love in First Corinthians
13, and his letters remain a primary influence in Christian thought.
Paul's confession of his own inner conflicts and struggles (Romans
7:19) make him an accessible figure with whom many can identify.

CONVERSATION SEVEN

St. Paul

What I most wish to change is how I saw Jesus and how I relayed that to people. I would not describe Jesus as being so separate from other human beings. I would have honored him, but I would not have made him the singular object of adoration. I would have given him full credit for my conversion, for he was a man of great compassion and depth, but I would have emphasized the fact that all people have the same essential nature as Jesus. I would have elaborated upon that to encourage people to celebrate their own lives and go more deeply inward to find their own Christ Spirit. The Christ Spirit, with which Jesus of Nazareth was endowed, is the presence of God within. It is the ideal man, the ideal woman.

—St. Paul

St. P: I am here. I am in the stream of Philip's thought and feeling, and it is easy to flow through him. We are grateful that we are able to bring truth in this way. This is St. Paul.

Some of you may think I have a pre-arranged script that I will say as I come through *(chuckle)*, but I would prefer that you not hold any concept about me. I would rather that you come to know me as I am, as a human being. The essence of who and what I am is love, and that is no different from your essence. I taught about this. I was not always so, but beneath the many layers of falsehood and things I needed to change, I found the fountain of divine love, ever pouring forth within me. If there is anything in me I could compare with Jesus, it was that. I found that fountain within him and within me. I sought to let all people I influenced know that, though not in these words. These are my words in this twenty-first century of Mother Earth.

Without further elaboration, I would like to go through your questions.

Dr. D: *Thank you. In your writings in 1 Corinthians 12:10, you wrote about gifts of the spirit. Could you tell us more about that?*

St. P: I have a much broader view now of the gifts of the spirit. These gifts are innate properties of human existence, not outside of reality or in any way "extracurricular." What I tried to say in my writing in Corinthians was that this is the natural state of human beings, not an unnatural state. The unnatural state is to be separated from these gifts, because they are the means by which to be aware of God and to perceive God.

As has been said, God is spirit, and those who worship God must worship him in spirit and truth. What do we mean when we say to worship God in spirit? Though some have interpreted the meaning to be "enthusiastic or praising God," we are not talking about that. We mean to say your *very essence* is spirit. You are a spirit in a physical body. You came to the earth as spirit, an energy form from the Father, to take on a body and exist on this earth for a period of time. You do this for the purpose of awakening, growing, and being educated spiritually, but your essence always was and always will be spirit. The essence of your spirit is the light of God. Others have implied this, but I speak of it directly. To worship God in spirit is to go deep inside and discover this light. It is not an abstract light, but one that contains all that God is within *you*. That is why I taught that you are the temples of God. I *knew* that. I could not put all of this into the words of your modern day as I am right now, but it is what I meant.

When you go into that divine garden of self, that beautiful place within, you do not just celebrate or experience God's love in a passive way. You experience the dynamics of deep emotional involvement. Indeed, the love of God will move you to the core of your being. That is when you are most fully alive. When you come back to the earth plane, out of your spiritual reverie with God within, you are a new person.

Many Christians claim to be reborn. What has happened is that they have been overshadowed by spirit. Spirit quickens the movement of energy, atoms, and molecules within the spirits and bodies of such individuals. It reveals the true self that always was and always will be, the divine self at the highest level, pushing away and casting off layers of negative energy. When people experience this, they are as new creatures, but not truly. What they have always been inwardly is now outwardly revealed. To worship God in spirit is to go inside and have a dynamic experience not many have had. This is why the earth still yearns for God.

The gifts of the spirit play various roles in enabling people to awaken, whether spirit is speaking through a person, as I am now, or using the instrumentality of a human being to dispense healing energies. Spirit may also use the higher perceptive faculties of a person to see into the future and to prophesy. All of these gifts help human beings to marry their lives to God's life. God is spirit and should be worshiped in spirit. God should be worshiped through the gifts of the spirit such as clairvoyance, clairaudience, and clairsentience. Through these gifts you can be aware of the spirit of God as part of you.

You cannot worship God through your physical senses, though you may look at the physical creation and see a reflection of God like a reflection in a mirror. The beauty of a flower is the same beauty that is within God who created it. The vastness of the universe reflects the endless possibilities within God and the endless existence of the eternal God.

To truly encounter God personally, face to face, you need to awaken your spiritual senses. I did teach you the gifts of the spirit, but not apart from the necessity of awakening to use them to worship and love God within. Everyone has gifts of the spirit to varying degrees, but the highest of all among them is love.

Much more could be said, and there could be volumes of books written, but the essential truth about gifts of the spirit is what I have spoken today.

Dr. D: *Can you comment on the hypnosis and channeling work you are now part of?*

St. P: I love this work, but not because I am one who benefits from it by being allowed to come through. I love it because it is moving us into the twenty-first century by combining spirituality with science, which must happen. God is the greatest electrician, biologist, chemist, and doctor that could ever be! God created everything having to do with the physicality of existence. Indeed, God has created all things through higher and lower mathematics, imbuing all with love. Through the work you are doing, you are trying to demonstrate the reality of all of this. I will not say prove, because people in the world today are astute. They read, attend lectures, and have television. You are addressing an audience where many are already attuned to what you are trying to do.

You are trying to demonstrate the reality of all of this by faithfully recording your observations and experience. From our point of view, its greatest value comes from bringing through higher truths. After all, you can demonstrate the validity of hypnosis on stage, as is already done in many places, but in this project you are bringing together a mediumistic person who is open to the influx of our energy and a skilled hypnotherapist who has worked with many people for years. Through this demonstration we are able to bring higher truth, and that is what matters. So what do I, Paul, think of it? I think it is wonderful, simply wonderful.

Dr. D: *Is there anything you would advise us to change in this process?*

St. P: No, because the best way to do anything is the natural way, meaning as you are so moved. That is what I did, though even today I am criticized. I was I, and I was not Jesus. I did what I felt moved to do, according to my own spiritual perception. I, too, was endowed with spiritual gifts. You can see through reading my letters that I had the ability to prophesy, and I had clairvoyance and clairaudience.

Taken as a whole, the work you are doing through your personalities, through the manifestation of Dolores and Philip, is what is right for you. The most important thing is to be yourselves.

Dr. D: *Your teachings laid the foundations for Christianity. If you could, would you change those teachings in any way?*

St. P: I have been trying to influence changes in some of my teachings, and this book may help some with that effort. Some of the most important things I wrote were left out or augmented. What I have spoken of at length today regarding God within was not fully included.

What I most wish to change is how I saw Jesus and how I relayed that to people. I would not describe Jesus as being so separate from other human beings. I would have honored him, but I would not have made him the singular object of adoration. Jesus was a man of great compassion and depth, but I would have emphasized the fact that all people have the same essential nature as he. I would have elaborated upon that to encourage people to celebrate their own lives and go more deeply inward to find their own Christ Spirit. The Christ Spirit, with which Jesus of Nazareth was endowed, is the presence of

God within. It exists in each of God's children. It is the ideal man; the ideal woman.

When Buddha, I, or even Jesus, who I understand is going to speak for this book, talks about this, we are referring to the fact that God already lives in each one. The core nature of all human beings everywhere always has been, is now, and always will be that of God, or God's presence. It is because of misunderstanding and ignorance through time that you on earth have lost this awareness of your inner selves. Those whom you call masters had the ability to find God within. They awakened to God's presence and became enlightened.

If he had the chance, Jesus himself would have taught more and more on this point. This would have helped people to understand what he meant when he said that when they saw him, they could see the Father. What Jesus would have taught is that you should reach that point in your own illumination or enlightenment where people see the Father when they look at you.

Lower nature has to do with this earth plane, but higher nature has to do with heaven. You came from heaven, and you are returning to heaven. Become aware of your divine self while still on earth, as Jesus did, and do not wait until you die to find God within. *That* is the part of my teaching that I would change.

Dr. D: *Can you tell us more about your personal experience as a human being?*

St. P: I have said some things along those lines already. To use a modern phrase *(chuckle)*, I am letting my hair down. It does no good to use pretense to try to blind people with a brilliant light by using a lot of high-minded theological verbiage. There is enough of that on earth. When a person is on his or her deathbed, none of those things have meaning. What does have meaning are the questions, "Did I love?" "How many people did I love?" "Was I loved?" "Who am I, and where am I going to go from this expression on the earth plane to the next plane?" People do not look back wanting to celebrate the elaborate expression of truths. They want to look upon their life in simple and real terms.

When I have this opportunity to express in this way, I want to say I am a human being just like you. I have lived a longer period of time, so I know more things than you know. From my vantage point, I know what is ahead of you and how to help you prepare for that, but I am like you. I have a need to love and be loved. It is the most central aspect of God, the need to love and be loved, and it is why God created all of this. All the elaborations, twists and turns of existence, facts, figures and information are just for this: You find yourself by loving yourself. You find yourself by loving other people. As you do that, God will automatically dawn within you as love.

You may read my words in scripture, and some of you may be in awe of them, but I tell you, it is when anyone is most real with us that we can become most real with ourselves. That is my intention.

Dr. D: *Can you tell us about your experience on the Road to Damascus?*

St. P: There is no need to elaborate, so I can tell you in a few sentences. My meeting with Jesus as I traveled to Damascus humbled me. The love that Jesus is and was at that time pierced me deeply. He awakened God's presence within me and enabled me to see my own divine self. When God's presence came into my awareness, I was never the same. Once that happens in any human being, that person is not the same. When you realize God, you cannot lose that realization. That is what Jesus did for me, and that is why I took up the cause. I knew his words were true. I knew he was a man of God and sent by God. I needed to know nothing else. My experience on the Road to Damascus put me on fire in my desire to help others to have the same revelation.

All that is really needed to change this world is for people, one by one, to be so awakened and so moved by spirit that they are motivated toward love, divine love, and goodness. That is what the love of Jesus did for me, and that is why I proclaimed him. As time unfolded, and as I grew spiritually, I found this same love within me, the same God presence. This is the true essence of my encounter with Jesus on the Road to Damascus.

Dr. D: *Would you please tell us about the spiritual dynamics within the early Christian Church?*

St. P: It was different from the Christian Church today. We did not have the ceremony and ritual and the pomp and circumstance. The Church is overly laden with these things today. Being in a beautiful environment does help people to feel the beauty within themselves, but what may be lost is the actual, personal communication with God. This goes back to the point that God is spirit, and those who worship him must worship him in spirit and truth. In our time, because of the great emphasis upon the spiritual senses, or gifts of the spirit, there was much greater allowance for spiritual phenomena, and it happened.

I wrote of speaking in tongues and prophesying. I wrote about the gifts of the spirit because those things came forth in our worship services. Someone would go into a trance and prophesy, and someone else would interpret. We *knew* about spiritual beings and how they were working with us. *I* knew, because I was clairvoyant. I could not have written about the gifts of the spirit if we had not experienced them. How could I? There were no books written about these things then. There was no esoteric tome to teach us. My understanding came out of my life experience, as did the awareness that love is most important.

To get back to the point of your question, in our services we would sit in a circle. There was no head. It was inevitable that someone would speak first or take leadership, but the point was to realize what we had in common—that all of us shared one spirit. We would imagine Jesus and do a kind of meditation, visualizing much as you do today. Spirit came and spoke through those among us who were psychic. Messages were given through the intelligence of those individuals or through the taking over of their vocal cords as I am doing right now. Certain truths were spoken through such people about individuals and about what God was trying to convey to everyone.

There were others who would be taken over by high spirit to predict the future and foretell what was going to happen. Some warned us of dangerous outcomes if we were not careful, especially with some of the people who persecuted us. Not much is written about this in the scriptures.

We sang, but not like you do today. Our worship services were more in keeping with spirit manifestation, including the spirit of Jesus, and with receiving spiritual guidance in this way. Yes, healings took place, and the impetus for that came from Jesus. We did *lay* hands on people, and they were spontaneously healed within the context of that experience. I cannot say more.

Dr. D: *How are you occupied in the spirit world?*

St. P: I am in that convocation about which others have spoken. I am in the ranks of spiritual masters because of the work I did on earth and because of the obvious responsibility I have toward those who embrace my words. I work with Christian leaders, though not all of them. I come to inspire them. I stand guard to protect. I come to people such as Philip and try to convey truths from my side.

My work and my words went far. There are countless millions of people who became Christians and who are Christians today because of my words. I have a responsibility to oversee those individuals, especially the Christian leadership, so I lend my energies there. I have spent time in the libraries of the spirit world writing out the proper portrayal of the history of my time. We must correct scripture or writings where that is needed, and I also do that. I could go on and on about that point.

I have a personal life, and I live that out as well. Particularly I enjoy fishing, boating, and those kinds of activities.

Dr. D: *As we ask everyone, is there anything I have not asked that you would like to say for the readers?*

St. P: No, I think not. I was standing here wondering whether or not there was more I wanted to say, but if there is more that needs to be said, you will both be impressed about that. I thank you from the bottom of my heart for this opportunity to come through to spend this time with you. This is St. Paul.

End of session.

ST. FRANCIS

St. Francis of Assisi (September 26, 1181—October 3, 1226) was born into a prosperous Italian family. In 1205, Francis had a vision that radically changed him, and he adopted a life of poverty, preaching repentance and caring for lepers and the poor. Wandering in the hills, he touched many hearts through his kind service and words of love. In 1209, Francis founded the Franciscan Order. That year, Clare of Assisi joined him, and in 1912, he established the order eventually called Poor Clares. Francis was said to have experienced the stigmata (wounds of Christ) in 1224 while praying and fasting. He dictated his spiritual testimony before he died and was soon pronounced a saint by Pope Gregory IX. Many consider his writings to have great religious and literary merit. His beautiful poem, *Canticle of the Sun*, expresses love for Brother Sun, Sister Moon, Mother Earth, and all creation.

CONVERSATION EIGHT

St. Francis

When you come to the spirit world, you will and will not be the same person. Though you retain memories, you become a much bigger person in this expanded universe than you could ever expect. You want to embrace all the stars and the planets and wrap your arms around all creation. That is the effect of being in the very presence of the one who created all of this. Your love is unbound. It flows freely because you have complete understanding.

—St. Francis

St. F: This is St. Francis. This atmosphere is wonderful. I am so happy and pleased that I have this instrument to come through. Beloved sister Dolores, thank you for making it possible for me to intercede in human history in this way. The love that I feel for you and earth, all mankind, is pouring forth from my heart center. There are waves of energy going out from that God presence within me. I was standing by, waiting to come through, and I am overjoyed with the Father's love to be able to be with you. There are many who are very close, including Clare who worked with me and other brothers and sisters. We have graduated to higher levels of awareness, but we retain our family feeling. In fact, it is stronger, because love is more powerful, more potent here.

We are allowing this span of time for you to ask your questions, that we may speak to each reader.

Dr. D: *Thank you. In retrospect, how do you feel about your life on earth?*

St. F: My life was sweet and bitter, but that's life, isn't it? Wouldn't you say that? Sweet and bitter are two sides of the same coin. As others have said, without darkness no one would have sought to illuminate the night and thus discover how to harness and use electricity. I am and I am not the same person as I was on earth. When you come to the spirit world, you will and will not be the same person. Though you retain memories, you become a much bigger person in this expanded universe than you could ever expect. You want to embrace all the stars and the planets and wrap your arms around all creation. That is the effect of being in the very presence of the one who created all of this. Your love is unbound. It flows freely because you have complete understanding.

When I look back to the ancient past of my life, it seems like a narrow cavity. I was young, and though I was primed for my life before I came into earthly existence, I was narrow. My emphasis was more upon suffering than joy. Still, I have to say that through suffering I found real joy. This was not superficial joy that comes from a full stomach or from physical love, but the joy that comes from bringing forth my own God presence, my own divinity. Through getting closer and closer to the God of the universe who is all love and all light, I shifted into that heightened state of awareness whereby I became more universal.

I knew I was being used by God, not only in my external life, but also in my dream life, my spiritual life. I would be caught up into spirit and go into such a deep state of union with God in love that I simply did not want to come back. It was because of my awareness of union with God that I aspired to lead people to conscientious and overt suffering through fasting, praying, wearing sack cloth, laboring, and serving the downtrodden and the lonely. Through suffering, I knew my life would yield to me existence in God as an experience, not just in theory. My life is one long continuum, as is your life. As you look back, you will see that everything has been there for a purpose, and you will cherish how God has interwoven all of your experiences into your life to perfect it. In the end, that is all God wants. That is all that God has in mind. I loved my life on earth. I still love it and am proud of it and how God used me. I give all the credit and the glory to God. That is my nature.

Dr. D: *Who is God to you?*

St. F: God is love, though he cannot be contained in any word, no matter how big it is. God is beyond comprehension. But God is also intimate. God is my own highest Self, and God is not separate from me. All that God is, I am. As long as I am in a physical body in finite form, there is a sense of limitation, but that will exist only until I come to understand and aspire toward my higher self, realized in God. I would encourage all people to imitate the life of Christ, as I sought to, because to Jesus, God was the all in all. Jesus knew God within himself and proclaimed this. His relationship was intimate as well as universal. Seek to imitate the life of Jesus, the life of anyone who has attained that level of spiritual awakening.

Dr. D: *Who is Jesus to you?*

St. F: The latter portion of my answer to the previous question says much about who I think Jesus is. I have met him, and to be in his presence is to be in the presence of absolute, unconditional love. There is not one ounce of judgment, only love. Love knows why you came to earth and that you must go through your life of suffering, your life of questioning. That is each soul's privilege, responsibility, and opportunity. There is no reason to judge others or judge self. What comes upon us comes by the will of God, though people may respond by thinking they are in charge. Because God is love, the outcome of every life is predicated upon the ideal of divine, unconditional love. God has only one thing in mind for you. In your higher self, you have only one thing in mind for you: Union with God, oneness with God, *joy* in oneness with God, and *peace* in oneness with God. That is all universal love has in mind for you.

No matter how many times you fall down and get up, there will be that final time you fall down and get up, if you understand what I am saying. There will be that last time. Do not give up. *Do not* give up. Never, never, never give up! Know that each step, whether it is toward falling down or toward getting up, is one step closer to God's ideal for you.

Dr. D: *What is your opinion of the way in which your work is being done on earth today?*

St. F: The word that stands out is "today." Those who took over my work, those brothers who sought to administer the work, have done a good job. After all, Popes have come out of my line to lead, operate, and administer the Catholic Church and its entire family across the globe.

We are most concerned that people ultimately understand what love is about. Marriage can be very important to the awakening of the soul. Altruistic love is altruistic love, but it is not always applicable or necessarily possible without the *intimacy* of love. There are those who were single during their lives on earth who, when they come here, wish they had married. This is because they can now see the reality of two people who have loved each other completely, as soul mates. I would challenge the leaders of the Catholic Church to look at this point. I would ask that they consider in the coming years that perhaps it could be a better way, a happier way, a more realistic way, to allow marriage of your priests and your nuns.

This flies in the face of doctrine, but doctrine is *man-made*. It is often thought that the will of the Holy Spirit descends into individuals and groups and influences certain decisions to be made. That may or may not be the case. Many times the voice of God has been left out. Many times, because of ignorance and prejudice, false ideas have come down as law, when they have nothing to do with the love of God. It is important for those who can to take up leadership to bring about changes. They should not do this in a rebellious or negative way, but should begin with prayer. In this way, they will be able to bring about changes to help any institution that is serving God to serve God better.

Dr. D: *The Catholic Church regards you as a saint. Is there anything you would like to say about that?*

St. F: Man's legislation does not make any difference. Because of my earthly record, men labeled me this way, but putting a word before my name did not make me a saint. There are many, many people who are hidden saints, and everyone has the capability of acquiring the same characteristics I had. My life stands out because I was a leader, because, yes, there were exemplary aspects, and because there were miracles.

Setting someone aside as being different from the lot of humanity is good on one hand because it gives people someone to look up to, but it is important that a saint be brought down from the altar to be among the people. Thus, the people may see and experience that they can do likewise. They can live the same kind of life. I taught that. I sought to make my brothers saints, in the universal meaning of saint. I taught them to love others unconditionally, to love others as they loved themselves, and to give their lives to others, even at the expense of their own lives. That is what I knew to be true and what I lived. I know those principles still hold up today because they came from God, and they are universal.

Dr. D: *You suffered greatly from stigmata. What was the origin of this experience?*

St. F: I did experience the stigmata, which originated through my faith. Faith is energy, and my faith in Jesus drew him to me. As has been said, it is the law of attraction that draws to us what we experience. I sought to imitate the life of Jesus, and I persisted willfully and relentlessly to be one with him. I drew out of his life many, many things I did not talk about, things that I felt through his heart in my own heart. So deep was my desire and so great my aspiration to be one with Jesus, that I became like him. I, too, came to love humanity as myself. The more I served the down and out, the lepers, the poverty-stricken, the deformed, the dregs of society, as you might call them, the more did my love grow, and the more I became like Jesus.

Because I was spiritually open, I could take on some of the energies of Jesus, which then manifested in my body. Because I would not go backward, and that love would not be altered, then the miracle of the stigmata happened again and again. Was it valuable? Yes. When people give their lives to a cause, they become that cause. When people look at that person, they can see the full embodiment of all that this cause represents. Jesus was the Christ, and the Christ is an archetype of a lover of humankind. Taking that on, he became all that a lover of humankind can become, including being one with God.

Dr. D: *If one wears a medallion with a picture of St. Francis, does this help or make a difference in one's spiritual life?*

St. F: Indeed, it makes a difference if it follows what I said before. If you are in earnest and truly want what religious life means, then you shall have it. The medallion will draw us to you. Again, it is because of the law of attraction. At the very least, you will receive the assistance of the holy ones who will usher you along according to your path instructions, your map, the things *you* must experience, the things you contracted for when you came to the earth plane. Just the wearing of things such as a medallion does not mean much, but if you wear them enough, you magnetize them with the kind of energy that you are. If your love is great enough, that particular piece of jewelry may be laid upon others, and that love will penetrate them and heal them. There is more than one example of that in human history. Again, it goes back to the condition of the heart. When you love, and love as God loves, you will attract to yourself mighty forces and make a difference both in your life and in the lives of others.

Dr. D: *Do you still consider yourself Catholic?*

St. F: I love your question! *(Laughter)* I think everything I have said up to this point will tell you where I stand. If you use the word "catholic" meaning universal, yes, I am a universal being. Am I caught up in the teachings of the Church? No, I am not. Do I respect them? Yes, to the degree that they are true. Do I help those who are involved with the Catholic Church? Without question!

But I do not help them exclusively. As I said in the beginning, all people are my brothers and sisters. I sought to love all people as myself, imitating Jesus. I sought that. I practiced that. That was my religion. I cannot be caught up in only one way of life or faith. All of them, when met with conscientiousness, bring about spiritual awakening. All of them!

Dr. D: *Is there anything else you would like to say at this time?*

St. F: I think we have covered everything. I just want you to know that right now there is a white dove above this room, which represents the spirit of God. God cannot be contained in one symbol, but I want you to know that the dove is here, as a symbol of God's love and blessing upon this experience. God bless you. This is St. Francis.

Dr. D: *God bless you. Thank you.*

End of session.

Comments:

PB: I felt so much love when St. Francis came through. My body was filled with electricity—this warmth—over and over. It almost brought me out of my trance.

Dr. D: *It got very hot, and I felt waves of heat. (The session was in January and the weather was rainy and cold.)*

Dr. D's Observation: *On this occasion, two sessions were completed in one sitting. For the first session, Philip's voice was very deep, strong, and* *vibrant. I felt a powerful energy, and Philip sat upright in the chair. I felt alert and energized the entire time. When St. Francis came through, Philip sat back, with his body completely relaxed. His voice became soft and quiet, and the energy in the room was filled with much love. As I experienced with Buddha, I wanted to go into meditation and become one with the energy.*

GEORGE WASHINGTON

George Washington (February 22, 1732—December 14, 1799) was a Virginia planter who was interested in military arts and surveying. He served in the House of Burgesses and was happily married to Martha Dandridge Custis. Like many other planters, Washington opposed Britain's policies toward the American colonies, and at the Second Continental Congress in 1775, he was elected Commander-in-Chief of the Continental Army. He led the American Revolution for six years.

Following the surrender of the British at Yorktown, Washington was elected the first President of the United States, serving from 1789 to 1797. Upon his retirement, he urged his countrymen to forswear excessive party and geographical distinctions and avoid long-term alliances with other countries. He retired to his beloved home, Mount Vernon, where he died at the age of sixty-seven.

CONVERSATION NINE

George Washington

In the final analysis, I want to tell all of you, including leaders, not to be selfish. Do not think only of self or only of your nation and its agenda. What does <u>humankind</u> need right now? What does your earth need right now? It is very obvious. The family of man needs to understand that it <u>is</u> a family and that all of its members are brothers and sisters. This family comes from love and, when enlightened, lives by love.

—George Washington

GW: I am here. This is George Washington. It is a great privilege for me to speak to you today. It is an honor that I take very seriously, even as my words were taken seriously when I was on earth as a president of your country.

You are doing a great work. If the two hemispheres of existence were truly one through this gift of mediumship, the world would be in much less trouble than it is. The idea for the activity you are under-taking was impressed upon you by us. The two of you were chosen to do this work together to demonstrate the reality and authenticity of spirit and the spirit world. Each of you is a half of a whole, with one of you serving as the medium and the other making it possible, through hypnosis, to bring the mind of the medium to a place where we can come through.

I speak on behalf of all those who come through in this process when I say you will find a thematic thread running through the information you are capturing from us. Our words have certain ideas and principles in common. It would be the same if ten or fifteen travelers went to a far off country and came back to tell their stories. They would tell about similar things using different expressions. As spiritual beings, we know the priorities of life. We also know what part of our lives will be invaluable to share in helping people on earth to progress.

I could talk to you about the grandeur of the spirit world or about energy as we experience it, but the primary purpose of this work is to enlighten people about the path to follow to attain the highest and best while they are on earth. Is there some pre-arranged decision about what each of us shall say? I don't intend to be a spokesperson, but there has been a certain degree of planning because this is the world of cause, and yours is the world of effect. There have been discussions, but there has been no effort to coordinate a comprehensive or detailed response to your questions.

I am sure some who read this will expect me to come through almost singing the "Star Spangled Banner," but I wanted my first words to bring clarity to how we see what you are doing. As I said, I feel honored to be able to participate.

I want to add one other thing: Rather than think of me as someone famous, I would prefer you think of me as your elder brother. That is who I am to each of you, more than I am someone who held the title of President of the United States.

Now, please ask your questions. As I said in the beginning, this is George Washington.

Dr. D: *Thank you. How is your time occupied in the spirit world?*

GW: Those of us who were leaders on earth tend to be leaders in the spirit world, and those who were part of governments on earth tend to be drawn toward governing here. I am part of a hierarchical government that is manifested by the co-mingling of leaders from many different backgrounds, including philosophers, world famous teachers, presidents of universities, and those from spiritual organizations. In their way, all of these leaders governed on the earth plane. Very important among them are those who were not famous but who loved in a magnanimous way. Their hearts were enlarged to embrace all humankind. Some of them lived far back into unwritten history, at the earliest beginnings of humanity on earth. They are at the helm of this universal, spiritual government.

In this government one person's ideas do not dominate those of another as happens in your world government on earth. The most important result of how we work is that our ideas coalesce so that we come up with the best one, the best and highest truth. Opinions are not a part of this sphere of existence, because the truth is obvious. It is all around us, in the energy, in the light, in the garments we wear, and in the overall energetic reality of the spirit world. We know the very truth of things, and there is no second guessing. A fact is a fact, and you cannot pretend something is different from what it is.

When we speak, we are aware of any dissonance between what we think and what is true, and we are always being corrected. It is not a punitive correction, but rather an automatic awareness through the reality of clear-sightedness. We present our ideas, concepts, and thoughts without any criticism, and they are shared as a contribution toward perfecting the final conclusion.

I am a part of this governing in the spirit world, and God is the intelligence that emanates through us to solidify in right thinking and right feeling. God is the all-pervasive, synthesizing, loving energy that moves through and among us. Above all, God's energy is personal; exceedingly, penetratingly personal.

Dr. D: *Do you have any advice you would like to give to the American people and its leaders?*

GW: I do not hold myself up as the supreme person to answer that question, but as George Washington, I will give my response.

My answer to your first question should tell you in part what would be most beneficial to you on earth. Governing should be done by seeking out the very truth of things. Where it is influenced and led based on party interests, divergent goals, and divergent ideas about how to reach those goals, then a clamoring to promote one's own idea or way of governing is inevitable. As humanity evolves, there will be less and less of an argument about what is right, because existence, by its very nature, yields its own answers. People cannot long go against universal principles and not suffer. When there is not adherence to the highest truths, your nation and world suffer. Even though you may try your best, you cannot find a true semblance of a perfect government on earth.

Thanks to the intercessory presence of spirit, your world has not gone awry to the extent that it has destroyed itself. Individually and collectively, we are there to help guide the destiny of planet earth. We see to it that the forces and ideas that could crush humankind are thwarted. In the unfolding of human history there are certain things that simply cannot be allowed to happen. Human beings may go to the brink of ultimate destruction, but they do not annihilate all of humanity. There are forces and causes behind the reality of human existence on earth that you cannot begin to understand. They play out for the good of all in influencing the ultimate outcome for humankind.

A child being disciplined may not be happy, but the child who is without discipline, without the structure and principles of guidance, will be even more miserable. Every movement on earth will come to bless humanity in the end. Even death is not the worst of lots in life. It may be a great blessing, because on this side there is greater opportunity to awaken quickly and work more knowledgably upon one's life.

In the final analysis, I want to tell all of you, including leaders, not to be selfish. Do not think only of self or only of your nation and its agenda. What does *humankind* need right now? What does your earth need right now? It is very obvious. The family of man needs to understand that it *is* a family and all of its members are brothers and sisters. This family comes from love and, when enlightened, lives by love. Where people live for the good of individuals and the whole, no one suffers and all prosper. This is possible only in a world governed by the truth of things and by unconditional love.

At the very least, live such lives as individuals. You cannot live another's life, and you cannot decide the fate of a nation, no matter who you are. What is set in motion is set in motion. But in your individual choices, live selflessly. In that sense, the Christ ideal of sacrificing yourself for the good of others is the best ideal. Though I tried to live that way, I was not perfect at it. Of course, I understand much better now than I did then.

Dr. D: *How closely is America following the plan that God had in mind at its inception?*

GW: While some decisions are absolutely providential and must be made a certain way, one often has choices in life. Where selfishness and party politics become more important than the truth, then you must look at those who govern and those who follow. The meaningful thing about democracy, though it is not yet ideal, is that the populace does govern its own destiny by voting. Is America following its destiny? Yes, in some cases, no in others.

The guarantee for your own individual safe journey is to be selfless and to follow your conscience. If you do that, you cannot go wrong in the end. As others before me have said, God is within. The still, and sometimes not so small, voice of God is better to listen to than the clamoring of the world. Those who live quietly that way will guarantee their own safe journey in this life and in the next.

Dr. D: *There is an account of your having a spiritual experience during your encampment at Valley Forge, indicating that our country will experience great suffering. What can you tell us about that?*

GW: People suffer in every period in human history, but God is always in charge. It is all so that each one may learn, because without suffering there is no awakening. The body itself has its own built-in warning system in that sometimes you have pain here or discomfort there. If a painful sensation continues, you know there is some need to be met in the body. It is not different for your nation or for the world. Where there is suffering, where there is squalor, where there is starvation, where there is war, those are the areas that need treatment. These conditions are the tell-tale signs that the body of humanity is ill. Without these signs, the illnesses will not be recognized and treated.

At best, society creates government programs to meet needs and lessen the problems in the body of humanity. When you ignore the problems and cease to hear the cry of the hungry, such ills persist and grow. When you ignore the gathering of negative forces in the world, you allow things to grow out of proportion and become unmanageable. Many know they should not ignore certain signs in their own bodies, and yet they do. There may come a time when the body can no longer endure this mistreatment or neglect. It is the same for our planet. As citizens of earth, none of you is without responsibility for its care, albeit in your own small way. If each of you would do your part, it would make a difference.

There is a record of my having a vision at Valley Forge, but it did not happen exactly as it is written. I could see the suffering of the nation occurring in the era in which you are now living; but sometimes prophecies are given because certain things must happen, and sometimes they are given as a warning, similar to my description of how the body gives warnings. If you recognize the need for treatment in certain areas of the world and address the problems with a certain caring to abate the suffering, such prophecies do not have to come true. Suffering does not have to grow into something bigger than it already is.

Your future is in the hands of all the people, leaders and followers alike. What you do individually and collectively will determine the outcomes for your nation and world. You will meet, coming toward you, the very things you have determined to be, reaping the seeds you have sown.

If I can touch even a few lives through this book, I want to take this opportunity. Be aware, the chance for me to speak in this way is so rare as to be almost non-existent, so I will do my best to take advantage of it.

Dr. D: *Given the ways in which America has changed, are there any changes you would like to see made to our Constitution?*

GW: What *are* the principles of existence and life? There are efforts to amend the Constitution, but there is not much I would change. I would be slow to amend it because it comes from a very high plane of the spirit world, indeed. The Declaration of Independence and the Constitution come from some of the highest masters in the spirit world who used their intercessory ability to greatly influence the content.

The Declaration of Independence was a declaration of freedom from a most despotic reign in England that had caused life in America to become very miserable. I was a part of all that, so I know. I fought against it, because of what I knew. As many philosophers have said, and life proves it, with freedom comes responsibility. The Constitution guides how that responsibility will be lived out, over time.

The declaring and maintenance of freedom is supreme in enabling human beings to come into their own. Freedom is what makes your land a great land. When you teach and achieve proper self governing, then principles of freedom are adhered to correctly. Each one takes responsibility, having the awareness through proper education, as to what is and what is not morally correct.

The whole world has an innate desire for the kind of governing America has. This shows that your land is a great land. I was very proud, more than I can say, to have been a president of America. Times change, and people change. But truth does not change; it just alters its expression according to the degree of enlightenment one has experienced.

Dr. D: *You have touched on this, but I will ask anyway, what do you think about our world in this twenty-first century?*

GW: Well, we are still here, and we are still helping out. That should tell you something about what we think of this world. It is necessary for us to be with you and for God to continue to guide the evolution of this planet. As has been said, this world is an object lesson, a school. As in any school, there are tests to pass to prove you are ready to go to the next level, and then you can evolve in the school. In all of life there are tests, passing tests, and evolving. This is the innate nature of all people and of all things. Your nation and the world are a part of this whole dynamic.

Dr. D: *Are you and Martha together in the spirit world?*

GW: Of course! You use the term "soul mates" in some circles on earth, and, yes, we are soul mates. There is a love between us that was not written about, but it was a deep, abiding love. That love was retained when we came to this side, and it continues to grow between us. While she did not participate in the governing aspect of my presidency, Martha was a very wise woman whose counsel I often sought in the quiet times we spent together. She knew when I was troubled. She knew my moods. She was also interested in the causes behind what I thought and felt as president, as her husband, and simply as a human being. God used her to help me. We were a good pair.

Dr. D: *Is there anything else about you as a human being that you would like the readers to know?*

GW: My answer is yes, many times over! I have been speaking in eternal terms from the highest levels of the spirit world and have not included personal information in answering your previous questions, but I want people to know I have retained my nature. It was one of sobriety and seriousness, but not without humor. I had a great sense of humor. I was a man who had feelings like all people. I was not given to following the lusts of my body, but in my younger days I was quickly attracted to beautiful women. Though I had discipline, this does not mean I did not indulge in thinking about such things. I was human. A part of the condition of being human is having emotions, but a part of being Godly is to direct those feelings, and that is what I tried to do.

I loved being out in nature, and that is why I loved being a surveyor. In those days, there were no highways, and there were no housing divisions. The land was so rich, so virgin, and so untouched that you could walk for days without seeing a house or another human being. I enjoyed that very much, and I am still a great lover of nature in the spirit world.

I have not even touched upon the subject of the care of Mother Earth, and that should be covered by someone from the spirit world who is a greater authority than I am. I am not suggesting this for your book, but it is an important matter.

I have talked primarily from the perspective of my role as a former president of your country, a citizen of the world, and an individual who is part of a governing body here in spirit. While that has been the focus of what I have talked about, in response to this question I have shared some personal information people may not know about me.

Dr. D: *Yes, thank you. Is there anything you would like to add to this communication?*

GW: No, it is enough, it is enough. I bring the conversation to a close with great hope for America and for the entire world. This is George Washington.

End of session.

Comment:

PB: In terms of content of the session, I don't know what he said because I couldn't hear his words, but my impression is that he spoke with authority and did not equivocate. His presence didn't tax me, though I can feel in my body that I'm different from how I was when I went under.

BLACK HAWK

Black Hawk (1767—October 3, 1838) was born in the village of Saukenuk in Illinois. His Sauk Indian tribe grew corn in the summer and moved west of the Mississippi River for the winter. During the War of 1812, Black Hawk fought on the side of the British, and in the 1832 Black Hawk War, he led a futile effort to retain control over Indian lands. He was captured, and many of his followers killed.

Following his release, Black Hawk was taken on a tour of the United States so he would see how strong the U.S. was and stop resisting its expansion. Until his death in 1835, he lived with his tribe along the Iowa River. He related the story of his life before he died, warning that white settlements west of the Mississippi River were a threat to Indians. His story, *The Autobiography of Black Hawk*, was published in 1853.

CONVERSATION TEN

Black Hawk

The truth is that your aunt is not dead, your mother is not dead, and your father is not dead. The truth is that you are a spiritual being. You are going to leave your body one day to come to the spiritual side. The truth is that as you love others so you become loved. The truth is that God is in all people, everywhere, and there are no exceptions.

—Black Hawk

BH: I am here. This is Black Hawk. I just walked through Philip. He is so open today. The more Philip unconsciously attunes himself to me, the more I can come through as I am. As you will notice, Dolores—may I call you Dolores? *(Most certainly.)* As I speak, there is always the energy or tone of Philip present, but that does not change the truth that comes through.

As has been said in this book, and we will continue to say it through all channels, all of you get inspiration and information through your minds and hearts as impressions. We are not concerned with whether or not you hear the tone of Philip's voice when I speak.

In other places in this book it will be explained that this is part of the phenomenon of channeling. The container determines the shape or mold of the liquid poured into it. If you heard me, some of you would say, "He doesn't sound very Native American to me!" *(Laughter)* You all have your stereotypes, you see.

I am Black Hawk. I am proud of my name, but I am not seeking any fame. I love working with this man. We have had some very, very good times together, and these experiences are the basis for love through familiarity. There has to be some basis for loving, and I love Philip very much because of the experiences we have shared. I am happy to be the Native American who takes care of him.

When he is in the trance state, as he is right now, I am usually the one to survey the whole space around him to make sure no lower energies or entities can come in and lodge themselves into his energy field or aura, as you call it. I am here to protect him under any circumstance. Most of you who are reading this book have Native Americans working with you among your many different guides and teachers. We are happy to do this, more than happy. It is not just a servant's position, but a protecting, healing position. It is an honor to do this.

Any of you coming over to the spirit world will find that this place is a world of service. The great ones among us are not those who are living in a mansion somewhere, though they may have a mansion, but they are the ones who are serving. Jesus is hailed as the greatest one because he gave the greatest service by giving his life. That is why he is exemplary. But even the Master Jesus is not in some kind of glorious place where others are sitting around and bowing to him. This is a world of service; a world that exists to meet needs of people when they come over and to meet needs of people still on earth. Philip had a need for someone like me within his mission as a medium, so I volunteered. I serve as his close spiritual protector.

This is my self-introduction. Now, you may ask your questions.

Dr. D: *Thank you. What role do you play in the execution of Philip's mediumship?*

BH: I have described some of that. I also help with the message-bearing, though he does not know that. From time to time, they let me field the energy or the information. I try to get Philip to break out of holding me in some rigid pattern in his mind, because it does not always fit. I do not even have to be in the same space with him, as I can protect him from a distance if I need to. When he is teaching mediumship to people, I am present to help with that because I am mediumistic. I have the gift of mediumship, which is something you bring with you when you come over to this place.

Not everyone has awakened to all the gifts of spirit when they come to the spirit world. There will be things to learn here, too. What you do not know, you do not know! It does not come by osmosis or magic. It comes more easily to us in the spirit world because we have no physical body to hinder or block us. For example, if you want to learn to play the piano here, there is no difference between seeing the note on the page and having the energy coursing its way down to your finger so you play the correct key. When you see the note, instantly your hand goes down, your finger goes down to the correct note. There is no lag time, and there is no space. There is no time between knowing and doing.

At times we have to be careful about that. When you first come over you do not realize, unless you have had the experience, that you can be mobilized by your mind. Think yourself somewhere, and you go there. If you do not watch your mind, and it runs off randomly, and you think of someone, you might find yourself in that person's home uninvited. Because you have been thinking about them so much, you just go there.

It is very interesting that we have to learn here, too. Some who have come here without the awareness or cultivation of mediumistic abilities learn how to do this work through mediums on earth. They learn how to interact with the physical world. Though I have mediumship abilities that came with me to this place, my primary work at this time is to protect Philip from lower or lesser entities.

Dr. D: *We hear many stories about Native American or Indian Spirit Guides working with white people on earth. Can you explain why this occurs?*

BH: This land was our land first. You have that song, "This land is my land." Not true. I am saying that light heartedly, but when the white man decided to take over this land, and when he crossed our plains and our mountains, we who were pushed out, we who struggled, took exception to that. That is why there were conflicts and wars. You would do the same things if someone invaded your land.

At first, Native Americans had no knowledge about the white man. He was a mystery: Where did he come from? What was he doing?

Why was he here? Why did he have that gun he was carrying? Before my people understood what a gun *was*, they saw it kill. They reacted with both awe and fear, and out of fear they also killed. They killed to protect themselves personally or to protect their tribes, because some white men had no compunction about killing them. Some white men wanted to get rid of the Native Americans in a perfunctory way because they were inconvenient.

The leaders of your nation passed certain laws and provisions by which the white man could be justified in killing Indians or in putting them in different places that you now call reservations. They reserved certain spaces, and we Indians were taken out of our natural settings and isolated. We were no longer able to roam as we had roamed, and that was very painful for us. If someone were to do it to you, you would feel the same thing.

How do you get over resentment? You can imagine that in the spirit world there are many Native Americans who have yet to get over their resentment toward the white man's injustice or unfairness. A story called "A Trail of Tears" was written about the experience Native Americans had when we were transported from one place to another, sometimes on foot, sometimes on horses, surrounded by your military scouts and soldiers. I am not saying this because I want to stir up resentment, hatred or conflict. I am explaining these things to you because you asked why we so often work with the white man.

Many of us on this side learned from masters who taught us how to get over negative energy and become free of resentment. Some of our teachers were our Native American chiefs who were also masters on earth. In the spirit world they taught us that the way to get rid of negative energy is to do things that create positive energy. By protecting, guiding, and helping the white man, the negative energy that was hurting us in spirit was dissipated or transformed. We actually came to love the white man and to see him as ourselves. He has a different skin color and different features, but our essence is the same. It is all God. The core energy of all of us and of everything is God. The energy that creates skin color is God. So the medicine we used was to serve, and when we did that, we also realized the value of service.

Some of us were primitive, but not all of us. We had spiritual revelations just like you. We had visitations from our primary guides, teachers, and loved ones. We were quite adept at that. Sometimes we had ceremonies to create openness within our psyche through which we had spiritual experiences, and these ceremonies were conducted with respect and reverence. Within many of our tribes, we were just as religious as you, but in our own way. We respected nature and communicated with spirit.

Yes, we had some beliefs that were inaccurate, just like you, but in essence we were not off track. We were on track. In our own spiritual experiences, God was nature, and God was also the Great Spirit. We were not without our own adeptness regarding these things. You surely can tell by the vocabulary I use that I am not a primitive individual who just walked his way through life ignorant and uneducated. Those kinds of stereotypes do not apply to most of us.

I am serving Philip, but not to get over resentment. I am long past that. No, I am serving him out of love, and I wanted to do this. I *wanted* to do this. It is my great joy to see how many people are helped through the work he is doing, and I feel part of that. When he comes over here, we will spend quite a bit of time talking and celebrating. It will be a great day for him and us. Can you imagine what it is like to work with a team of people for so long, helping people to make transitions, understand life after death, channel, give messages from above, and bring God in? All that and more we have done together. It has been a great joy; a great, great joy.

I could not help but personalize my experience with Philip because I feel an affinity, affection, love, and appreciation for him. Some of the things he has gone through in terms of suffering are similar to what my people experienced. By that, I mean that he also has had to learn to serve in order to grow spiritually.

This life is a kaleidoscope in which multiple facets of God can be seen. The Great Spirit is manifested in endless ways and in endless forms. If you fixate upon any one of them and say it is the truth, then you will turn around and learn something else is the truth. Finally, you see that life is a big diamond with many facets, and God is a *cosmic* diamond with many facets.

We Native Americans knew God was a being of multiple manifestations, and we learned that from nature. All one has to do is look at the wide, wide variety of flowers, plants, trees, and animals. Even the topography of the earth, with its undulations and hills, speaks greatly of the variety of God's being. There is green. There is desert. There are vast, vast realities that we observed as we traveled across the country, learning about different territories as we moved. We migrated for crops as we became more aware of the need for that. We learned. To Native Americans, this whole nation was just one great book of learning; and we passed our knowledge down through our traditions.

We knew much more than you may suspect. *Primitive* is a word that does not apply to us except with regard to the outer form of its meaning. We did live primitively in that we lived simply, as did the early white settler. But in terms of our nature, potential, and our own spirituality, we were not primitive. It is only a lack of knowledge and experience with us that has hidden that fact from the white man.

We are deeply spiritual, meaning we celebrate the presence of God manifested in all beings everywhere in all of creation, including the stars, the sun, the moon, and more. We know that all of space is God. Space is not a minus, but a plus. It is not the absence of something, but the presence of something. Space is the presence of God.

I gave a long answer, but I wanted to say all of this to get it out of my heart. This book is not just about cold facts. I know you want to know about us personally. I am a different person than when I first started working with Philip, and I am also a very different person from who I was during the time I was on earth. I now love others as myself.

Dr. D: *You said Native Americans learned lessons through the white man's taking over Indian lands. What did the white man learn?*

BH: The white man is still learning, and this is partly why your nation is undergoing some of the things it is going through now. You have to learn to love others as yourself. If the white man had loved us as he loved himself, there is no way he could have mistreated us. In some areas, some Native Americans are still so mistreated that there is unmitigated suffering and isolation. This is taking its toll psychologically and emotionally upon Native Americans to the point that some are quite dysfunctional or withdrawn and do not even want to be Native American. This is especially true for some of the young people.

The white man must learn that might does not make right. He cannot just go and do something or take over something just because he wants to do that for the nation. He must learn to think on a world scale. Human beings are members of one family.

Yes, there was fighting among the Native Americans, but as a whole we were peaceful with each other. Not all tribes were warring or had characteristics of anger, hate, distrust, or other negative energy. Until a new world view comes and until you become a world citizen, loving all people *everywhere* as yourself, no matter who they are, conflict and war will continue. You must learn not to center upon "God Bless America" alone, but God Bless the world, *all* people everywhere. Any leader who dares to call himself a leader must be capable of putting himself in another's place. He must be able to empathize with others, to have compassion for others, and to lead from that wisdom. Such leadership is very, very different from the ordinary, self-centered, or one-nation leadership.

You are very fortunate in this nation, because you do have the wise among you who are helping to keep things afloat. Native Americans on this side are also a part of helping to keep things afloat because our people are a part of the nation, too. We do not want this country to go under, because our people will also suffer. We do not want any negative prophecies to be fulfilled. We are working overtime to help with adjustments and changes.

Dr. D: *Would you explain the dynamics of mediumship from your perspective?*

BH: I said earlier that we had revelations, meaning we had mediums among our people. You can read about our revelations and prophecies. There was a tradition and a manifestation of mediumship among us, but I do not see it in the same way as I did before I became more enlightened about it. From my perspective, people are used as mediums because they are needed for that purpose. I am most happy when the truth can come through, and people can receive and understand it. The truth is that your aunt is not dead, your mother is not dead, and your father is not dead. The truth is that you are a spiritual being. You are going to leave your body one day to come to the spiritual side. The truth is that as you love others, so you become loved. The truth is that God is in all people, everywhere, and there are no exceptions.

The purpose of this life is to awaken to the reality that God is within; God is your center of self. This is the most important thing you can come to understand in this lifetime, for it is the purpose for which you came. Everything else is secondary. You came in order to know God within and to experience that in reality in your daily life. For me, that is what mediumship is about—that and more.

The higher the truth that comes through, the greater the value of the mediumship. I am channeling through Philip as you ask about mediumship, and he is an energy field. There are receptors in this energy field that pick up the vibrations, whether they are visual, auditory, or otherwise. They can also reflect feeling or emotion. These vibrations flow into Philip and go through a process within the mechanism you call mind. Then Philip simply pours out what I am pouring into him. He is quite passive during this process, as you can see. His arms are still. His body has not moved from this position the whole time we have talked. Sometimes Philip's upper torso or head moves. That happens when I am getting closest to him and when I am most excited or enthusiastic about what I am saying. This energy spills over into Philip and moves his physical being. That is how it happens.

The more subtle mediumship is the kind that you have experienced many times. Energy flows into you, and you are not cognizant of the entity who is present. You feel chills. You feel the flow of energy in you and through you. In that way you validate the authenticity or the presence of spirit, or you validate an idea. I cannot say more on mediumship at this point.

Dr. D: *How are you occupied in the spirit world, other than working with Philip?*

BH: I am a teacher. I teach other people how to do what I do, and this includes the full array of the things I have talked about. All of us on this side want to learn as much as possible about our real self and how to become aware of it. We enjoy the celebration of life, because God's presence here is so obvious. There is no arguing about whether there is a God or not. There is a constant flow of energy present, and we bask in it. We celebrate it. We love it. We may not always talk about it, but it is just an all-pervasive joy and peace that you do not have on earth. It puts everything in perfect order and perfect perspective.

I sit in classes, as there are always new things to learn. I love to paint, and I paint with light here. Philip is so impressed to paint because that energy pours over into him from me, plus he has the gift to do it. Painting with light is very different from painting with tempera paints, watercolors, or oils, though we can use those paints if we want to have that experience. It is not impossible. I love to paint things in nature. I also love to travel, as others do. I love to get together with my own people, though I am not in a tribe. I am a universal being, so I am with people from all walks of life and all backgrounds at a high level of spirituality. I no longer personally identify primarily with being Native American. My outward configuration may appear that way, but inwardly, as I say, I am a universal being.

It has been a pleasure to be with you today. This is my first chance to speak through this medium at length and to speak about my own heart in this way. You have to know heaven is a place where we all speak our hearts. We bear each other's burdens, and we celebrate each other's joys.

This is Black Hawk.

Dr. D: *Thank you so much for coming.*

End of session.

HARRIET TUBMAN

Harriet Tubman (circa 1820—March 10, 1913) was born Araminta Ross, a slave in Dorchester County, Maryland. She suffered severe beatings as a child, sustaining permanent brain damage, and she saw several siblings sold away from her family. In 1844, she married a free black man, John Tubman, but he declined to go with her when she escaped to Philadelphia in 1849. Eventually, she left that marriage.

Tubman was active in the Underground Railroad and led dozens of slaves to freedom. She was a friend and supporter of Frederick Douglas and John Brown. She served as a cook, nurse, and scout for the Union Army during the Civil War and later worked for women's suffrage. She cared for her elderly parents, relatives, and friends in a home built on land she bought in Auburn, New York. In 1869, she married a brick mason, Nelson Davis, and adopted a daughter, Gertie.

A devout Christian, Tubman had lifelong mystical experiences and said she could hear God speaking to her directly. She lived in near poverty much of her life and died in 1913 in a home for elderly African Americans built on land she donated for the facility. Today she is one of the best known and most respected women in U.S. history.

CONVERSATION ELEVEN

Harriet Tubman

When you come to identify yourself, not by color, language, or culture, but by being the son or daughter of God, then you are free. I don't live looking at these external things, and I wish the world would not do this either. If each person could stand before the other, race to race, language to language, culture to culture, and feel and experience the divine reality of every human being, the light of God in each one, then earth would become heaven.

—Harriet Tubman

HT: Yes, I'm here. It took you awhile to get Philip down. He was running around today, and his nerves needed this longer introduction.

Dr. D: *It does take longer sometimes. Thank you so much for coming.*

HT: It is my joy. I feel so lucky and privileged to be here, and I thank you; I thank you.

Dr. D: *We are honored to have you present with us among the other special people featured in this book.*

HT: I'm honored to step into this lovely energy you have created for us and to have this person to come through. I understand from our discussions here in the spirit world that you have some questions you want to ask me.

Dr. D: *Yes, I do. Please tell us anything you would like us to know about your life in the spirit world, including your home, your surroundings, and what you are doing now.*

HT: Most of all, I want people to know I am happy. I am no longer a slave, and I do not have a slave mentality. Earth was meant to be a place of trial, and many people don't get that. They don't understand that the earth is a school where there are tests so individuals can learn to know themselves; to pass the grade. When you come here as I did, after life's labor, it is impossible to find the words to express the difference between the two worlds. I found so much freedom here, and I found limitless possibilities.

I was not educated on earth except by my life experience, but that was so rich that I learned to deeply appreciate a broad array of things. I was an adventurer, so I dared to do things others did not dare to do, and this created for me a place in the spirit world that matched that expression. The realm I now live in is vast, but I didn't create it alone. People of a nature and experience similar to mine are dwelling in this sphere in the spirit world, so I have many heroic friends in this space.

As far as my home goes, words fail me to explain it, except to say it reflects my character. I was a simple person, but I cared about others.

No one had to teach me to care because it came out of my soul. I felt deep, deep compassion for others. When you suffer so much under the hands of someone else, it feels like your whole life is squeezed out of you to the point you can't even breathe unless they give you permission. You feel so hemmed in and blocked. I broke out of that because I was determined not to allow someone else to master my life. I wanted to be the master of my own life, which is God's plan.

My place of living in the spirit world is actually not so big, and I would not feel comfortable in a mansion. My home is beautiful, and it reflects my deeds on earth, my loves on earth, and what I did with my life on earth. All of this is reflected here in many ways— in the topography, the vegetation, the animals, the plants, and the materials used to build my particular house. Those who have selflessly given themselves to humanity and have had such a will that they mastered themselves completely, live in houses made of precious stones. Some live in houses made of diamonds and other jewels because these stones, and the mineral kingdom in general, represent will. The animal kingdom represents love, and the plant kingdom represents truth. I leave it to the reader's imagination as to what it would be like.

I carry on in many ways. I have dear friends here, and we get together just as you do on earth. Because of my nature and the focus of my life on earth, I am also part of a vanguard that seeks to win freedom, not just for America or just for black people, but for *all* who are enslaved. They may be enslaved by human beings, habits, or any number of other limitations. We work, in your earth time, around the clock for this cause.

Do I have recreation time? Of course. You can't spend eternity without it, any more than you can spend life on earth without it. Like many in the spirit world, I enjoy the exploration of nature, spending time in the woods and in the gardens, because all of that speaks to us so clearly. It speaks to you too, but not as clearly as it does here. We are re-invigorated as we walk the paths in beautiful, divine forests or bask in the sunlight. Light and color are everywhere. They revive our souls, and we are touched in every atom of our beings. It is easy to get out of the earth vibrations when we come here, because we just shake them off.

Am I coming through all right? *(You are doing wonderfully.)*

Dr. D: *Some say we become glorious but impersonal beings in the spirit world. Are our races, languages, and cultures retained? Are family and community identity retained?*

HT: You have asked several questions in one, so I will answer by breaking it down. As far as coming over to the spirit world and being a glorious being goes, there *is* glory here. There are emanations of light, and beings who have been here for countless numbers of years are light itself. I am light itself. We are all light. Even now, when you are still in your physical body, you are light. You are made of light. You are the emanation of light because you are a direct ray from the great central sun or God. You are always connected to that reality we call God.

When you come over, what you have done with your life will determine how much of that presence of God within you can shine forth. If your life has been blocked by the misuse of your energies, then you will not shine with the bright light that you would if you had served others and lived unselfishly, using your life energies most constructively for the betterment of self, others, and the world. How you appear in spirit depends on what you have done with your life.

As far as race is concerned, of course it continues. First, race is not only of the skin, but also of the mind. When I came here, I retained all the virtues and good aspects of my culture and my people. To tell you the truth, some of the highest beings in the spirit world are of my race because they suffered and overcame so much throughout history.

As far as family and community go, love is the means of drawing people together on earth, and it is the same here. Communities exist in form; that is, there are buildings, houses and neighborhoods. Everything on the earth plane is also here, but some of the people who were in a neighborhood on earth are not in that neighborhood in the spirit world. Neighbors live together here who are from the same level of accomplishment or level of spiritual growth. They may have done more with their lives than other people from their neighborhoods on earth. In the real sense of the word, in the spirit world, neighborhoods are made up of people who have loved life, loved God, and loved others to the same degree. They have a similar understanding about life, self, and God.

There is a truth to the fact that Catholics are with Catholics, Protestants are with Protestants, and so on, especially in some realms; but in the highest levels you will find the spiritual masters, people who often did not know each other on earth. The masters are, in fact, attracted to each other to the point where they make up neighborhoods or communities because they have the same degree of love and feel a common bond. Have I made myself understood?

Dr. D: *Yes, thank you very much. Is it too difficult for you to talk about painful things in your life on earth as a slave or the arduous task of leading hundreds of people through the Underground Railroad to freedom in the North?*

HT: *(Crying)*

Dr. D: *If this is too hard, we can go to the next question.*

HT: I'm okay. It's just that I feel temporarily overcome by some of my memories. I have been here in the spirit world nearly a hundred years, so I have worked through much of that pain, but you cannot live where people are treated so inhumanely without being affected. When I remember it all, I am still sensitive about the suffering I observed. People were treated like animals. They were taken from their mates, their parents, and other family members and often beaten for even a small infraction. Some of that remembrance is still in me, still in my heart, but for the most part, I have learned how to forgive.

I was a Christian who had experiences with God, so I knew if I could forgive people, somehow I would be freed from the negative side of my life. I worked on that both on earth and when I came here. I was quite effective in forgiving people because, as my record will show, once I set my mind to do something, I do not stop. After all, forgiveness is not about the other person. It's about you. It is about learning to free yourself from negative energies so *you* can go on living in a loving and positive way. Isn't that true?

Another thing is that there is still much enslavement on earth. Some people are slaves to food, some to sex, some to alcohol, and some to tobacco. Everyone comes to earth to be caught up in different things and learn lessons. Through my suffering, I learned of myself, and I learned more and more of God. If I had not suffered as I did, then I could not be where I am now. Through my suffering, I found my strengths and my weaknesses. I found the ability to overcome my weaknesses by magnifying my strengths.

As you probably know, I made many trips from the North to the South, always in great danger, but I did not allow myself to dwell on that. I had great faith in God because I had a high level of awareness. The voice of God spoke to me, and I followed what God directed. This helped me to find my way so that I lived with courage and determination and not in fear. I lived mostly in faith, and through doing that, I had a realization of who I am. I am still Harriet, but I am an expanded Harriet. I discovered there is a Christ light in each one of us, the brilliant light of God's presence.

We are all indeed the sons and daughters of God. When you see things in this larger perspective, you understand that people are playing roles and carrying out their lives on earth to do the things they came to do and learn the things they came to learn. You see that people become liberated to the degree they take initiative to be liberated. You understand that people's lives, in the long run, are often the better for their suffering, especially when they can take it positively. I did that.

So yes, I am choked up to think back on my life. As you could see, tears came to my eyes through Philip, and there was a moment when I found it hard to speak; but in the ultimate sense I am okay. You should feel free to ask me the questions you want to ask me. I will probably not be bothered again to the point that I shed tears.

Dr. D: *Among the people in this book, you are unique as an African American who was held in captivity as a slave. Can you share your thoughts about your experiences?*

HT: As I said before, we're all enslaved by something, if only by certain thoughts, fears, or worries that plague us over and over. As far as being black goes, there are many races on earth that are non-white. As I said, race is about mentality. Among my people there are those who are very refined, highly educated, very spiritual, and very saintly. At the other end of the spectrum, you will find those who have not yet awakened to their own divinity and beauty, and there is everyone between these two extremes. The same extremes are in the white race, the red race, and the yellow race, and you will find this true around the world.

When you come to identify yourself, not by color, language, or culture, but by being the son or daughter of God, then you are free. I don't live looking at these external things, and I wish the world would not do this either. If each person could stand before the other, race to race, language to language, culture to culture, and feel and experience the divine reality of every human being, the light of God in each one *(becoming tearful)*, then earth would become heaven.

Dr. D: *Please take a moment to rest.*

HT: For me to come through and express my emotions to such a full degree is a blessing for me. These energies I am feeling on the earth plane revive memories, but they also revive the love I experienced on earth, and it gives me a kind of longing.

Over and above that, because of my present mission and purpose in the spirit world, my heart is always dwelling with those I work with on this point: If only you on earth knew that you are all brothers and sisters from one love, and that you are all going through life's struggles in order to return to God!

Dr. D: *Are you ready to continue?*

HT: Oh please, yes. I'm waiting with bated breath!

Dr. D: *Can you describe some of your earthly experiences and observations so we can better understand the suffering of your people?*

HT: The first word that comes to me is *fear*. As slaves, we lived in constant fear. We never knew when, but any hour of night or day, our life could be changed completely. We could be sold off without being asked. We could have our children taken from us without one bit of consideration of our love for our child. We were treated like cattle, numbered like cattle, and chained up like cattle. We were thought of as inferior because we came from cultures that were not understood, and our skin color was different.

Even in this situation, though, I overcame my suffering. The more I saw the day-to-day reality of what it meant to be a slave, in my life and in the lives of those surrounding me, the more it stirred up within me the clarity and determination to remove myself from it. And so I did.

Those who used their enslavement as a stepping stone to carefully, prayerfully, and even cleverly remove themselves from it became stronger to overcome. When I finally found freedom, I was more disciplined in my personal life than the average person. In the grand scheme of things in eternity, I am better off and more a master of myself than many people who lived a life of freedom and luxury. Does that make sense to you? *(Yes.)* So, here I am, greatly blessed.

Dear friends, your life lasts for *eternity*, not just for thirty, forty, or fifty years on earth. Your time on earth is a very fortunate time, if you understand that instead of complaining about your suffering you can overcome it by using it to learn. Because of my suffering, I learned I would never, ever treat another person the way I was treated. In that sense, I learned how to love unconditionally; something my masters on earth could never do. They loved money, power, and recognition, and because of that, they became enslaved by their own appetites. They are the ones who are in darkness here in the spirit world, in the grip of their own lack of self-mastery, lack of compassion, and lack of love. Some of the worst are in the darkest part of the spirit world, and they will be there yet for many hundreds of years.

So who was the slave, and who was the master? Who won freedom, and who became the slave? You have it all backwards on earth. That is why Jesus said, "Blessed are the meek. Blessed are the peacemakers." You bless yourself as you bless others, and that is the secret. In the end, I could forgive my masters because they were actually enabling me to become greater than I would have been had I not been a slave.

Dr. D: *At a video store some time ago, Philip saw a movie about the life of Rosa Parks and was suddenly overcome with tears and chills. He heard a voice behind him say loud and clear, "I was the spirit guide for Rosa Parks." He immediately discerned that it was you, Harriet Tubman, and that you were telling the truth. This visitation led us to know with great certainty that you were to be in this book. Would you please share with us more about that moment with Philip and your work with Rosa Parks?*

HT: Yes. That was history in the making! I was sent to Philip that day for the dual purpose of helping him understand what I was doing in connection to the earth plane and impressing him to include me in the book. I did not personally choose myself to be included or to speak to Philip that day in the bookstore without the direction of the higher masters. Philip had been thinking of me among several others to include in the book, and the masters were trying to impress him with that information. Finally they had to *double* impress him, so I came that day, and he heard me clearly.

When I was on earth, I had the experience of going back and forth between the North and the South, especially in Maryland, to bring people to freedom. This gave me great, great understanding, wisdom, and merit, so I became an authority on how to think, feel, and act to win freedom. This put me in a position to work with people like Rosa Parks.

My work with Rosa was in keeping with all that I have already said to you about my concern and the concern of others like me in the spirit world. We are working to help mankind to win freedom on a scale running everywhere from the individual person to the nation. We are doing this centered not *only* on race, but on the whole spectrum of things that hinder people and keep them from knowing themselves, knowing God, and being free.

Dr. D: *America elected the first African American in American history in 2008 and re-elected him in 2012. Could you share with us how you and others in the spirit world view this?*

HT: I'm actually *not* excited simply because Americans elected a black president. He could be white, red, or any color. According to God's plan, those who should lead are always those who are wisest and most loving, so color has nothing to do with it. What I *am* excited about is the attitude of acceptance that his election represented. It was a big step forward for your country, and there is a great sense of relief in the spirit world because of this. As America goes, the world will go. That is the kind of influence you have. Because a black person was elected president, people of other cultures and colors throughout the world can now relate more with your country and culture, which in the past has been almost exclusively led by the white race, as has also been true in England. This is one world—one humanity—and color should not matter.

Because of how things are on earth, there is a lack of understanding and experience in these areas. Suffering will go on as long as people do not look at such things from the perspective that I have shared here. Your country will go on, and the earth will continue to turn, but suffering will continue. Rather than getting caught up in personalities, including those of persons in political office, work on *yourselves*. If everyone would do that, including all of those elected to political office, and come into the mentality that I am speaking of, you would have righteous leaders who are the wisest and most loving, and heaven would come on earth.

Dr. D: *You were referred to as the Moses of your people, and you were obedient to the voice of God in making all of your decisions, especially during the long treks to bring slaves to the North. It is written that you were also a prophet, foretelling things to come. Would you please comment on the role of divine guidance in your life?*

HT: It remains the most important thing in my life. While it is said I was hit on the head as a child and this brought about certain infirmities, this experience is *not* the origin of my spirituality. What is not known is that even from childhood I had a perception of things not seen. The blow on the head only hastened the day of my greater spiritual awakening and the full opening of my spiritual senses. My receiving that blow also paid a physiological and spiritual price that increased my position of merit. Having such a sharp blow to my head caused God, in his love and compassion, to draw even closer to me. Knowing me better than I knew myself, he knew I would change the history of black people in America.

Change had to start somewhere, and I was not the only one to bring it about. There were many doing the kind of work I did, but I was singled out to do the particular things I did. God drew close to me to use me. Once I got here and spoke with the masters, I became aware of my own God presence, and I understood. I realized I was not little Harriet Tubman, but cosmic Harriet Tubman. You all are cosmic, but until you awaken to it, you cannot function that way.

Yes, I was able to prophesy. When you do the kind of work I did, God is obliged to help you. When you give everything to others and don't think of yourself, you are indeed providing a mirror for God to see himself, because he does the same thing all the time. He gives of himself without thought of himself. I was doubly empowered because it was my nature to be determined. Fueled by all I experienced from childhood up to that time, my determination was to liberate myself and as many of my people as I could. Therefore, God invested so much in me, and I obeyed. We had a working relationship that helped me to save myself and many others.

I am, to this day, grateful beyond words for this reality in my life. To the world, I was a homely person. I did not dress well. I was rather masculine and strong of muscle because of how I was treated as a slave and what I had to do, and I didn't have the womanly wiles of some women. What I did have was the heart and the mind to do what I did. And I did it.

When I came to the spirit world, I understood how and why things happened as they did, and I had no regret. I do not suffer here at all because of the life I led on earth. The suffering I experienced on earth became a springboard for my salvation.

Dr. D: *You are one of America's great heroines. As a result of your sacrificial and exemplary life on earth, how were you greeted when you arrived in the world of spirit?*

HT: In life, I was not aware of my true self, and most slaves were not aware of themselves, because they were always at task, never knowing what was going to happen next. I spent most of my life helping to free slaves in the South, and I was busy raising funds to get money for my next trip, my next trip, and my next trip to the South to bring people to the North. I worked at jobs to earn money when I couldn't get money another way, and I was always ready to go to the next thing. When I was not working on my cause, I was resting because I was exhausted. I nearly burned myself out to the point where my health suffered. I was kept strong, beyond the power of my body, through the power of my mind and the spiritual energies around me. I prayed, but it was always about my mission, and there was no time in my life to really think of myself.

When I came to the spirit world, I spent the first hours in tears, crying floods and floods of tears of gratitude for the overwhelming reality of the welcoming love I felt from the masters, including the Master Jesus. There are simply no words to explain that love or that welcome.

I would encourage anyone who is reading this book to think about all I have said. Know that you and I are not so different. We are eternal beings who take our walk on earth, seeking to realize ourselves. When you realize yourself, you will realize everything in God. Then you are free.

Please don't squander or waste your time, but use it wisely for the things that truly count. Then you can move up to be in the ranks of the ones who are most celebrated in the spirit world—those who were unselfish in life; those who loved others with a heart and a mind that blessed them with the very presence of God.

Dr. D: *Is there anything else you would like to share that I have not asked about?*

HT: Only that I am deeply touched by both the efforts you are making and by the fact that you have been so considerate in your questions. Each of us needs to be considered as a unique human being. We need to know that the love going between us is personal and genuine. That is the nature of God, and that is the nature of the great ones. I am so thankful I could come today and spend this time with you. There is much more I could say, but this is enough. God bless you. This is Harriet Tubman.

End of session.

ABRAHAM LINCOLN

Abraham Lincoln (February 12, 1809—April 15, 1865) was the 16th President of the United States, serving from 1861 through 1865 as a Republican opposed to the expansion of slavery. During the American Civil War, he issued the Emancipation Proclamation in 1863 and promoted the passage of the Thirteenth Amendment to the Constitution. Lincoln is remembered for his powerful, influential, and inspirational words, and his Gettysburg Address is cherished as one of the greatest public speeches in American history. Lincoln strongly supported a policy of generous treatment of the defeated Confederacy to promote national reconciliation. His assassination in 1865 made him an American martyr for the ideals of freedom and unity. Because of his eloquence, integrity, and the dramatic times in which he lived and died, Lincoln has had a lasting influence on U.S. politics and the American imagination.

CONVERSATION TWELVE

Abraham Lincoln

By seeking to heal individuals and your land, you inadvertently heal yourself.

—*Abraham Lincoln*

Comment:

Dr. D: *I could feel the energy of Abraham Lincoln wanting to come through, so the hypnosis induction was brief prior to this session.*

AL: Yes, I am here now. As most know, my face appears on the smallest coin used in the United States, the penny. As a point of focus, the image of a penny is now being suspended in front of Philip. I have been eagerly waiting since he perceived my presence earlier this morning. I am here to engage my thoughts and feelings in this experience, and there are many eager to do this. It should be no surprise to either of you that people of stature would want to come through. When we were on earth we wanted to be heard, we *were* heard, and we influenced others. We carried that desire with us to the spirit world. Our influence is of a different nature now because it is amply backed by an awareness we did not have on the earth plane.

I am so happy, Dolores, that I can come through. When he comes out of this state, I want you to greet Philip for me and thank him for allowing me to be here. I was so pleased that he heard me when I communicated my desire to be included. You have no idea how exhilarating it is to get into the earth energies in this way. There are many on earth to whom I can be close, but what the two of you are doing in enabling us to come through this kind of channel is rare. There is a celebratory feeling here when something like this happens, and I am grateful to be a part of it. It is humbling for me to be selected from among others to impart my thinking and feeling.

We would like to have many trained as mediums, so we could come through to bring the truth that could make a difference. Such truth trickles through now, compared to what could come through if more people were trained. I want to encourage Philip to continue what he is doing and to keep moving in the direction of training others to do what he does. We are helping with that.

As you can well imagine, and I am allowed to say this, your book is already written here. That should bring a smile to your face. It is hard to explain what it means to say your book is already written, but everything that is of the spirit pre-exists its appearance on the earth plane. With God there is no time, and all things are known. You are but instruments for the manifestation of the truth God wants to bring through the personalities who are speaking in this way.

I know you have questions, as you have had with each soul who has come. We are very aware of all of this. I am ready for any questions you have.

Dr. D: *How do you feel this book will help humanity?*

AL: As has been said by others who have spoken, it will not help all people, but there are those who are hungering for truth at this level. There is already an intention that the book will touch their lives, and so it shall. Man is not complete, not whole, not fully alive, because he does not have all the truth. It is like existing without certain limbs or faculties. When I say "man," I mean man and woman, and I do not want to offend women who are reading this.

The spirit world is the ever-present, ever-guiding center of life energy. God, that electrical, phenomenal force of love, is always pouring through the spirit world, spiritual entities, and spiritual phenomena of all sorts to bring truth to earth. Especially during the last two decades, many on earth are writing about these things. Known and not known to them, they are instruments for bringing through higher truth.

When Philip began this work, much less was known about the spirit world, but now there is an outpouring of phenomena. Mediums, channelers, philosophical teachers, and writers with this interest are all being used and inspired. All the information is important, but I am interested in the fundamentals, because people need a specific path to walk to get to a specific point. They must know and apply the actual principles of spiritual life and spiritual growth. If their interests are too scattered, and they are simply curious, they may find they do not arrive at the highest level of spiritual attainment.

Your book will be among other books being written, but it will captivate the imagination of many. In each generation people have wanted to know, "What did those who lived prior to us think and do? What were they really like? What are they doing now?" People are curious about relatives who have passed on, but they are also interested in those who were famous on the earth. This is true in your country more than in others, but it is a rather universal interest. Why? It goes with the territory of being human, because you are all destined to come to the spirit world.

You are an eternal being who is simply in a physical body from which you will one day depart. This is well known, at least theoretically, because it is spoken of in scripture and in literature around the world. Human beings have an innate desire to know what is beyond life on earth. According to personality, life experience and the role each plays, we in the spirit world are cooperating with you by pouring out information through various individuals.

I realize that I gave a long answer to your question, but because I have the rare opportunity of having the door open between the two worlds, it is natural for me to pour out as much information as possible.

Dr. D: *You came to Philip this morning asking to be included in this book. You told him you would like to talk about religion in the spirit world. What would you like to say?*

AL: Well, well, he got it. He heard me!

I believed in God on earth, but I was a universal person with a universal mind. When I was a child I had experiences with spirit world, though I did not write or speak about this. Ultimately, I was involved with spiritual phenomena in my presidency, and this was absolutely, unequivocally important. Without it, I would not have been the same person, and I could not have done the work I did.

You may disregard spirit as "spooks," treating us as if we do not exist. You can pretend you know all things and are capable of living by yourselves, but that is simply not the truth. We all need each other. Life is about the family of man, not the individual. We are all from one parent and one origin. The more we defer to the reality of where we came from and where we are going in terms of our spiritual life, the quicker we are going to come into enlightenment as to the whole picture and our individual part in it.

Religion is man-made. Is it inspired by God? It is to a certain extent, but man's undisciplined imagination, combined with ego, has created within religion limitations that are simply not applicable to the truth. Those who come to this side with a spiritual perspective have a bigger picture, but those who are religious tend to cling to an organizational kind of awareness. By magnetic attraction, they unwittingly seek out affiliation with the religion they adhered to while on the earth. You will find them still gathering in a congregation. They are not without cognizance, but they will go to services until they realize what is really intended by religion; to go inside of self and find God. This is what scripture refers to when it says we are temples of God.

Where does God truly dwell? He dwells in every atom of the universe. God is a lover of mankind and also a scientist. His energy runs the whole gamut of creation and is found in every atom. Rather than limiting God to being inside of some kind of text or to coming through one figure, one should realize that God is equally present in every person. The light in each person is equal to the light in every other person. What varies is how much this light can shine into the consciousness of individuals. This determines how much they can know their own divinity, their own spiritual reality.

When there is a lack of knowledge and life experience, ignorance blocks the way and keeps a person from awakening to God within. Once you have met God within yourself, what else is there? Once you have tasted sugar, you will always know what sugar tastes like. Once you have tasted God, truly tasted God within, you will always know what God is like and what the experience of God is. It is as natural as breathing.

If you were completely different from God, God could have nothing to do with you, in the same way that water and oil cannot mix; but you are *not* different. The element of love exists in both you and God, and the need to express love creates the basis upon which God and humankind can become one. As you extend yourself into that energy within, you become an expanded human being, as Jesus was. Through the consciousness of God within you, you are able to know the things that God knows, and you become a universal person. In the spirit world that is the goal—to become a universal person, breaking the bonds of spiritual ignorance to soar into the cosmic awareness that God is all things. God is everywhere at all times, including within you. If you could but see, you are a radiation of light from God, the universal light from whom all light is derived.

Those in the realms of light in the spirit world know this. It is obvious because it is a continual conscious and unconscious experience. Those in realms removed from plentiful light do not know. Their ignorance blocks them from such awareness. In fact, the darkness they live in is but an outer manifestation of their inner ignorance.

Not all on the earth plane are ready to climb the rungs of spiritual attainment and awaken to the reality of who and what they are, to get out of the darkness of the shadow of ignorance. But to those who are ready, I would say to soar toward that ideal, and it shall happen. It shall come to pass. The magnetic reality of the universe will bring to you the things you focus upon. If you long to be a universal being, whether or not you understand what that is, you will. If you can imagine knowing God personally and becoming an expanded being in the energy of God, and if that is where you put your focus, then it shall happen. The universe, God, or whatever you may call it, will respond. You will reach the apex of life.

I am more than enthusiastic about all of this, and I was that kind of being when I was on earth. Otherwise, I could not have done what I did or been who I was philosophically. It was not a pretense but the very nature of my being to be imbued with humility. I did not tell others about the experiences I had that caused me to bend easily to a power greater than myself.

I wanted to come through because my words are different from what other speakers have said, though there is some overlap. What I say reflects my own vocabulary and experience. What will the overall result be? Each part of this book is valuable, but what we say taken as a whole will have an impact upon the consciousness of those who read it. They will walk away saying, "Hmmm, I didn't know that," or "I thought that was true," or "That is meaningful to me," or "I feel more awakened to the reality of the existence of spirit world." The book will enable us to come close to the reader, and this will help each one along the way toward the pursuit of God and self, that is *Self* with a capital "S."

Dr. D: *Do you wish to make any comment about your untimely death?*

AL: *No* death is untimely, dear. Death happens to each of us exactly at the appointed hour and in the appointed way. Would I like to have stayed longer on earth? Yes, given my idea of what life is. But once I settled in, I understood why I had to come here when I did. My work was over. I had brought the Emancipation Proclamation, and I paid a price for it. Once I had done that, I graduated into the spirit world, and I was ready.

Did I miss the earth plane? Not at all! It was a relief to be in the spirit world. I still had to face responsibilities, but I had greater understanding as to the cause and effect behind everything that had happened on earth, particularly in America, during my presidency. Once you come here, you have the bigger picture, though it does not just come automatically to every individual. You have to be ready for it, open to it, and evolved highly enough to understand it.

Many mourned my death, and we find such mourning to be human nature. If elephants can mourn their dead, we could ask, why not human beings? Such mourning is necessary for individuals on earth for cathartic purposes. It allows them to bring out and expiate their grief, so new energy can come in, and they can move on and up. I do not in any way eschew the experience of mourning. It is necessary for many.

I did not suffer, in that there was no pain. After I was shot, I was totally unconscious and out of my body. I could see people rushing about, worried, whereas I was very calm and did not feel concerned. I was already attended by those teachers who had worked with me, some of the great ones from ancient times, particularly from the Greek civilization. I was already being apprised of what my life was about and why I was moving into the spirit world. It was not done hurriedly, but more quickly than you could imagine. By the time I had taken my last breath, much was already assembled in my life on the other side so I could move on. That was the nature of my life.

Yes, I missed people on earth. I would not be human if I did not have those feelings. I found I could visit again and again, so I did visit, and I do.

Dr. D: *Can you give us any insight into the future of America?*

AL: Well, you know, life is cyclic. *(Chuckle)*

People become victims of their own thinking. If they but knew *how much* they are victims of their own thinking! They draw to themselves what they are. This is true for individuals, and as individuals go, so goes the nation. Criticism, infighting, and the news media's publishing of all the sordid details of people's lives only generate negative energy and cause a disturbance within the national character and organism. Yes, indeed, America is in a bad way because of that. The negative energy is a huge thought form over your country, and prayer energy is needed to neutralize it.

Prayer truly provides the kind of energy needed to neutralize the negative energy within the self of many. By sending love out to individuals, again by the law of attraction, you draw love back to yourself. By seeking to heal individuals and your land, you inadvertently heal yourself. That is the point of such prayer. All I can say, all that I am allowed to say, is this: As the energy changes within more than a few individuals, then the energy within the whole nation will change, affecting all people.

We cannot interfere with those who hold fast to certain concepts or ideologies as though they were religion, and sometimes that kind of energy blocks progression. Your nation needs much prayer, and so does the world as a whole. You are in error, though, if you think this world was intended to be perfect. It is through the vicissitudes of life that you learn and grow. It is by suffering that you seek to find the solution to suffering. Many are now bending their knees before

God to ask for help who have not done so for some time. Many are praying in desperation. What has happened to your nation is for a purpose higher than you can understand. I would urge all people everywhere to think loving thoughts of themselves and others. Be quick to forgive self and quick to forgive others for their mistakes. It is when you become earthbound and bound by negative thinking that you create war within self and ultimately in the world.

I say nothing new, but you asked me about the state of your nation. Know that those who are in charge are not always in charge. It is often those praying ardently behind the scenes who are in charge. Those who have the greater wisdom are funneling and focusing the energy, not just influencing your nation, but the world at large. Master teachers in the spirit world are working in this way to guide each of you and all of humanity, working with you individually and collectively.

Dr. D: *Is there anything you can tell us about the reality of the soul before it enters into the physical body?*

AL: Intelligence begins with the beginning of God, and God always was. Those are the only words I can use to explain the reality of God. You could not comprehend an explanation of God from the higher realms, from our perspective. You would be like a 4th grader trying to understand higher math. There is a continuum: The science of math exists from the beginning to the end of the universe, and God exists throughout all of creation. Divine intelligence brought forth all of the ideals that exist in physical and spiritual form. Everything that is came from God, including your body and soul.

Prior to your entrance into the human world on earth, there is a plan well thought out by the masters, in consultation with you. When you come to the earth plane, you are already enlightened. You are aflame with the light of God. The life that is in God is in you, because without that life, you cannot be, either in the physical or spiritual reality. It is all God. It is by entering into the physical body that the process of covering up that light begins. The journey into ignorance begins with the first cry, which you call suffering. Through this process, you seek to find the way to overcome suffering. That is what eventually awakens you to the divine self within. You realize you are not your body, you are not your thinking, you are not your mind, and you are not your feelings.

You are the God presence, emanating forever and ever from within you, as the flame of life, divine intelligence, divine love, and divine will. This comes with you into the earth plane, and you eventually awaken to it, either on earth or in the spirit world. Then you are set free. You awaken and know from where you came and to where you are returning. It is a full cycle.

God manifests in the finite form of an individual to experience the limitations of the earth plane. This causes the individual to seek to break through and go beyond such limitations. That is the quest and the struggle of the human soul. When there is enough earnestness behind such questing, again by the law of attraction, you attract the God presence from out of self. That is the coming of the kingdom of heaven on earth of which Jesus spoke. *That* is the awakening. Then the search is over. Then you can live in total peace, totally detached from the earth plane, and at any point leave to come back to the source. I cannot say more on this point.

Dr. D: *It has been said that we choose our parents prior to coming into our new birth. Is this accurate? If so, do things sometimes go awry after this choice is made?*

AL: It is true. On all points, it is true. Even so, the choice is made for the purpose of eventually awakening enough so you are able to overcome all problematic situations. If there is no darkness, there is no light. If there had been no night on earth, there would have been no need to invent the light bulb. It was the need and desire to illuminate the night that caused the search for a way to do this. Through the struggle you undertake as a soul, starting by struggling with the body and with human relationships, you come into your own.

If individuals understand why they struggle and why they need to be earnest in overcoming, that gem of truth alone will make the reading of this book invaluable. I am not the first to say it, nor will I be the last. I am making a point that has been echoing down through eons of time: *Man's extremity is God's opportunity.*

Dr. D: *What role are you now playing in the spirit world?*

AL: I still have concerns about the awakening of people. As you can tell from my words and my spiritual energy, I seek to go to the etiology, the source, of human suffering.

I am also part of a universal government. The desire to govern, in and of itself, is a good thing, but many on earth govern in error because of ignorance. Politics is an outer manifestation reflecting an inner reality. Governing must be conducted with love and truth. That is why I am driving home the necessity of being of pure soul, of seeking the highest truth and manifesting divine love that sees and treats others as self. That simply does not exist today in governments on earth. It is an ideal of government in America, but it is not practiced. That is why America and other countries are in trouble and why the world is in a state of turbulence, nearly bursting open with hate, anger, and bitterness.

I work with a universal government through the hierarchy of the spirit world, seeking to influence leaders, followers, and all people on earth through the multiple streams of consciousness here. Those of the higher realms of the spirit world also teach and influence those in lesser realms.

Yes, we know how to govern better. We know how to win elections, raise funds, and all of that, but those activities are secondary to one's motivation in leadership. As we approximate the Christ Spirit, with total and unconditional love of the people, sacrificing our lives in seeking to bring the highest truth on the earth plane, we will change the world. That is what I am about, as are others who have sought the truth of things.

Dr. D: *It is well documented that you and your wife, Mary, held sessions with mediums. Is this accurate? If so, would you like to say more about this?*

AL: It is completely accurate. You can read about this if you wish to do the research. No further comment is needed, because the facts are available on the earth plane, and I seek to bring in new information.

I totally embrace the idea of spirit communication within the context of right education and right application. In the hands of those who are not enlightened and educated, spirit communication can be misleading or harmful by drawing in lower entities that can damage a person's mental and emotional faculties. In the right hands, with the right teachers, it is appropriate for people to interface with the spirit world, because it is God's original intention that the two worlds are one.

The evolution of the planet is dependent upon the interaction of the spiritual and physical worlds. Communication can happen through direct contact such as you are having now, through revelation, and through inspiration given for scientific advances or artistic expressions. Through all of these means, interaction between the two worlds is legitimate and needed to bring man to the next level of spiritual awakening and attainment.

Dr. D: *In a reading Philip did for me several months ago, Thomas Jefferson came and said that our book will be like a new Declaration of Independence. Could you elaborate on that?*

AL: Because this book will declare higher truth, there will be decreased dependency upon lesser truth or ignorance. This will free many minds to pursue the spirit world through understanding the dynamic going on between you and us. People will have a new sense of freedom in doing this.

Many on earth adhere to teachings that have been applicable in the evolution of human life on earth, but there is a need to evolve into higher awareness. It is much like the difference between the Ten Commandments that Moses received and the two commandments that Jesus gave. If you truly live by the two commandments, to love God with all your heart, mind, and soul, and to love your neighbor as yourself, the Ten Commandments will be less needed, because they will be automatically followed.

Once you understand that the highest expression of religion is to love and serve others as yourself, you have evolved from a complex system of religious ideas and teachings to the Golden Rule, and this is all that is necessary. When you love others as self, many things that bother you will fall away. Selfishness and greed will fall away. You will not be able to treat others in a selfish way, as you would not treat yourself that way. It is vitally important for humanity to awaken individually and collectively to the knowledge and practice of higher and simpler truth and to embrace the religion of love as a universal principle.

Dr. D: *Is there anything else you would like to add?*

AL: I am very happy, because I determine to be. True happiness depends upon inner, not outer circumstances. If you practice going inward and take the time to discover your real self, you will find it is impregnated by the love of God and that it basks eternally in that love. Happiness is a part of that discovery. I did not seek happiness on earth as much as I sought peace. When you know what life is truly about, why you came on earth, and what you are to accomplish, you can make a breakthrough into *Self.* Then you desire or need nothing else in order to be happy.

I have no need for anything but myself, because all I need is contained in me. Most importantly, divine love is contained in me, as it is in all people, through time and eternity. Awakening to that reality is what life is about.

Go in peace, all. I am so very happy that I could come through today and share my thoughts with the beloved family of mankind. This is Abraham Lincoln.

End of session.

DANIEL DAVID PALMER

Daniel David Palmer (March 7, 1845—October 20, 1913) was the founder of chiropractic medicine. He was born near Toronto, Canada, and later moved with his family to the United States. While he worked at various jobs in Iowa, he became a self-taught student of anatomy with a keen interest in healing modalities, including osteopathy.

Dr. Palmer was spiritually inspired to develop chiropractic methods. He believed that impaired nerve flow was the cause of most disease and that a properly aligned spinal column was necessary to optimize nerve flow and good health. He founded the Palmer School of Chiropractic in 1897. After selling his school to his son, B.J. Palmer, he moved to the West Coast and developed chiropractic educational programs in a number of other states. He died at the age of sixty-eight from typhoid fever.

CONVERSATION THIRTEEN

Daniel David Palmer

Through meditation and prayer, particularly through meditation, you can consciously tune into the energy of God and bring it forth in yourself. This will bring about not only physical and mental changes, but also soul changes or spiritual changes. It will bring about healing. Once you touch the great energy of God at the highest and deepest part of your being, you are never the same.

—Daniel David Palmer

Dr. P: I am here. This is Dr. Palmer. Can you hear me? *(Yes, you are coming through just fine.)* We appreciate the process of your taking Philip deeper and deeper. For a few moments he was actually at rest, and he needed that. Your guides were guiding you, and you intuitively tuned in well to their guidance. I want you to know that and to keep trusting that you are doing a good job.

I want to be of service as much as possible. I am excited about this opportunity to speak, because our job and our desire is to free people on earth from ignorance about life after death—the continuation of life. I work with Philip for the purpose of his mediumship, but for me the most important point is that I am able to help other people through my cooperation with him. That is the reward.

Through Philip's work, we can help not only those on earth who are on the telephone with him or sitting before him, but also individuals on this side, by coordinating our work with them. As Philip gives a reading, ancestors and immediate family in the spirit world come and observe, sometimes participate, and learn. That is another important benefit.

I know you have a list of questions. I prompted some of them through the mind of Philip, and I would say that about a third of the questions are about things I wanted to address. The rest of them were written under the auspices of you and Philip. I would like to go directly to your questions.

Dr. D: *Please describe yourself and tell us more about who you are.*

Dr. P: I am filled with love. Philip does not always think that, because I am independent, and his communication with me has not been as strong as it has been with some of his other guides. I am Dr. Daniel David Palmer, the founder of chiropractic medicine on the face of the earth. There are those who learned how to manipulate the skeletal structure before I did, but theirs was private work and was not widely available to the public.

I wrote a tome on chiropractic medicine that became like a bible or source reference for many chiropractors. After working with patients over a period of time, I founded what is now the Palmer

College of Chiropractic, which is still in existence. My work was based on knowledge that came from working with patients and trying different approaches, but I was also spiritually open. That is how I first intuited the possibility of manipulation of the skeletal system, particularly the spinal column, to help people.

I studied the effects of my techniques and developed research papers of my own. I kept track of results and recorded the science of what I discovered through experiments. I also recorded what was given to me by spirit. You might say I was chiropractic medium. I could clairvoyantly see into the body and manipulate the spinal column to where it needed to be both by touch and intuition. I could look into the body and see where there were subluxations or pressures on certain vertebrae and help bring about adjustments in that way. I pioneered a field that had not been developed before I went into it. Today chiropractic medicine is as commonly available as regular medicine.

Dr. D: *What do you see as your "claim to fame"?*

Dr. P: I laughed when Philip came up with that question, because he knows my personality. He knows I am not orthodox in the sense that I am not going to say the typical thing. I could not have done what I did with chiropractic work had I been just like everyone else. I had to bring what I had to bring, and I am the same way now as I was when I was on earth. In that sense, I get bored with the repetition of things, so it would have not been enough for me to do only chiropractic work. I had to do more, and one of the things I did was to teach other people how to do what I could do.

My claim to fame is that I am the founder and teacher of chiropractic medicine. In the medical field now, bone manipulation or chiropractic is often used in conjunction with orthodox medicine because people have experienced the benefits. In studying the body more deeply in medical school, students can see the primary importance of the spinal column. They can see that electrical nerve energy comes from the brain through the spinal column and out to various areas and organs of the body. They can understand that if this electrical energy is not flowing steadily and correctly, the body's cells and organs cannot get a sufficient amount of it and will become impaired and dysfunctional. It is very important to understand that there are electrically charged ions flowing throughout the body that affect its overall functioning and health.

Dr. D: *What kinds of things are you doing in your life on the other side?*

Dr. P: I do many things. Interspersed with work, I have the chance to travel, which I did not get to enjoy on earth, and to rest. I still work with my schools on earth, and I inspire leaders and students. I do this because chiropractic medicine was my work on earth, and I am responsible for both the good results and the mistakes made based on my teaching. I help to bring new understandings I did not teach on earth because I did not get a complete revelation at that time.

Others have augmented or changed some of what I taught in my practice, and it was correct for them to do that. This is in keeping with the need to perfect a methodology that I was not able to completely do, and it will be more and more perfected. There will be a deeper and higher understanding as years go on. Chiropractors have now incorporated other knowledge into the field of chiropractic medicine, and that is good. It is most important. From this side, I help with the operation of my schools and with the continual expansion of knowledge.

On this side of life, I also work at a hospital teaching many students about mental healing and how to use the mind to heal oneself and others, to be channels for healing energy. I help to teach students how to use their own minds and energies to help others. Here we know directly that we have a certain power because we are able to tap into cosmic, universal energy. When we do, we are magnified in our usefulness and purpose.

Of course, I spend time with the masters, and I am considered a master within my field. If I were not, I could not work with Saint Germain, Kathryn Kuhlman, and Black Hawk. We are on a par with each other, to use that earthly term. We have mastery in our own particular fields, and mine on earth was chiropractic and healing. My work carries on in laboratories where I continue to experiment. In that way, I work as I did on earth, but on a more advanced level.

I also teach about how to communicate with God within and how each one can come into that awareness. Not everyone who comes over is ready for that, so we have classes to help people awaken. I help Philip with his classes and the work he is doing to help people help themselves.

I enjoy nature. That is one thing all of us here enjoy. It is intoxicating to walk out into the woods and to have a baby fawn come up and lick your hand and not be at all afraid or a mother bear come and rub her head up against you, filled with love, while her cubs play at your feet. It is an amazing joy to experience these things, and I wish I could convey the whole reality of everything we have here. No words are adequate to tell you about the magnificent, supreme beauty we experience in the realms of the spirit world where I live.

I have my own garden with my home. I love to work with master horticulturists here to create some of the rarest flowers and the most beautiful garden. My small garden does not need tending as gardens do on earth because everything here is in divine, perfect order. My garden gets enough nutrients, water, and light so that it does not need for me to do anything.

We create our home before we arrive in the spirit world, so there were already flowers in my garden when I came over. The wonderful thing is that the flowers bloom and bloom and bloom! Many flowers that were in my garden when I came here are still blooming, and the petals have not fallen off. There is a sustaining power that enables all things to be continuously alive for as long as we want them. If I desire it to happen, something I no longer want will just disappear, and something new will come.

I have covered much about what I do and about my life here. Though I have not said everything, it is enough for now.

Dr. D: *Is there anything about chiropractic medicine human beings do not know that they need to know at this time?*

Dr. P: People need to fully understand the flow of energy throughout the body and how vitally important it is to maintain a flexible backbone. If that flexibility is not maintained as one ages, the backbone can push on nerves, causing pain and restricting the flow of energy to certain organs. The result will be determined by where the impaired nerve is, meaning through which vertebra it passes. People on earth have physical problems that result from there being insufficient electrical energy to enliven and keep healthy the cells within an organ or an area of the body. There is a correlation between not having sufficient energy and diseases of the body.

Dr. D: *How did you discover the area of chiropractic medicine on earth?*

Dr. P: I had a natural curiosity about the human body from about the age of twelve, and I had impressions about it because I was spiritually open. I had dreams and experiences out of the body where I learned from the masters that I would be the channel to bring chiropractic medicine to the earth. God knows it has paid off and has gone a long way toward helping millions of people every year. God led me gradually to see clairvoyantly what chiropractic medicine was, in the dream state and through my meetings with the masters, but it had to be brought to the earth plane on a practical level. It had to be applied and refined.

I was chosen not only to bring the revelation of chiropractic medicine, but to help perfect it. Because I had this natural inclination and a certain natural healing ability, I was right at home with what I was doing. I never regretted a thing I did. I was only happy and proud to have brought chiropractic medicine to the earth plane. I did not want to unduly proclaim things about myself, so I did not do that, but I was happy that healing could take place through my offering on earth.

Dr. D: *You have worked with Philip for many years. Can you tell us more about that?*

Dr. P: Well, it is now going on thirty years that I have been working with Philip. The work is not static, but there is a certain kind of conforming to an order because of the way in which this medium works. He has an orderly mind, and that has helped him to come this far. He has been doing things step by step and stage by stage. He had a general and slow entrance into his mediumship. He struggled with being confident that I was there, but he was very able to attune to me. Once he had enough experiences over time, he could become more confident about my presence.

It takes practice to learn anything new, including learning to ice skate, dance, sing, write, or develop any talent. It is a matter of taking your time and gaining skill and confidence little by little. Through the learning process there is a gradual awakening and a growing knowledge of how everything operates related to this talent of mediumship.

Today, I am like Philip's left hand—an integral part of what he does, not only in attending to him in every aspect of his earthly life, but also in being in his energy field. I am like an extension of him for the sake of the people who come to him. It is hard to tell, as it is with Saint Germain, where I begin and he ends. There is a considerable oneness that can be established when we work with one medium over a long period of time.

I initially impressed Philip with my words and ideas. From time to time I would talk to him through his writing on paper and in other ways about how I was working with him. There came a day when I was no longer a stranger to him, when he readily accepted me. We began to work together, and we have done so ever since.

When Philip is reading for an individual, we are aware of this, and we impress him about this individual in terms of their medical needs. Within his own body, his own soul, his own intuitiveness, his own sensitivity, Philip will pick up information and tell people they need healing in a particular area of the body. Individuals will often confirm this is so. I impress Philip either through audible voice, clairvoyance, or both to help him in this process.

I also seek to directly help the individual who is struggling. I go to the person, and Philip will often see me standing behind him or her. I usually stand to Philip's left and behind the client. I do manipulation of the energy of the spinal column and other parts of the body during the reading. This helps to bring about the healing process and make a positive difference in that person's body.

Dr. D: *Others have talked about energy from their perspective. Is there anything you would like to add about energy?*

Dr. P: I was here and heard the comments you refer to, though I do not completely remember all that was said. I could go into recall here and get that information, but I will simply tell you my own experience.

Energy is really God. The essence of all that is, is God. We can heighten that energy in ourselves and direct it toward other people by the conscious inclusion of divine love. To love all people as ourselves, that is God's love. Because we all came from God, God loves us as himself. We are emanations from God, and God loves us because we came from him. Parents cannot help but love the child that comes from them, and God loves us in that way.

God's energy is everywhere. In the spirit world, we tap into it as the source of all life. It is as if God's love runs through our veins and through our minds. It is the essence of all of life. It is what enables life to be and to go on, and that includes our own lives. This precious, precious energy, while it is everywhere, needs to be treated with a certain level of respect and devotion because it is holy. This includes your own life, the life of a family and the life of humanity in general.

This question about energy is very important. Energy is not a cold thing. Yes, conceptually it seems cold, but experientially the energy you put out is the energy you get back. Because of this, you want to make sure you are truly attuned to the influx of energy from God. Through meditation and prayer, particularly through meditation, you can consciously tune into the energy of God and bring it forth in yourself. This will bring about not only physical and mental changes, but also spiritual changes. It will bring about healing. Once you touch the great energy of God at the highest and deepest part of your being, you are never the same.

That is how Jesus was touched by this energy, and I do say energy. Jesus was so deeply touched, to such an extent, by this energy, this ever-present love, this divine being ever flowing in all of us, that he fell in love with God from childhood. We all have this experience to some degree, don't we? That is, we feel the presence of God. We may not put a label on it, and we may not truly recognize that it is something objective coming from outside of us and flowing into us, but that does not matter. Whether we recognize it or not, God continues to flow in love toward all beings everywhere. That is the energy of God. I am speaking about a different facet of the same energy others have spoken of, from a different direction. It is all one energy. It is all God and God's love.

Dr. D: *From time to time, Philip has experienced that you stand beside him while he is lying down or in a recliner, and you cause energy to course through his body. Can you explain what is happening when you do this?*

Dr. P: It is a radiation of the divine love that I have been speaking of. It may not be called that, but its source is that, and it pours through me as it pours through every living being. Because of his plentiful service to others, Philip has been close to burning out, like anything that gets used and used, unless it is well taken care of and maintained, and has a period of time when it is not being used. I have come to him at those times out of compassion. I am capable of working with the spine, and I have sent the energy back and forth, up and down his spine. He feels this wave going through him and sees me, usually standing to his left, while I work. He sometimes falls asleep, and that is perfect, because I can then work on him even more deeply. This has all been done for the reviving of his energies.

Dr. D: *This book is to demonstrate how hypnosis and channeling can work together. What role do you and other spirit guides play when I am putting Philip in a hypnotic state?*

Dr. P: We cooperate by holding Philip in a kind of overshadowing light or energy. Again I use that word energy, divine love, source, or whatever you want to call it. We create and maintain a matrix of energy around him and through him. We maintain its purity, integrity, its steady flow of energy, and its perfection. In that matrix of energy you are included. You are part of the equation, and we include you. We could not do otherwise.

As you progress in knowing your routine and the way you work, you tune in unconsciously, and sometimes consciously, to the extent you know what to do next. We help, as do your guides and teachers, to impart information to you, and you get it quite correctly. That is why your practice is successful and why you are able to do the work you are doing right now.

Other guides, such as Black Hawk, will be there to protect Philip and the energy field around him. This prevents any lower energies from coming into him that could distort the information coming through him or do harm to him.

We pray. It is not prayer as you would think of in terms of formal prayer, but a steady concentration of our mental and emotional energies upon the work at hand. It is sacred work. For us there is no other work than sacred work. It is all God. It is all for God as we understand him.

Dr. D: *Do you have any personal comments that would help those who are reading this book?*

Dr. P: If you do nothing else in this lifetime, come to know yourself. Many who come to the spirit world are masters of great fields of work who have a deep love for what they did on earth. They are sometimes the same ones who are in classes here, learning about discovering themselves. It can be more easily done here, and we all continue to seek to find God within and what that means. Just because we are in the spirit world, this does not mean everything is totally obvious to us. We still have to ask questions. Information may be more readily available and easier to get, but the mind has to be stimulated to ask questions. There has to be a hunger to know.

Some on earth are successful financially in business or in getting their degrees and so on, but they are not successful in knowing themselves or in loving themselves and other people. Knowing self has a broad meaning. It does not mean knowing yourself in the narrow sense of the word, your earthly self, but coming to know your expanded self, your own God presence. The manifestation of God is within *you.* If you do not discover this experientially while you are on earth, then when you come here you will be wanting. You will not be as close to the direct energy of God, both inwardly and outwardly, as you would have been if you had taken the time to do the things I am talking about.

That's it! Are you satisfied with my answer? *(Chuckle)*

Dr. D: *Yes, thank you. I have a question that just came up. The palms of my hands have been itching since you have been speaking. Can you explain this?*

Dr. P: Of course. As we have told you, you have to trust your own mediumship. There is healing energy where I am present. That energy is pervasive in the whole matrix of energy in this room, because I am a healer. When I did the chiropractic work, I did not just manipulate the bones, the skeletal structure, and the vertebrae. There was healing energy coming through me. Anyone who has compassion automatically draws from the energy of God within them to help other people. You have that same healing power. You do it through hypnosis, but it also comes out when you are near someone like me. There are many other healers here today as well. Kathryn Kuhlman and Black Hawk are healers. Others are also participating in this matrix of energy, and you are picking up some of our vibrations. Is that helpful?

Dr. D: *Yes. Thank you, and thank you very much for being here.*

Dr. P: I must add that we do not want the reader to believe just anything and everything or to believe what we say just because we are coming through and talking. We want you to look at the information, *really* look at it, not just on the surface. We would like you to go out and have your own experience. Prove or disprove the truths we are telling you.

The purpose of this book is multiple, as everyone will know when it comes out. We do not want you to accept what you read at face value. I would challenge you to sit in meditation on a daily basis for a substantial period of time, perhaps three or four months. Go inside. Work with the energies that you are inside, and see if you do not awaken to your own spiritual self and thus to God's presence within. Through this, see if you do not also awaken to the presence of many of us who work with you.

The revelation that came through me for chiropractic work was of little value if I only applied it to other people. I was constantly giving compassion to others by helping to eliminate pain, but I also needed to go inside and discover my own value, my own beauty, and work on that. If I did not heal myself and take care of myself, then what was I doing? The healer is worthy of being healed.

Those of you who are reading this book are worthy of awakening to your own spiritual gifts as well. This is why I would challenge you to find a teacher. Do not work with just anyone, really search. When you search with all your heart you will find that teacher, and when you do, sit with this person. Go inside, as I say, and learn the things we learned, the things we are trying to teach here.

This book will be of little value if you read it only with curiosity. It will be of little value, even if your curiosity is satisfied, but you do not act. I am not a passive person when it comes to these things. If people know me, they know that I am very energetic. That is my personality, but it is also what I used in my work. I challenge you because I challenge myself.

If you look at my book you will see it is very thick. You have to know I worked hard to get that information, to bring it through, not only by insight, intuition, and cognition, but also through knowledge based on experimentation. You have to have all of these in your life.

So do not just take in this information I am giving to you today. Do not just receive the insight, but go out and get your own experience.

That is all from Dr. Palmer today. God bless you all.

End of session.

ALBERT EINSTEIN

Albert Einstein (March 14, 1879—April 18, 1955) was a German-born physicist known for his theory of relativity and his famous formula, $E = mc^2$. His contributions also include the conception of a unified field theory. Einstein won the Nobel Prize in Physics in 1921. He produced many scientific papers as well as geopolitical writings. He also wrote works that shed light on his philosophy, and his co-authors included Sigmund Freud ("Why War?" in 1933). Named "Person of the Century" by *Time* magazine, Einstein is regarded by many as the greatest physicist of all time.

CONVERSATION FOURTEEN

Albert Einstein

Love, the essence of God everywhere, holds everything together. That is what holds life together, that is what holds the atom together, and that is what energy is.

—Albert Einstein

Comment:

Dr. D: *Because this was one of the first sessions conducted, I initially called on Saint Germain to convey Albert Einstein's message. But Einstein soon took over Philip's vocal cords to speak directly. Ultimately, all of those who came through Philip while he was under hypnosis spoke in this way.*

SG: This is Saint Germain. Philip is a little tired today, but we will do our best to bring you truth. I am pleased that you and Philip have this friendship. Your paths were meant to converge for your mutual spiritual benefit and so you could work together as you are doing now.

Albert Einstein is here, standing to your right, just as others have stood in this veil of energy. Though he has a serious look on his face, he has a twinkle in his eye and is quite youthful looking. Before I came in to speak, he said to me, "They all think of me as hunched over with my hair messed up. They will not recognize me because I now stand tall, and my hair is combed." *(Chuckle)*

The questions you have for Mr. Einstein were inspired by him, and he is eager to share information with you. I don't know if he will be able to get into these energies, and he is not yet sure he wants to do that because it requires an adjustment. He will let you know. Because I am quite accustomed to it, I do it readily, and it is not uncomfortable for me. You have to understand that a narrowing down of energies is necessary for us to come into this passageway called "Philip." This is not always appealing, because we are expanded beings. You are an expanded being too, but people on earth have been confined to their bodies for a purpose. It provides you with the opportunity to develop discipline, structure, self-control, and self-mastery. The body helps you to develop spiritually. It can mislead a person, but it helps more than it misleads, as you can see in this process. You are not entirely confined, as you go out of the body at times, but you remain connected to it.

Let us get to Mr. Einstein.

AE: Saint Germain calls me "Mr. Einstein." *(Chuckle)* I appreciate that, but I like to be called "Albert" because it is a friendly thing, and I am, you might say, as comfortable as an old shoe here. The masters here are all that way, unpretentious and not out to impress anyone. They are focused on being a presence of love and pursuing the truth. In the spirit world you cannot avoid truth, because it faces you wherever you turn.

As brother Saint Germain has helped me to adjust, I am here in Philip's energies, but not to the degree he is. Saint Germain's rapport with Philip is much deeper because of the many years they have been together, but I will do my best to bring the information you are seeking. Right now, please imagine in your mind that I am outside of Philip, using him as a medium by projecting my presence into his auric field, through his mind, and out of his vocal cords. I do not have to be totally within him for this to happen, though the more he opens himself up to me, and the more I work with him, the more this would be possible. You will note that the degree to which I am in him is the degree to which his voice changes. At this point, there is not much of a difference in the voice, correct? *(There is a slight change.)* There is a little bit, but it is marginal.

A change in his voice is not important. I am bringing this information for the reader's sake, because we want to put this experience into reality. We are not trying to make this a "holy book" or something to be thought of as sacred. We are interested in *what is going on here* between you and me and the spirit world. We want to explain how information can be channeled accurately to help all people move further along the path of spirituality toward their common destiny. From my point of view, the destiny of humankind is union with divine love, the highest thought, and the highest feeling.

Dr. D: *Thank you. Where are you in the spirit world?*

AE: Well, right now, I am here with you *(chuckle)*, so this is where my focus is; but because the mind is free in the spirit world, I can be mindful of things going on in many spheres at the same time.

I work in a lab. In your wildest imaginings, you could not comprehend what that means because, rather than mixing chemicals for various experiments, we work with light and energy. We still try things out, but everything is known. Information is filtered to us from higher consciousness or higher masters. They deliver answers through flashing insights into our awareness, showing us, for example, where one thing could be combined well with another. We also have our own God consciousness, and we can tap into that source, or universal energy, so we do not have to struggle to find answers.

The greatest struggle comes in trying to bring inventions to earth. Television is a prime example. Many scientists gathered in the spirit world to work on the idea of television before it came to the earth plane, but it already existed in the mind of God. Television existed side by side with the dinosaur, if you understand what I am saying. It was just a matter of time to create the earthly environment to bring forth everything, dinosaurs first and television later. *(Laughter)* Some of the work happened in Russia and other places, but in the western world, Filo T. Farnsworth was the primary target of efforts by the spirit world to pass ideas to earth about television. Creating a device that could pick up energy waves and translate them into pictures on a tube was extremely complicated and took a lot of thought, but Filo T. Farnsworth was impressed by the spirit world in such a way that he could pick up the ideas. He had a brilliance or genius about him when he came to the earth plane. You might say Mr. Farnsworth was born to invent the television.

I went off the point of your question as to where I am in the spirit world, but telling you that I work in a lab made me think of labs in general and how things such as television are created here first. That led to my explaining how information flows from the world of spirit to earth. I hope this gives you a little glimpse into how this happens, though there is much more information I could share.

I work with scientists who are some of the greatest thinkers. You might say we are in an area that is holy, to use religious language. To us, "holy" means everyone has equal affection and respect for one another, and there is peace among us. There is no arguing or fighting because we are all seeking the truth. That is what scientists do, isn't it? Though it can be the cause of arguments, we enjoy personality because we understand that variety is not only the spice of life, it *is* life. Eternity would be exceedingly boring without variety, wouldn't it? *(Laughter)* One of the things you find intriguing in what we are doing now is the variety of spirits and messages coming through. Variety exists not just to do away with boredom. The human mind is ever expanding, wanting to know more and more, so as to be free. We thrive on knowing more. It is our basic drive.

I am in various buildings that represent different periods of science and different inventions. Everything is here, from Hippocrates' period of time in Greece up to your modern times.

We actually have an Intel factory here. Can you believe that? *Whatever* exists on the earth plane exists here *first*. Do inventors and entrepreneurs leave their bodies at night to consult and work with us here? They surely do! Do we inspire them by communicating our ideas and encouragement through their waking thoughts? Yes! How do you think they come up with some of the genius in their work? They are vehicles for the influx of God's creativity or new thought, particularly in the electronic world.

Creative people visit the spirit world in their dreams or in their imaginings to learn from the masters. They learn not only about innovations relating to their companies but also about how to manage their new technology and the wealth gained from it for the betterment of the planet. Those endowed with such creative talent are not endowed for self. They may partake of their wealth, but they are more blessed if they use it for the raising of humanity. Individuals who have been given the ability to generate money, sustain that wealth, and use it to make the earth a better place, are among the great souls.

Intel, General Electric and all of your companies exist in the spirit world. There are also big factories, though they are not the same as they are on earth. For example, there is no need for General Motors to assemble cars here. In the lesser realms, they *do* assemble cars because people think life is the same in spirit as it is on the physical plane. Sometimes people cannot differentiate between the two worlds and even think they are still in the physical world. For this reason, they create cars throughout the day and drive them off the assembly line in their mind. Where do they go? People drive them, but only as far as their imagination will take them. But there is an end to that, too. People can only go as high as their understanding, so when they arrive here, they will experience reality according to their existing concepts.

When I say "lesser realms," I am not talking about dark realms, but about realms close to the earth plane that resemble earth, where people have not evolved enough to understand the difference between material and spiritual life. For example, there may be someone who enjoyed flying planes for a hobby or was a commercial airline pilot on earth but who has not yet awakened to the full reality of spirit. Such people will go into the spiritual realm that is consistent with their ideas about reality.

If these people go to an airport in that realm, they will be able to climb into an airplane and take off, but when they try to fly beyond a certain point, the plane will simply not go further. It will, by itself, turn around, as though it is hitting an invisible wall. Roads, also, will go only so far before turning back to the source from which they came. People will not be able to go beyond their vibratory level. A first grade student cannot become a senior without going through all the grades in between. While on earth, people can only go as high as their understanding takes them, and they will experience things according to their perception. So it is here.

Our purpose is to give you as much material as possible. You can sift through it and edit as you choose, but we are aware that people on the earth plane will be fascinated, educated, and helped by this information. The larger the context of your book, the more people will be well satisfied when they finish reading it. It is not that I have a plan to help you write your book. I am trying to be as broad as possible in answering your questions and yet respond specifically to what you have asked.

As for my personal life, I do not live in a big place because that is not my style. My house is pretty, though, with clapboard siding and a brown shingle roof. It is like a house you might find in an area like Maine or in the northeastern part of America. It is located on a piece of land I chose, though not consciously. It was chosen for me because it reflects who I am as a person. I could change it, but I like it the way it is. There are many flowers, mountains, streams, and a variety of animals, including deer; all things I enjoyed on earth. It is a beautiful place.

Inside the house are prizes I won. These are not literal prizes, but representations of my accomplishments. My home is rather utilitarian, because I am that kind of person. It is a very comfortable place, and you would feel at home in it. As you walk in, you might think, "Oh, this is the home of Albert Einstein," because the vibration you feel is a reflection of my soul.

You cannot separate soul from dwelling place or from the particular space or realm in which we exist. Some of you would ask, "How high is it? How close are you to God?" I would say to everyone, in the spirit world God is apparent. Wherever there is light, dim or bright, it is all God's energy; all God's presence. Where I am, the energy of God is the central sun, and it shines quite brightly. I had my ups and downs, and I took exceptions to things, but, generally, I was a good and moral person. Those characteristics put me in a good place. I really don't think about these things so much because here, as on earth, my mind is on the search for truth.

I am a creator, or as some of you might say, a co-creator. I am pleased and eager to work with other scientists as we put our ideas together to create things. You would be amazed and happy to see all the inventions yet to be impressed upon the right person's mind so they can come through to the earth plane. Some of them you would find unbelievable, but they will come in time.

As a personality, I don't just stick my nose in books and sit at a lab table discussing the science of being or the science of creation. I enjoy nature, including fishing, traveling, and just sitting down to socialize. Anytime I want to do those things, I do them. I am giving you a full answer to the question of where I am in the spirit world, and I hope it lends interest within the context of your whole book.

Dr. D: *Based on what you know now, can you tell us more about the atom?*

AE: *Adam*, as in Adam and Eve, or *atom*, as in the creation of things? *(Laughter)* What would you like to know?

Dr. D: *What do you know about the atom that you were not aware of while you were on earth?*

AE: We are aware of things in existence that pertain more to source than the atom. The atom comes from thought. Thought itself is a kind of atom, which you might call a thought atom, thought-tron, or something like that. Everyone puts thoughts forward, and the manifestation of thought energy is through the instrumentation of the atom. Without the atom, nothing can manifest.

God is invisible energy, but he *is* energy, and he is outside of his creation. The painter of the picture does not wind up on the canvas in the picture. He creates the picture and stands outside of it. God created everything on the canvas of life, but he is *outside* of it. He is a part of it in the same way the energy of the artist is a part of the picture he paints. Energies of the artist manifest in the picture in symbolic form but also literally. The flow of energy becomes a part of the picture, not only in the fibers of the canvas but in the color and in everything.

Someone who is sensitive could touch an object and pick up many things about its creator. In the same way, when you look at a flower on earth, you can pick up many things on a logical or intuitive level as to what the character of God is. Many things could be inferred about God by the reality of the rose. Looking at a rose, or even smelling its fragrance, you know God is sweet and beautiful. God's heart is one of love. The thorns may reflect that God also has discrimination and is just. No matter how beautiful it is, if you pick up a rose, you must be mindful of the thorns or you could prick yourself. Justice rules the world, and those thorns are a reflection of justice or of keeping things in order. At the same time, God is a being; a character of such untold beauty that one cannot even put it into words. Do you see?

I learned on earth that $E = mc^2$. This equation says everything about the essence of the reality of mechanics, chemistry, and science of the atom. We learned on earth how to multiply, divide, and harness this energy, and we do the same thing in the spirit world. When we want something to form in a solid way, we use thought to cause it to coalesce. Through the use of my mind—thoughts, mind-trons, thought-trons, or whatever you want to call them—I can cause to flow out in front of me the configuration of something I have imagined.

Pictures in our minds are like blueprints, in our energy existence or in our thought-trons, of what we want to manifest. Based on this blueprint, we can take the energy around us and use our thoughts to form the configuration, model, or objective manifestation of what we have thought. We can look at the object in front of us. Because we can create in this way, we understand how God used his own mind to solidify that which was ethereal and invisible. What existed in God's thoughts, he projected outward.

You do this on earth in a similar way. If you have an idea of something you want to create as a custom piece of furniture in your home, you think in your mind, "I would like it to be this way, this color, at this height, to fit in here," and so on. Then you pick up pen or pencil and draw it. Let us take, for example, the making of a dresser for a bedroom. Every dresser you have seen was in someone's mind before it was created. Everything on earth originated in a thought form first. The process is not different here. It is just that you are in the physical body, so you cannot just think about it and see it in a three-dimensional way as we can. Only the masters on the earth plane can do that.

In the spirit world, we learn how to use the atom in a finite and practical way, and we are able to be very observant. We can go down to the nth degree and enter *into* an atom. That experience is a part of our existence, much like your experience of walking out into the sun. You do not analyze it. You just enjoy it. Here, we do not look at energy only in scientific terms or just to analyze it while working in the lab. Life would be very boring for us if that were the case. Instead, we celebrate life by being in it. We enjoy basking in all the beauty because it is energizing to us. It is our reality.

We would be hard pressed to put into words the feeling we have when we sit by a lake, look at a beautiful tree in blossom, or walk on a path in the woods, because everything here is so very much alive. This is true for you on earth too, but we are much more sensitive to it. When we walk among trees, animals, and lakes and look at the sky, we become one with our surroundings. Then we are exalted, fulfilled, enriched, and joyful. We have a feeling that can only be described as the kingdom of heaven within. We are in heaven within as we partake of all that surrounds us. I spend my time in this way, in addition to the work I do in the lab with other scientists and inventors.

You have yet to truly understand the atom because you do not have the things on earth that would make it possible to explain it to you. You have to be in the spirit world to really understand the atom because this is where it originated. Earth itself resulted from the right application of energy through manipulation of the atom.

Dr. D: *Can you explain how energy works in relation to the atom?*

AE: The science of energy is based on attraction. Energy flows where it is attracted. There are magnetic charges of positive and negative energy, and everything works according to the science of one thing flowing to another that complements it. Where there is a minus, a plus will be attracted. In the atom, the nucleus is positive, and the electrons flowing around the nucleus are negative. The science relating to the atom understands this complementary association. This is a part of what makes it possible for things to be. The Taoist ideas relating to complementary relationships are true.

How do you raise your own energy to a higher frequency of existence? Raise your love. Dwell on love. Truth helps, because it disciplines and directs love, but love is the purpose of life. The more we have it, the more we want it. It is addictive and meant to be that way. As the essence of all energy, love flows throughout the entire creation. It is the glue that holds everything together.

Atoms of love, thought-trons of love, mind-trons of love, are the basis for existence. Perceptive individuals on earth already know this. Nothing could exist without love, because everything was created out of love, through love, and for love. God is a being of love. God *is*. He objectifies himself through creation so that he can appreciate himself.

The energy between what God is and what God sees outside of himself could be called love. Energy is love. It has been called by various names on the earth plane, but its essence is love. When scientists analyze the atom trying to understand the basis upon which it exists, they cannot find it, because it is love, which cannot be measured or quantified. It must be experienced. We can say it is an emotion or we can say it is energy; but it must be experienced.

Love exists objectively, even as oxygen and sunshine exist, all flowing out from God. Love is the essence of life, the spark that made life want to be. For what other purpose would life exist? Even birds and other animals fall in love. You recognize the element of love when you hear a bird calling for its mate in the spring. Love is the essence in the heart of that bird, though he is unaware of it because he does not have that kind of consciousness. The essence of love is there; the desire and the need to love and be loved.

When you look at birds sitting together in a birdcage, whether you are watching parakeets or cockatoos, you will see them nuzzle each other. They will rub their beaks together, and the energy of affection goes back and forth between the two. Atoms of love are flowing, thought-trons or mind-trons of love. Love, the essence of God everywhere, holds everything together. That is what holds life together, that is what holds the atom together, and *that* is what energy is.

Dr. D: *Can you give us information about channeling, where the energy of spirit comes into the physical body?*

AE: Wherever there is a need, wherever there is receptivity like an open container ready to be filled, there energy will flow in. When you create a vacuum, you are creating a minus where a plus will flow in. On earth there is a need for channeling, but for what purpose? Did man just think it up? No, it is from God. All receptors on earth are created by God to receive the influx of whatever is to be there. Plants have a need to absorb water. That is a minus that creates a vacuum, as it represents the absence of something. Water rains down and flows into that space so the plant can survive and thrive.

From a scientific point of view, there is a need for people on earth to be fed higher and higher truth. When they do not receive this, they do not grow. In your record of human history, there are children who have grown up among animals, and some are in that situation even today. Such children simply cannot grow intellectually and emotionally unless they are "fed" higher understanding. Children must be educated. In this situation, the human being is a minus, and God can create a reality, a plus, to complement that minus. The educational system came about as a plus to fill the vacuum existing in human beings because of their need for higher knowledge; their need to learn.

So it is with channeling. There is a need for man to have the information we bring through. More than one invention has come to earth as the result of an individual sitting and wondering how to take care of a problem. There was a vacuum on earth, a minus. This made it possible for us to channel into the mind information to help that person think about and invent a means to solve that problem.

At one time, earth was covered with outdoor privies or toilets. There had been no invention of the modern toilet in a warm space with a flush valve, a toilet seat, and all that goes into the operation of a toilet today. I use this mundane example to illustrate there was a *need* for something that did not exist. The toilet was needed on earth for comfort, but also for health reasons, to make it possible to flush away impurities and control disease. Here again was a minus or vacuum, the need for something to solve a human problem on earth for higher, better living. Someone from our side placed the idea of the toilet into the mind of someone on earth. That person provided the minus, and spirit provided the plus.

Of course, we in spirit cannot create new products or inventions without the energy, intelligence, and determination of those on earth. Cooperation between the two spheres is necessary before a new idea can become physical reality.

Energy by itself is like an amoeba. It needs form to fulfill its purpose. Atoms are attracted to an idea and flow into it from thought. In the spirit world, atoms flow outward into the projected creation of the idea, where we can examine it, look at it, and make sure our concept is perfect. After much testing is done in relation to its value—how it will interface with the earth plane and whether or not it can be realistically created on earth—we find the person through whom the idea can come.

When I was on earth, I happened to be the instrument for understanding $E = mc^2$. I was a target for those in the spirit world because I had a searching mind and asked questions, thereby creating a vacuum. Someone came in spirit to answer those questions, so the information flowed into my mind, whether I was aware of this or not, and I "saw" it. During my life on earth, I think I even referred to my experience as being something like a vision. Some of the information was not from my cognitive thinking, but came as a result of reflection and of "seeing" something that I knew did not come from me, but through me.

The whole earth plane is replete with needs, and we come to meet those needs. Through the minds of people on earth, and with their cooperation, we channel information and energy through in the form of ideas, pictures, illustrations, and blueprints. Their collaboration and action are necessary, so the rest is up to them.

Frank Lloyd Wright may have thought he invented his ideas about structures and how to create a home. Those who have looked at his work know he has a certain approach to design and there are common elements within his buildings. When you look at one of them, you can say with some certainty that this is a Frank Lloyd Wright house or building because his work reflects his personality. He was a man of structure and solid thinking who wanted to create buildings that were lasting, utilitarian, and beautiful, so his work incorporates these elements. The essence of the ideas for his work, as well as the expansion of the ideas, came from the spirit world. All we need do is plant a seed of an idea in the right mind, and it will take root and grow until it becomes reality.

All of you receive inspiration from spirit. The energy flows in, channeled through minds and hearts, and through the whole reality of a human being, even as I am channeling now through Philip. The personality of Albert Einstein is behind all this and bringing the information in. However it may appear to the reader, this *is* the truth of it.

This puts everything into perspective, doesn't it? Saint Germain has explained in his way, and I am bringing in another facet of truth, another way to explain things.

Dr. D: *Can you tell us how and where the universe was formed?*

AE: Do you have an eternity? *(Chuckle)* That is a big assignment! If I were to think I understand it all, I would be at the height of arrogance, because I don't. I know what I know, and that is not very different from some things I have already explained.

Everything *is*, because God always *was*. Because you see the sun rising and setting, and you know the earth is turning, you have watches and calendars and think of life in a linear way. Life is not three-dimensional or four-dimensional, but *multi-* dimensional. We impress many people to write about this from various points of view, explaining, for example, quantum physics. The concepts in quantum physics provide the objective explanation of the creation and evolution of things. We understand the equations and the whole science of it. We understand it. It is a part of who God is. Everything always was, you see. Everything always was.

On the earth plane, a favorite saying of spiritual teachers is, "Go within. All the answers are within." This does not mean you suddenly have all the answers. You have to work, probe, and spend enough time to merit the answers. You have to have an open heart and mind so you become a minus, and we can fill in that minus with our plus. Again, this does not mean that you on earth are just empty vessels, waiting for our input. You are as creative as we are, but we have more advanced knowledge. We channel it through so you can combine it with your own knowledge and talent and create something beautiful or useful.

Why is it true that all the answers are within? This is because the mind of each person partakes of the mind of God, which is infinite. The mind of God contains everything, either as an idea or in solid form. The great ones who have reached the level of perception of the mind of God, of the presence of God in a holistic way, say everything is contained in God. There is nothing that will ever be or ever was that was not already in God, because God is everything. This makes sense, doesn't it? God is everything, and God is every *thing*. You cannot confine God to G-O-D. You have to define God by using the word *infinite*, a concept your earthly mind cannot wrap itself around.

The highest level of mind is called the superconscious mind by some of you. We use different labels here, but it's fine to use that term when we talk about people on earth. When you go into the superconscious mind, the real self, or the divine self, you will find your mind has no limitations. The superconscious mind is the corridor leading to the mind of God, and when you go to that level, you will see that everything is one. This is not new information, but it is relevant to your question about how the universe came about. The universe always was, and it always will be.

Energy cannot be created or destroyed; it only can be transformed. God is the source of all energy, the source of all ideas, the transformative power. When you become a master at the highest level, you are able to be like God and use that source energy to do whatever you want as long as what you do is moral and based upon true love and goodness. There is no real separation between humanity and God. Only ignorance draws a line in the sand and says, "This is what I know, and this is what I don't know." The truth is that you can know everything.

The universe was created out of the thought of God, the womb of God. It is held in earth time by the very nature of God. God's nature is not static, but what God loves, God wills into existence. What God wills into existence remains until God does not will it. God's will is perpetual, so it is not as if God has to hold something up in the air. God is will, and God is love. Everything obeys, follows, exists, and is maintained because of the reality of God. God is the creative principle. After creating everything, God is the one who holds everything together. In essence, it is all *love*.

God loved beyond measure and beyond consciousness and so gave birth to everything automatically. Everything just flowed out of God. There was no necessity of forethought, as God *is* trees, God *is* birds, and God *is* the open sky. God is the engine in the car and the gasoline in the engine. God is the river that runs through the land and the land through which the river runs. God is the fish in the river. God is the teeth in your mouth and the toenails on your toes. God is the baby. God is the sperm, and God is the egg that created the baby. God is the love behind all things. God *is* all things.

You say that God is everywhere, and when you really think about it, that means God is everything. There is no separation. I am as much God coming through Philip as Philip is God, as you are God, as the tape recorder is God, just manifesting being. God and his being-ness are everything. God does not need to *do* anything. Of course, God enjoys everything, even as a woman enjoys her reflection in the mirror. If you take the mirror away, the woman still exists and does not need the mirror in order to be. God does not need human beings or creation to be. God is, always was, and always will be, perpetually so. That is my answer to your question.

I am sure scientifically-oriented readers may take exception to some of what I say. As is true of everyone, when I came here, I was stunned—absolutely flabbergasted—by what I did *not* know. But what I am telling you is what I now believe or know to be true.

You may think you know Jesus, but you do not really know him unless you attribute to him knowledge of modern times. With this knowledge, what kind of a man would he be? He would not be the man he was when he wore his sandals and robe and walked with the fishermen. He may appear that way to people who have that image of him, but he is more modern than you are. He speaks very capably, incorporating modern vocabulary. He is not trapped in a time warp of the past, because life in the spirit world is progressive.

We are as up-to-date as people on earth and beyond, because the cause of life is here. The idea of man started in the mind of God, on the spiritual, invisible plane, and then manifested in objective form. Everything that will ever be is already known here, though much of what is known is hidden from us. This is because, if we know something prematurely, we fail to focus on what is right in front of us, and that is what we need to do in order to understand and grow.

There is a lot of material in this chapter, and I am so pleased I can come to the earth plane to share all of this with you. I am not a hand in the puppet of Philip Burley. I am energy itself, manifested in the character and name of Albert Einstein. I am manifesting this way for the sake of all who would find meaning and value in my words. We must put life in a larger context. Life is not just science and it is not just religion. It is all of that but still more than that.

Dr. D: *Is humanity on some kind of a timeline in terms of our existence on the earth?*

AE: Much of what I have said up to this point responds to that question. Humanity is not on a timeline other than to say life evolves and is progressive by intention. The acorn is not intended to be an acorn for the rest of its existence. Those that fall to the ground and take root are not intended to become just a little tree, but a huge oak tree, a greatly-expanded manifestation. Humanity is inevitably on that kind of timeline, meaning people are meant to be and meant to grow into greater consciousness. They are meant to understand and gain awareness through consciousness and use that awareness in multiple ways to *become*. That *becoming* is infinite. Humanity will always be growing, changing, meeting new challenges, and progressing upward and outward. It is the very nature of being human.

We came from God, and we say we are in the image and likeness of God. God cannot be contained in one little body, so each of us is created to expand to the degree we become one with God. In becoming one with God, we must become what? We must become totally expanded. That is what the superconscious mind is all about, to enable each of us to tap into our *full* reality.

Many people are aghast when they come to this side and learn how small-minded and narrow their perceptions have been. They find out what they missed on earth by not being expanded, not being more curious, not getting out of the status quo, not searching more, and not having a great adventure in life. They find they have limited themselves. The principle of growth, of becoming, is a central, controlling principle. It is there for each one to walk upon like a train moves upon a track. It serves as a timeline, not in the sense of time as you think of it on earth, but in the sense that humanity is evolving, ever reaching to higher and higher levels of understanding, being, and doing.

Dr. D: *Is the physical world as we know it coming to an end?*

AE: Oh, dear me, what a question! How many years has earth existed? Most people live less than one hundred years, so what can they know about something that has been around for billions of years? People know what they know in a lifetime, but there is so much more to know outside of their experience. That is why there is eternity and why it is necessary to remain humble. You should be open to higher understanding and not have fixed ideas such as, "Oh, I already know everything," or, "I believe this, so this is true." Such people are doing a great disservice to themselves.

For example, you may worship and love Jesus in the context of your present-day religion, whatever it is. But do you ever stop to think that Jesus may want to share more than just what is in the Bible or what is in your daily life or in the Sunday service? Do you ever think Jesus may want to sit down and talk to you about the far-reaching realities of life? Very few people think in those terms. Many believe that they do not have the right to know such things.

You asked whether or not the earth is coming to an end. No, it is not. Even your scriptures say the earth remains forever. The scientist would ask, "Well, what is forever?" To a finite being, a million years is beyond comprehension, even as a million dollars could be beyond the comprehension of some. The idea of a billion, trillion or gazillion years is far beyond an individual's comprehension. In the cycle of life, which is short compared to the existence of God, a human being cannot know very much. This is why eternal growth, education, and ever-expanding understanding are important.

You may have heard stories about all kinds of phenomena and people predicting this and that, but the earth is not coming to an end. It is the womb of God in this galaxy. The existence of earth is necessary, because it is a place for us to narrow down our lives long enough to master self that we may master all of life and become God-like. Each of you has chosen to come to the earth plane because you want to narrow life down, to be a finite being long enough to learn all you can, which is endless. You have come to earth particularly to learn about your own character, your own selfhood, and what that means. The more deeply you go into the reality of self, the more you realize you are not limited. You are limited only by your thoughts, but not by reality as expressed by and through God. God is infinite, and you are intended to be infinite. You are intended to be an ever-expanding being.

The earth is the schoolroom, a learning place. My words are not original, but this is very important. The athlete may be capable of doing many things in life, but if he wants to learn to be a winner and to master himself, he needs to master a particular sport, whether it is track, basketball, baseball, or any other sport on earth. By focusing on a sport he masters it and thus masters himself. Life is narrowed down for this purpose. What is the mastering of something but learning to focus energy in a specific way, in a specific area, long enough to understand it and take dominion over it? The hardest thing to master is self. It is easy to learn to drive a car compared to driving oneself, isn't it? Each of us came to earth to master himself. But God is the supreme master of all energy, of all life, and I emphasize this: *We are not different from God.*

Dr. D: *Do people affect physical events such as earthquakes, tornadoes, and hurricanes?*

AE: Thought is energy, and similar thoughts are magnetically drawn to each other. When enough energy is gathered, and enough negative thoughts are focused on the same thing or the same person, energy can flow in that direction and do harm. This is why voodoo works. If an individual has enough hate toward another person and sends it forth with the will to harm, then it will reach that person and do damage. This is why those in the spirit world, and those on earth who understand this, caution parents to be careful about what they say, or even think, around their child. They have the power through the energy of thoughts and words to lift up or put down; to give hope or kill hope.

Man's misuse of energy can create thought-form conglomerates that become massive enough to affect both the earth and the atmosphere. Is it all because of man? No, but much of it is. Whether your scientists or your politicians or whoever is in charge want to accept it or not, there is a direct correlation between the fuels being used on earth, their manifestation in the atmosphere, and the warming trend. This can result in catastrophic realities such as floods, breaking down of your icebergs, an increase in quantities of water once solidified in ice form, and an increase in pollutants that will bring about greater health hazards and a consequent decline of health.

I did not come through with an agenda, but to ignore this reality is only to ask for future tragedies. It is much like a doctor telling you that you have a cancerous tumor in your lung. You may wish to ignore the reality, but the day will come when you will not be able to ignore it because it will kill you. I think I have made my point.

Dr. D: *You have come through before with information for me, both when I was doing hypnosis with Philip and through another spiritual sensitive years ago. What is the reason for this?*

AE: Well, dear one, I came into your life with the knowledge that this day was coming for the greater purpose of humanity. We will not say that your book is going to become a best seller, though it may. The intent is to give the truth for those who are ready for it, and there are many. We are not discouraging you by saying that. We are simply saying there is a higher and deeper reason for the book, and the information in it will reach those whom it is supposed to reach.

I came because it was known that you would be examining the relationship between the science of your work and the spirit of your work. The two are not separate, as you know. When you use your voice, which is vibratory, to give words to influence and make suggestions to the conscious and subconscious mind of a client in front of you, that is science. It is science when you choose the right words, paced in a certain way, and when you use the countdown. All of this becomes a conditioning reality for the conscious and subconscious mind of the individual. It is science when a child falls asleep as the mother sings a lullaby. Sleep does not come because of pure sentiment or because of specific lyrics. The energy of the lullaby, in essence, is peace, depending on the song. It is sung for the very purpose of calming, bringing peace, or encouraging rest when the child is restless. Because it is all vibratory, it is science.

As a scientist, I am interfacing with your work, though I now consider myself more of a spiritualist than a scientist. You can understand why. Life is not as dependent upon the science of things as it is upon the soul or spirit of each human being. *That* is the essence of life, the important point. You can create all the beautiful things you want to on earth, including all kinds of inventions that we bring through to you, but if the hearts of people are not made more pure, and elevated to a higher level of unconditional love, one for the other, what is your earth going to become, regardless of all the inventions?

The work you are doing is important, and that is why I am with you. It is an assignment for both of us. Neither of us knows the outcome, but we do know the input can be helpful to those who are searching for answers.

Dr. D: *Thank you so much for taking this time.*

AE: You are very welcome. It is a privilege. I am so happy I have this instrument to come through. This is Albert Einstein.

End of session.

Comment:

Dr. D: *Philip took a deep breath and immediately came out of hypnosis before I could count him up. He said, "I came out. This is the first time this has happened. I just came out, I guess because I'm so fresh. He brought so much energy." In speaking to Philip several days later, he said he was energized for two days after the channeling and needed less sleep than usual.*

SRI PARAMAHANSA YOGANANDA

Paramahansa Yogananda (January 5, 1893—March 7, 1952) brought meditation, Kriya Yoga, and an understanding of Hinduism to America. He was born Mukunda Lal Ghosh to a Bengali family in Grakhpur, Uttar Pradesh, India. During his early years, he visited saints, scientists, and artists, seeking an enlightened teacher. At the age of seventeen, he met Swami Sri Yukteswar Giri, who became his primary spiritual teacher. While a university student, Yogananda studied at Sri Yukteswar's ashram in Serampore and took formal vows into the monastic Swami Order in 1915. In 1920, he moved to America and founded the Self-Realization Fellowship. He toured the country, speaking before thousands of Americans.

Yogananda taught that intuitive knowing of God within is more important than belief, and that human suffering comes from identifying too closely with this life rather than with God. His influential work continues today through meditation centers and temples throughout the world.

CONVERSATION FIFTEEN

Sri Paramahansa Yogananda

What will open the golden door to the heart of God? It is passionate love and earnestness; knocking and knocking until the door opens and letting God know that you want this peace, this love—that you want God—more than anything, whether or not you understand God.

—*Sri Paramahansa Yogananda*

PY: This is Paramahansa Yogananda. Blessings to you and to all who are reading these words. This bridge through whom I am speaking provides a rare opportunity by allowing the masters of various spiritual realms to share our lives with those still on earth. We are grateful to have this instrument to come through. We can come in peace, without reluctance.

I come in quietly because I am in a contemplative mood, not wishing to overwhelm anyone with my presence. God and truth are most important, not personality. It would suit me to come back as a voice without a name, but many are curious about me and still in need of answers, so I can use my name to draw people to what I have to say.

I am busy, as I was on earth, but I do take time for my own realization. As many of you know, and more than we would want, the vibration on earth in certain areas is not very positive; so when I spend time helping people in the lesser vibration of earth, I sometimes come back needing to be uplifted myself. At these times, I go into a place to sit quietly and attune myself to the presence of God within. While I do not have to do this, I experience an exquisite higher reality when I do, as happens with similar practices on earth. The experience is greatly heightened in the spirit world.

I made this introductory statement to set the stage and get myself more accurately and finely attuned to the earth plane and to Philip's vibration, but by God's wish and will, I am here to answer questions.

Dr. D: *Thank you. Who is God to you?*

PY: I call God Father and Mother because the energy coming from God is like that of both. God's energy includes the unconditional love of the mother and the strong, consistent guidance of the father to create within us the will to accomplish what we started out to do. These two forces are needed, and God manifests in that way.

Those who have read my autobiography know I had profound, personal, and exquisite realizations of God while on the earth. My writing came from that place within where I met with the God presence, God in me. From that energy I wrote about God, life, and spiritual topics. I came to the spiritual plane fully equipped to continue living in union with God, so it was not as if I stepped into some place and became filled with something. When you enter the spirit world, God is already within you, because God is everywhere.

Because of my life on earth—what I did, how I lived, how I sought God, and how I interacted with God—I brought a high degree of awareness with me into the spiritual plane. If there is a change, it is in the quality of my experience. Now that I am not encumbered by the energies and limitations of my physical body, I am able to experience God more profoundly and more broadly than ever. I can comprehend more fully what I experienced of God in lesser ways while still in my body.

As has been said by many, *God is love.* When you love people with all your heart, you cannot help but find God. My highest endeavor on earth was to love others as myself. I did not have enemies. There may have been those who quietly opposed me from a distance, but I personally did not hold negative feelings toward anyone. I was a teacher, and I sometimes brought my students up short to cause them to see how they were hurting themselves and their own growth. Sometimes I appeared rather stern, but that was another expression of love.

Those with whom I worked were being tested, not as to their love for me, but as to their love for life and God. I knew from experience what it took to bring awareness of God to the disciple, and that was my greatest concern. My desire was for each individual to experience God as I did, not through my personality, but through directly knowing God within. I knew people could have this experience when their awareness was elevated and their egos not there. That which was already in them could become manifest.

In my writings, you will read of my adoration of God, of the presence of God, because that is what I experienced and wanted others to experience. In that sense, I am fundamentally the same and have not changed. Many on earth have fallen in love with the material world, but such things are no substitute for experience with our Heavenly Father.

Dr. D: *From your perspective in the spirit world, how do you see your work on earth?*

PY: As a universal master, my aim is to enable *all* of God's children to grow gradually into an understanding and awareness of their own divinity and awaken to the reality of God within. To know God is to know self, and to know self is to know God. Once a person discovers God within, it is enough. The individual can then expand outwardly and continue to grow in an intimate, personal relationship with God. Being in a group may carry a person along as the waves and movement of the river carry a boat, but the waves are just a means to the end. Any genuine teaching or organization includes the understanding that it is a means, and not the end in itself.

Teachings within organized groups tend to become formal religions over time, and this can bring about exclusivity; so I would encourage maximum openness and tolerance to avoid rigid spiritual, religious, or political hierarchies. Some degree of organization is necessary in creating form, however, and those who are guiding my fellowship are aware that exclusivity is not the way of God. So, on the whole, what I taught on earth is being held together.

I do not follow every person's life in detail but seek to show by the example of my life what direction to go in and how to live. On this plane I am known as a master among masters in the spiritual line from which I descended, and many of you know about this. Because I am a world master, my work is with the world. I am as much concerned about the world and people from all faiths and walks of life as I am about my own organization. People would expect that of me because I was already a universal master before I passed on. I wrote books and kept my organization together, but with an eye toward appealing to all people. I taught many things that were original, but also things that were spoken of and taught by others.

Dr. D: *Is there anything else you want to say about your teachings?*

PY: There are no mistakes in life, so I do not look back and say I should have taught or done this or that. I did what I did because that is how I was moved for the purposes at that time. For example, I was celibate, as were those closest to me. Our dedicated, single-minded focus of spiritual energy created a beautiful aura of healing, inspiration, and love. In the presence of God there is great light in such a fellowship, but when a group is comprised of couples similarly dedicated, there is also a great light.

The individual reflects masculine and feminine aspects of God, but a husband and wife together may do so even more, especially when they become co-creators with God in creating offspring. Once

I came to this side and saw the results of *genuine* marriage, in retrospect I would have taught more about marriage as a path toward knowing God.

I know this may surprise some who call me master, but I hope they will understand that life is progressive, and truth forever evolving. You know what you know until you know something higher or greater. If you no longer search beyond a teaching or listen for the quiet utterance of God's guidance within the inner reality of yourself, this will hold back your spiritual growth. Learn all you can from what I said and the people who are sharing it on my behalf. Just do not be afraid—in faith, love, and trust—to look even higher.

The relationship with God is the ultimate relationship, and my teachings are aligned with this reality. God is infinite, and God's love is beyond comprehension unless you come to meet him in an intimate way so your understanding can expand. This is what I mean when I tell you to search beyond my teachings. Do not throw out what I taught, but use my teachings as a stepping stone.

Dr. D: *In your work, you placed a great emphasis upon meditation. Can you expand on what you have said about this practice?*

PY: God is everywhere and everything. Everything that is, was, or will be is God. One energy radiates out to create and sustain multiple forms through which God is manifested, and this is the creative principle. Individuals do not have the ability to know or experience the higher dimensions of closeness to God through the physical life alone. Ego must be kept out of the way. You must detach from what you think should happen and allow to happen what is supposed to happen. There are a number of methodologies one can use to do this, and I taught Kriya Yoga to raise a person's awareness or vibration because I found it to be a direct line to God as opposed to more circuitous paths.

Even if you have everything in life, you may ask yourself, "What is missing? Why is it that I am not happy?" What is it without which each man, woman, and child is incomplete? It is not the intellectual realization of God, but the heart-to-heart love experience with God. God is at the core of life, love, and peace. If you go into the state of adoration of God, not passively, but stating your desire to know God, you will be able to examine your heart and find what has been missing.

The heart of God, who is infinite, invisible spirit, is moved by your adoration and longing. How do you let anyone know you love them? By sitting idly in peace? No, you must let them know by your actions. The more earnestly you want to know God, the more you will bring forth God, who is already in you. What will open the golden door to the heart of God? It is passionate love and earnestness; knocking and knocking until the door opens and letting God know you want this peace, this love—that you want God—more than anything, whether or not you understand God.

I have said these things before in various ways, but I want to add the energy of my own earnestness, excitement, and passion. The experience of God is not just an intellectual experience. Yes, it enters into the portals of the mind, because without intellectual understanding no experience can be comprehended, but I want to go beyond that. I want to emphasize how much God loves us and how much the very core of each person is infused fully and completely with the presence of God!

Love yourself passionately. Fall in love with yourself. I do not mean your looks, money, or fame, but your own core energies, your own gift of life, your own creative principle. Be humble in your adoration and filled with gratitude in loving yourself. This will bring out the God presence in you, and you will transcend all to know you are God. More than anything else I have said, this is the essential information I want to bring through. What I was sent to earth to do was to contribute to humanity's awareness of God, desire to know God, and ability to open the door to the heart of God.

You can tell by the atmosphere in this room that the God presence is here. We did not bring it here or cause it; it was already here. When you are magnetically charged with passion for God, this magnetism draws God into your awareness and into the atmosphere around you.

There is no place to go but inward. Do not cry, "God come to me!" but rather plead for God to come out of you and your own consciousness. After all, in the end, we find it is God who is searching for God. But until you understand the motives behind God's act of creation, it is hard to understand how God could be looking for God.

Dr. D: *What can you tell us about the interaction of spirit with those still on earth?*

PY: If my words thus far have not given you the answer to that question, you will never understand. *(Chuckle)* The purpose of spirit interaction with those on earth is to bring the truth and love of God and also to help people on earth to become aware of the spirit world. When that happens, they may find hope and catch a vision that inspires them to prepare whole-heartedly for the day when they come to the spirit side.

Dr. D: *Many masters are in the spirit world. Are there any with whom you especially work?*

PY: There is an assembly of masters, and each one has a unique personality and assignment. Jesus' approach to God was different from mine, as was that of Mohammed and others. We have walked our paths, but we meet at the same place, and that is in the heart of God. Those masters work together whose teachings are of such a caliber so as to have genuinely awakened man to God.

In the spirit world, there are various levels of teachings and God awareness. Masters with the highest understanding from learning and living what they taught are completely aware of their oneness with God. Those in the highest realm taught of God at the highest level, and they also *realized* God. In spiritual spheres beneath them are those who understood God intellectually but did not experience God within themselves to the same degree. Still, they are responsible for bringing people closer to God, and they are also masters in their own right.

I am associated with many masters. On earth, you do not have an understanding or awareness of all of them, for there are more than you could imagine. Think of it! How many have come on earth who have been obscure, unknown, and not included in any history book? It is not just those with famous names who reach mastery of self. Such masters find God by transcending ego and attachments to the earth plane and by longing earnestly, with love, for God.

God exists in all of creation and can be found everywhere within it, especially within human beings. The master of masters is one who teaches and demonstrates that God is love, unconditional love; that God is the source of all life. God is never, *never* separated from that which he creates.

Dr. D: *When you made your transition to the other side, what surprised you most?*

PY: I loved God with all my heart, but my concept was not broad enough. Wherever you find yourself wandering in the desert of life, and whatever road you find your feet upon, *that is your path*. It was not always correct for me to call people to follow my path. Some suffered because they could not go my way; and because they believed it was the only way, they thought they could not get to heaven. The true master must teach that where you are *is* your path, and there can be no such thing as being off the path. Jesus said, "In my Father's house there are many mansions." If that is so, there must be many streets leading to those mansions. There are many paths, many roads, and many highways to get to one's assigned destination. It is all written on the scroll of life within self.

Dr. D: *Could there be a better path for someone than the path the person is currently on?*

PY: I have answered that question. Wherever you are *is* your path. Do we understand each other? If you find yourself questioning your path, this questioning is also part of your path. Your path is speaking to you through whatever appears and keeps appearing, and through whatever you are continuously prodded to do. If your path appears to take you somewhere else, to another way of doing things on your way to higher knowledge, then that is also a part of your path.

Wherever you are, whatever is happening to you at this moment, on this day, these are the things you are to learn from. This is your life. The quicker you have this awareness, the happier you will be in being you, where you are. You will know you came to earth to experience self realization through seeing yourself reflected in all things around you and learning from all things.

It is for the perfection of the soul that suffering takes place. It is for the perfection of the soul that every aspect of the path exists, wherever it takes us, wandering through dark valleys at night, up to the mountaintop by day, or any place in between. It is all reflecting back to you, giving you the opportunity to see yourself in order to correct yourself. It also helps to take you to the place where no change is needed.

Dr. D: *You have shared much information, but is there anything more you would like to say?*

PY: I want people to know I am substantially here, working through this instrument. You may question or doubt some of the specific points I have made, but I am here, fully present, and fully cognizant of what is going on. I know the value and purpose of this process of these two individuals sharing their gifts to write this book. This is seen by us in spirit as a grand opportunity to peel away the shadows, the darkness, and the ignorance that abound regarding spirit interaction with the earth plane and life after death.

What holds me here is the magnetism of this opportunity. As a teacher of truth, I could not fail to come. I was compelled to come by the very *nature* of truth, which causes us to want to go higher and higher and know more and more. I have come for the benefit of many and for myself. I too am in need of growth because life itself is eternal expansion. Eternity would be very boring if people were doing the same thing over and over, thinking the same way without searching for more, and following blindly without question.

Look into yourselves to find the truth. Respect your life and your own path. Know that each of you, wherever you are, is being closely guided by those wonderful guides and teachers in spirit who have been assigned to you, drawn to you, or both.

Thank you so much for allowing me this opportunity to visit with those still on earth at this time. This is Yogananda. God bless you all.

End of session.

Comment:

Dr. D: *My experience in this session was similar to my experience when Buddha came through. With Yogananda, the energy was serene and loving, and I felt as though I wanted to meditate. There was a similar contrast between the energy in this session and some of the others, where I felt the energy as exuberant and active.*

EDGAR CAYCE

Edgar Cayce (March 18, 1877—January 3, 1945) was a psychic healer born near Hopkinsville, Kentucky. He spent his later years in Virginia Beach, Virginia. Cayce was known as "The Sleeping Prophet" because of his practice of going into a trance with the assistance of a hypnotist to channel answers to questions. During his early years as a psychic, he gave free readings to people who needed healing and relied on voluntary donations to help support his family. Later, encouraged by some who came to him for readings, he gave information about the lost continent of Atlantis and other esoteric topics.

Cayce's prophecies made him a celebrity toward the end of his life, but he remained a devout Christian who believed healing was the most important aspect of his work. Since his death in 1945, Edgar Cayce Centers have been established in twenty-five countries. The Association for Research and Enlightenment (ARE) in Virginia Beach, Virginia, serves as the headquarters for documents and activities related to his life and work.

CONVERSATION SIXTEEN

Edgar Cayce

If only the leaders of the world would create a United Nations centered on spiritual principles, where the first thing they do prior to making decisions for a nation or a people is to meditate. Then they could become cognizant of the influx of spirit and higher guidance as to how to solve world problems. All would know that they are brothers and sisters and that not one person on earth is greater or lesser than another. This would level out the playing field of life and would allow God and divine spirit to permeate the entire existence of earth.

—Edgar Cayce

EC: I am already present. He is an easy being to get into. How are you today? It is so good to be back on earth, even with its rough-and-tumble energies. Because of what you are doing here, there is much of the God presence in this atmosphere, and it is palpable. Thank you for inviting me. We can start anytime you want to, as I am more than ready and willing. This is Edgar Cayce.

Dr. D: *Thank you. Just prior to a session with Philip two days ago, he told me you appeared to his right side. Was there a particular reason you did that, even though you were not scheduled to speak that day?*

EC: Actually, it is no different from being next up to bat. When the batter is up, ready to strike the ball, there is someone waiting in line to be up next. I was to be up next, and it is no more complicated than that. Also, I am assisting in all of this. I am probably more eager than you are for this information to come through, as it is part of my legacy. Wherever people are genuinely doing this kind of work I am there, because it is part of my mission or assignment. I am unwittingly drawn to aid in bringing awareness of this phenomenon to people on earth.

Channeling has existed throughout all of human history, whether or not there is a record of it. There have always been those who are channels for the voice of spirit, the voice of God. Such work will continue forever in the human race out of actual necessity, based on the principle that everything in your world comes from the spirit world. The earth and the spirit world are one, and the earth is our baby. To take care of earth's inhabitants requires that we come into the nursery, into the schoolroom, into the home, into the world of human opportunity. Though you may not feel us with you when you are depleted from overwork or suffering from some problem with the body or mind, we come with eager desire to serve and to make the world a better place.

If we did not come from our side to make a positive difference by educating and uplifting you and enhancing your awareness, you would still have to deal with certain situations when you come to this side. This would be more difficult because the body is a necessary part of the energy for change and growth until you reach the point where there is no further need for change.

I'm not only up to bat, I'm batting. (*Chuckle*) Throw me another ball!

Dr. D: *Your name is associated with having pioneered the phenomenon of channeling in the contemporary world. Because of your efforts and considerable published works, we are quite interested in what you have to say about the channeling work Philip and I are doing.*

EC: In my introductory remarks, I spoke about the necessity for this kind of work. Channeling is a part of the reality of the whole of humanity, whether or not it is called that by those who observe life and write history. It is difficult to impress individuals on earth with the fact that we are present because the spirit world is invisible to the physical eye. It is difficult to impress those who are not receptive and even those who *are* receptive if they are not yet spiritually awakened or developed.

Philip and others like him can perceive us. From the Oracle of Delphi to Ezekiel, from the School of Prophets to Native American medicine men, all are part of the manifestation of a particular type of human being who exists on the earth plane for this purpose. People with this ability have appeared throughout human history. Since God is invisible to human awareness, how could God otherwise filter through, especially with things as they are at the present time? Do you understand what I am saying? (*Yes.*) Doubt as much as you want to, anyone reading this material, but it is a fact.

There are many who have come repeatedly to listen to wisdom coming through a medium, prophet, oracle, or shaman. What such people have done for individuals, their people, their cultures, and civilization is not always recorded or widely known. To ignore it and write it out of history would be a great disservice to God, the author of this experience. Channeling, spiritual manifestation, and man's perception and awareness of these phenomena are all part of God's very plan.

We are more interested in getting information through directly to an individual who needs it than to have to use mediums to do it. People often receive information from us without being consciously aware of us. When we get information through this way, people pick it up as their own thoughts. Until the advent of greater awakening, this is the means we have to use. That is okay because it seems natural for most people. To tune into us, to perceive us, and to deal with us on an ongoing basis, hour by hour and minute by minute, could be distracting to some.

Though they may be dormant and not fully awakened, the faculties for perceiving the spirit world are present in each person reading this. Each one could become a channel, if only for the benefit of the self. In the world to come, there will be a greater practice of meditation, hypnosis, self-hypnosis, and other means of opening the spiritual senses that you already have. You are already a physical and *spiritual* being. Through your spiritual senses, even if only on a subconscious level, you are aware of being touched by us.

Those who approach all of this from a left-brained, intellectual point of view will have a problem because there are people claiming to do spiritual channeling who are actually channeling their own ideas, concepts, or personality. They are, in fact, channeling themselves. We advise anyone seeking to do this kind of work to get proper training. As you can read in biographical information about me, I was inclined to be spiritually open from birth.

A person who is spiritually open without proper training may experience untamed energy and must be guided as to how to channel the energy properly. By discerning who has had appropriate training, one can distinguish the genuine channeler from those who are not genuine. Even those who are not initially genuine can become legitimate if they practice with a good teacher.

I am not saying the whole earth should be covered with channelers or mediums. When many public channelers bring divergent information about the same subject matter, it leads to confusion and is of little or no help to society. The more objective among you have a more astute approach to mediumship. The most important reason to have such a gift is to get information from us that you need for yourself. Channeling plays a significant role in the evolution of individuals as well as the planet.

One of the reasons I was included in this experience is that I was a legitimate, well-established medium about whom much has been written and read, so I am able to bring some clarity to this topic. We do not care how many copies of this book you sell or how many people read it. We are trying to give objective truth that can filter down into the minds of many people on earth. This will bring about an evolution of consciousness, including an increased appreciation of this gift and its use.

I am greatly moved that you are doing this. To be able to participate in this work and to have my voice heard again on earth is a dream come true for me. Because I invested my whole self in what I did, it means a great deal to me personally. I went to such extremes of giving that I sometimes depleted my own energies. I gave to the nth degree. I loved people and loved giving them truth, particularly when it made a significant difference in overcoming health issues. Nothing could have made me happier. It also gave me joy to bring through the dearly departed during wartime. I could bring solace, comfort, and closure to those who came to me to find out about their soldier son or someone else who had passed over. To do this for people is a great work, and it is under appreciated.

Can you feel, as I can, the very beautiful presence of spirit here? Isn't it wonderful? This is spirit. Embodied or not, the essence of all spirit is love. In saying "all spirit," I include those who are incorporated in this kind of work. I am exceedingly embodied in Philip at this moment and am able to come through with great clarity. It is quite unusual to get this kind of clarity, but it is possible because Philip is willing and practiced. He prepared himself diligently, knowing I was coming. Undoubtedly, he and I have more in common than he has with anyone else who has come through him, so it is easier for me to use his faculties, establish this rapport, and settle into his body.

I wanted to bring this up because the energy is so palpable. I can't think of a better word. The energy is *palpable*, and you are feeling it.

Dr. D: *When you say you have more in common with Philip than some of the other speakers have, what are you referring to exactly?*

EC: I am referring to the fact that both of us are channels. To be a conscious channel for spirit is to take a unique position. The others who have spoken or will speak to you for this book were channels in different ways, but most were not conscious of this while they were on earth. One was more aware of spirit and spirit manifestations than she made known to the world, and I am speaking of Mother Teresa.

Dr. D: *You said some people are channeling themselves and not acting as true channels for spirit. How can one distinguish between channeling oneself as opposed to channeling spirit?*

EC: True channeling is the ability, by training and/or by birth, to get out of the way. Ego is at the center of being in the way, as it creates attachment. Ego has to do with your singular idea of yourself. When you can give that up, we can overshadow you and impregnate your consciousness and the organism of your whole body with our presence. Philip is demonstrating that now. If you think of it in simple terms, it is easier to understand. If you want to run a train on a certain track, and there is a train already there, you have to move the first train out of the way before the new train can come in. If a container is already filled, you have to remove what is already in it to put in a new object. I would not discourage anyone from seeking to be used by God for the higher purpose of being a channel, but get adequate and correct training.

With those who just spontaneously begin to speak and say they are channeling spirit, the ultimate way to test this is to consider the truth of what they say. In the end, your book will have value, not because of the array of famous personalities who come through, but by the truth they bring.

Whether or not it is of this nature, every book has a theme or plot, a central thread around which everything is built. There is a particular thread of truth you will find running throughout this book. There are a number of threads of truth, but there is a central one.

Dr. D: *We are interested in your own experience in channeling. What was the induction process, and what did you experience with the entity who spoke through you? Could you please share with us more about your channeling experience?*

EC: Yes, I can easily respond because it happened so many times. I must say that even when I was a child, the reality of my spiritual life and physical organism was such that I was receptive to spirit and had an above average ability to perceive spiritual things. I was born with this destiny. As a child, when I first began understanding my mind, I could place a book under my pillow and be able to recite its contents the next day. This demonstrated to my parents that I had considerable ability, and it made me aware of that too. Even though I did not objectively understand what was happening to me, I knew

I should watch this gift and that it was not ordinary. Following my early experiences, my openness expanded and grew to the point where I could be used more and more.

Though there are times when you think you are totally isolated, none of you stands alone. The spiritual and physical worlds are one, even as your spirit and body are one. The two worlds are always interacting, even when you are not aware of us. The communication that happens is spirit to spirit. *You* are not your body; *you* are spirit, and your spirit is embodied in a physical form while you are on the earth plane. You cannot be a living being on earth if your spirit has vacated the vehicle of the body. That's what "death" is. Life is predicated upon the ongoing interaction between spirit and body.

In my channeling, I worked with hypnosis. It is a conditioning process, and through conditioning and practice you can learn the principles necessary to raise your consciousness. The human mind has a wide range of vibratory levels, and it is able to achieve low and high frequencies, something like tuning a radio dial to various frequencies to find different stations broadcasting. Right now, as you are listening to me, you are broadcasting in a lower frequency on the dial of your mind. You can raise the level of your awareness until you reach the highest frequency on the dial of your mind. Then you can dial in God.

Isn't this meaningful? Doesn't it clarify, for all time and all purposes, the reality of how to become aware of us? Doesn't it clarify the reality of meditation and how meditation allows for gradual awakening to higher and higher levels of spirituality within yourself? This is why I wanted to come and speak.

Gradually I learned how to get to those higher levels of my mind and my consciousness very rapidly. I could get out of the way so that spirit, the entity that worked with me, could come through. There was nothing about it that was uncomfortable or peculiar, even as breathing is not uncomfortable or peculiar. It was that easy.

When a cloud comes between the earth and the sun, it casts a shadow upon the earth. As the cloud moves, the shadow moves—quietly, almost imperceptibly. Like the sun, the God presence shines forever and ever upon humanity. It allowed me to be like a beautiful white cloud casting a shadow that quietly moved into the physicality of Philip Burley, and here I am. It is beautiful and simple. How *much* we want humanity to understand this reality! It is hard not to go on and on, but I know time and space are limited when it comes to publishing a book, so I think I will stop here.

Dr. D: *You have answered the next question, but I will ask it in case you want to say more about it. What role did the hypnotist play in your channeling?*

EC: When you put Philip under hypnosis, you are the anchoring point for us. Spirit is working through your energies, your own spirit or soul, your own being, your own intelligence. You are overshadowed by those who are working with you to augment and amplify your energies. Since you are also mediumistic to a certain extent, from time to time you can feel that overshadowing, can't you? *(Yes.)* When you are working with people, sometimes you know what questions to ask without having foreknowledge about their situations. The questions come into your mind, and you just know how to guide them to deepen their awareness and cause them to go to a higher level. That is the influence of spirit, and you are the anchoring point.

It is my experience that the hypnotist, at least in the beginning, is vital. Consciously or unconsciously, the hypnotist knows how to tune up and tune in the person being hypnotized. The hypnotist knows how to raise that person's consciousness, using the "dial" of that person's own mind. The give and take between you and Philip forms a basis upon which we can come in and do our work. The two of you are greater in this synergistic relationship than you are as individuals. On that foundation, we work.

This information should help hypnotists who are looking for greater exploration in the use of hypnosis. It will encourage them to step out. I do not mean they should necessarily write books or have entities come through as I am doing now, though they can if they want to. It will assist them more to help souls to realize the fullness, the *fullness*, of self. You say on earth that you use only ten percent of your brain. If that is the case, then what percent of your soul, your spirit, do you think you use? You use only a tiny part, a fraction, compared to what you *could* use if you were more imbued with this gift of spiritual perception.

Dr. D: *How did you progress from having someone hypnotizing you to using self-hypnosis?*

EC: I think I have explained that. It happens through the modulating of consciousness and the raising of the frequency of the mind and emotions. One separates from the earth plane that magnetically pulls us to its heavier vibration. That is why it is effective to use uplifting words in hypnosis or in meditation, and to imagine seeing in the mind's eye a beautiful vista or hearing the sound of sweet music. It takes you to a level of yourself that is unattached to the earth, where you can have that higher experience called a spiritual experience. Right now, most people are having an experience of attachment to the earth to the extent that they are not able to get outside of the mundane and gross aspects of the physical world. That is why they suffer.

If only the leaders of the world would create a United Nations centered on spiritual principles, where the first thing they do prior to making decisions for a nation or a people is to meditate. Then they could become cognizant of the influx of spirit and higher guidance as to how to solve world problems. All would know they are brothers and sisters and there is no one on earth who is greater or lesser than another. This would level out the playing field of life and allow God and divine spirit to permeate the entire existence of earth.

Why do you think the idea of churches, temples, mosques, and other gathering places came into existence? That was not man's idea initially. Providence was behind their development for the purpose of bringing attention to that which is divine. In the future, it will happen as I have said. It will not happen tomorrow or the next day, but eventually it will come. A true United Nations, with one world centered on spiritual values that are understood by all and practiced worldwide, *will* exist. Your book will lend information that will help further such a cause to some degree. When the mind is on war, the mind is *at* war. When the mind is on God and spirit, the mind contains God and is spiritualized.

Dr. D: *There is a wide range of information being channeled today, everything from reincarnation to UFOs. If what we are reading about is true channeling, could you explain why we see such divergent information?*

EC: Thank you. I appreciate and respect your desire for an answer to this question. As I said earlier, some are channeling themselves and the information is based purely on opinion. It is the responsibility of individuals who hear or read such material to use the truth within them to discern the degree of truth that exists in any work. You must also know the channeler. When you encounter or read about such people ask, what is their record? How have they lived their life? What are their motives? This often can be discerned by considering the body of material that the person has published.

God allows all of this to happen, not because of the wide variety of interests, but because of the wide variety of needs. As the Zodiac shows, there are different types of people born under different circumstances, and they do not all perceive things the same way. Not everyone relates exactly the same way to the experience of God. Each person is on a different path and at a different place on the mountain of life, and each one sees reality differently.

To some, God is purely light. To some, God is truth. To some, God is love, divine love. In order to lead people, individually and collectively, a variety of channelers is necessary. According to the truth within you, as your own imagination leads you, and using the criteria I have spoken of, discern what is legitimate within any book or channeled information. Read from an objective point of view, and don't be swept up in something just because it feels good. If what you read or hear can stand the test of objectivity, aside from your emotional response, then it probably is a reflection of truth.

The most important truth is the truth you perceive about yourself in your own mind. That is the most trustworthy source of truth as you progress on the spiritual path of your life. Whether or not there are UFOs, whether or not there is reincarnation, none of these things is important when it comes to soul-centered issues for you. When you arrive in the spirit world, what you will be looking at first is your own character, which is *all* you will bring with you. Your spiritual tenor, vibration, and appearance will reflect the essence of your mind and heart.

Dr. D: *What is your mission in the spirit world?*

EC: With whom would you expect me to be working in the spirit world? *(God?)* Yes, God is innately a part of this world. To describe God in the spirit world is to describe personality filled with unconditional love. God is personal. But who are the spiritual beings with whom you would expect me to be working, not by name, but by mission? I am working with a hierarchy of people who are interested in the field I have been speaking about.

As you can imagine, ours is an international, universal effort that includes individuals from around the world. While they were on earth, some were channelers, some taught channelers, some were hypnotists, some were doctors, and some were therapists. All were aware of some form of spirituality and its objective manifestation, and they experienced this in various ways, including contact with spiritual entities or through the phenomenon of hypnosis. Sometimes when a client was under hypnosis, a separate voice came out of that person so that the hypnotist knew spirit was speaking.

I am one of the masters in the spirit world because of the skill I exhibited on earth and because I attained levels of knowledge to the degree that I can help teach other people. There are classrooms here, outdoors in nature or in buildings, depending upon the needs and preferences relating to the topic. If I want to talk about spirituality as it relates to the creation, we may hold our class in various outdoor places. In our immediate vicinity we can then directly experience the manifestation of the energy and innate intelligence present in the creation.

That's all I have for today. I have gone to great lengths to answer your questions in detail, and I hope the reader can appreciate the information given. It all needs to be said, and it should help, not hinder, the reader, don't you think?

Dr. D: *Thank you. Were you surprised at anything when you first arrived in the spirit world?*

EC: I was surprised at how much I didn't know! *(Chuckle)* How infinitesimal was my knowledge! When I saw how much knowledge was available, I saw it would take me an eternity to learn, and I am still learning. That is the great thing about God. God is the source of love in multiple manifestations, exhibiting endless knowledge. That is what makes for eternity and what makes for the joy of eternity.

Dr. D: *Is there anything you would like to share at this time that has not been covered?*

EC: I want to greet those still living on earth who remember me. Thank you for your efforts to make known to the world my life experience and what came out of it. I often visit the library in Virginia, and I am proud of what we have done together and where my work has led. I am especially pleased that many have been helped to understand me and the phenomena of spiritual mediumship and channeling. It was not easy for me to leave, as I was thoroughly caught up in my work and in the service I could provide to others. In a healthy sense, I am still drawn to that wonderful spot where you have put up a kind of monument to the work we did together on earth, and I am very much indebted to all those who are carrying on. Thank you. This is Edgar Cayce.

End of session.

KATHRYN KUHLMAN

Kathryn Kuhlman (May 9, 1907—February 20, 1976) was born in Concordia, Missouri. She became a born-again Christian at the age of fourteen and started preaching at the age of fifteen. Kuhlman was well known through her extensive healing work and her long-running radio and television ministries. She was at times a controversial figure because of challenges by skeptics and a brief marriage to a fellow evangelist who left his wife to be with her.

Because her unwavering belief that healings occurred by the power of the Holy Spirit, she repeatedly gave all credit to God for any healings claimed. In 1972, she was granted an honorary doctorate by Oral Roberts University. She died at the age of sixty-eight following heart surgery. The Kathryn Kuhlman Foundation was closed in 2016.

CONVERSATION SEVENTEEN

Kathryn Kuhlman

Look at all the great ones. They are not great because they sought to be great. Through their suffering, their own God presence came forth. They discovered what worked and did not work, and their innate qualities were brought forward. A refined self was born out of the caldron of suffering.

—Kathryn Kuhlman

KK: This is Kathryn Kuhlman. I am here, enjoying what you are doing. We are all standing around watching you with your artistry, as you bring through Philip's energies those of us who have been working with him for some time. As you are aware, I was very close to you this morning.

By the providence of this experience, I wanted to put in my two cents worth. My thoughts are not totally original, because anyone who knows anything about healing knows about energy. Healing is about the proper use of energy—speeding it up, slowing it down, or transforming it by using the natural reality of the human organism or of the animal organism, for that matter.

I could speak without difficulty for many hours about the topic of healing, and I know that is what you want me to talk about. Before going to the questions that you have prepared for me, I want to talk a little about Philip and my coming through him. He is open in his approach to mediumship. His adult mind is there, so he does not believe just anything, but he is receptive to our influence, especially things he sees and hears spiritually.

Philip is a channel who operates most effectively by our flashing information to his clairvoyance or spiritual sight, and he is receptive to our input. Many of you see, but don't see; meaning that to a degree you are spiritually attuned to our presence, but it evades your detection due to your lack of experience and training related to such phenomena.

When you were thinking about the work you and Philip are doing, during a certain opening of your awareness I had the opportunity to pop in and impress you, get your attention, and cause you to think about me. I could enter into that focus of energy and suggest to you in my own words the idea of my coming in today. You picked this up in your thoughts, and so here I am. The ease with which we can move in and out of an individual is in direct relationship to the essential attitude one has toward these things. It is hard for a non-believer to get even a modicum of information from us. We do slip in and channel through, but the more receptive one is, by inclination from birth or through training and exposure, the more we are able to work through that individual.

Rather than to take more time, I am going to remain here and listen to your questions. To the best of my ability, I will answer them. Am I coming through okay? *(You're coming through wonderfully.)*

You have the same childlike nature Philip has. The further you go in this work, the more you will find you are not only going to write books; you will be more and more attuned to us as a channel. We will write through you, impress you, and inspire you, and you will become increasingly aware that you are being used as a channel. You will be aware that we are there and coming through you. You have your own set of guides and teachers, and they are working nicely with you; but for this process, Philip's group and your group have married our souls together. We are working as a circle around both of you, guiding this endeavor.

Now, please feel free to ask me whatever questions you would like to ask.

Dr. D: *Thank you. How can people develop or increase their gifts of healing?*

KK: For anyone to be adept at healing, there are a number of attributes that are most important:

No Attachment: The first thing is to have no attachment to how all this happens or to the outcome of it. Truly, a channel is one who is open, though not without intelligence, values, and concerns. We would not try to work with a blank slate or with someone who is not somehow prepared.

I have spoken about Philip's childlike nature, which means he is open, with the ability to live in the moment. I am streaming through Philip, impressing him, and using his vocal cords and physical body. This is possible through the great focus of my energy into his energy combined with his passive presence. His passivity is not pure passivity, but trained focus, so I am able to pass through him without barriers and without much difficulty. Barriers could be fear, ego attachment to the outcome, preconceptions about how all of this should happen, or undue curiosity about the dynamics or mechanics of it. It is a simple procedure. When you open yourself in this way, you are most receptive to our energies.

Sympathy: The second thing anyone adept at healing must have is sympathy. In its fullest sense, the word "channel" means an opening for those of us in spirit to pass through. Such individuals are wired in a certain way, and there are realities of the body, mind and spirit that enable us to do higher and better work. There must be no blockage to the energy passing through. If you walk through a hospital ward and your heart is not moved by the suffering of individuals there, you probably are not a candidate for healing work. From early childhood I had a hard time because I was so aware of other people's suffering. I did not speak about it at the time, and not much is written about me on this point, but I was very concerned and easily picked up the pain and uneasiness accompanying another's illness, including their mental depression. Because I was a *joyful* person, I could slough it off, so I was not morose or heavy hearted; but because of my sensitivity, I picked up other people's problems and healing needs. Such sympathy is an aspect of love.

Empathy: Empathy exists when one has passed through similar circumstances and can feel with others what they are going through. This quality is also needed to be able to heal. I know you are going to ask a question about Jesus, so I will not go into this in depth, but Jesus *suffered* as a child and throughout his whole life, not just because he was different, but because of the way in which he was built. No one could have undertaken that miraculous position without having special aspects to his being, personality, character, body, thought and feeling. He had such a close and personal connection with God. Jesus says in a scripture that he felt virtue leave from him when someone touched him. That is, energy left him. His whole being was such that he could immediately empathize and sympathize. He suffered in such a way and at such depth that he became a being who could not *help* but feel empathy with others. He is the greatest healer of all because of that.

Compassion: Compassion is necessary for the healer. When I worked, tears often came to my eyes because of the compassion I felt for the person in front of me. I had to walk a fine line so I would not feel too much. The people before me had sometimes experienced so much suffering, so many abnormalities, and what seemed to be such extreme, unfair situations in the body or in the mind that healing energy was drawn through me as a channel, causing me to immediately want to reach out, touch, and relieve the person of their particular illness or difficulty. Genuine compassion is required to attract healing energy to come through.

Wonder: In doing healing work, it is important to have a sense of wonder, wanting to know the answers to the mysteries of life. One could not do what any effective healer does without marveling at what happens. While almost in a trance-like state, I would be filled with energy, and when I simply touched someone or came near someone, that person would pass out. This was not my doing, and I had little or nothing to do with it. I was simply a conduit for the energy that passed through me to individuals. They also had their own energy fields that would be touched by spirit through electrical forces that you on earth cannot yet understand.

The phenomenon that I am speaking about is similar to how lightning courses its way through the atmosphere and touches the earth. It can be very dangerous and can kill someone, but through its proper application by spirit doctors and teachers, particularly doctors who helped to manipulate this energy in a cooperative way with me, the person would be touched and effectively treated. Electric energy would revive, normalize, and balance out the energies and remove spiritual, emotional, and mental residue. It would realign the whole physical organism, as well as the relationship between the spirit and body, bringing everything into proper alignment.

These are some of the characteristics that are necessary for healing work.

Dr. D: *How do you actually connect with or get into the energy of another person for the purpose of channeling?*

KK: It is not so different in principle from the way you plug an electric appliance into a circuit of energy. The field of energy you and I are in is one and the same. It is an extension of God's love, which manifests as white light. Some say it is the glue that holds all things together. It is the energy that makes it possible for the atom to exist and hold its configuration. Using electrical terms, the medium or channeler becomes a minus and, as a spiritual being, I become a plus. You have put this gentleman in trance, so he is very passive, and this makes him more receptive to our energies. You will note that when people are in deep meditation, they often get revelation. When they are deep in prayer, a very quiet whispering prayer, they will have visions and other spiritual experiences. This can happen because of the raising of your vibration or frequency to meet us halfway as we lower ours. There must also be a certain amount of receptivity to our presence, a focusing of energy, but passively so. The image that comes to mind is a cup that simply sits there, open to being filled.

Right now, Philip is filled with me in the sense that I have engaged my positive and active energies into his negative and passive energies, and I am using him. I do not mean I am using him in some negative way, any more than you are doing something negative when you plug an appliance into an electric current. It is just the combining of two elements by which phenomena can happen. I am doing this by using his mental, emotional, and physical faculties, but he will not remember this. In his passive state the information just passes through him. It may be stored in his subconscious mind, so he may be able to recall it through hypnosis with your particular expertise. In his conscious mind, however, because he is in this passive state allowing me to come through, it does not register and does not stay there. It is like air just passing through a tube or through the heating or cooling system in your home. The passageway is there to receive that energy and allow it to do what it will do.

That is the science of it in my words. Someone with an engineering degree would probably use different language, but essentially that is how it happens. It is far more complex than that, but if I tried to explain it further that would only confuse the issue, because the realities here are not the same as those on earth. Until you come here, you cannot know or understand them, let alone experience them.

Dr. D: *At what point do you choose to work through someone on earth?*

KK: That someone will be a healer is known before the person comes to the earth plane. I am not always personally aware of such people, though I may be. I was still alive when Philip was born, but I was not aware that I would one day work with someone on the earth plane in the way I am doing with him. Though I did not share it publicly, I knew experientially there were spirits who returned and cooperated with individuals on earth. I had the experience when I was touched by spirit. I perceived a differentiation between the energy field in my own being and the energy of spirit. I went into a trance-like state, which is not static, but is a level of openness that helps one to receive energy.

On this side, they say it was known that I would do what I did before I came into the earth plane. It is what I came to do. This is not different from anyone else who becomes a true healer. There are those who dabble in healing and those who use their own energy to heal, but we are not talking about that level of healing. We are talking about receptivity to being a channel *for* and working *with* the healing energy coming in from the highest levels of existence. This healing energy comes from God, the Holy Spirit, and spiritual beings who are able to use this energy as rays of light.

I came into Philip's life when he first began this work, and that is another story. I had to get his attention first, but this was far in advance of a very distinct and specific encounter that he had with me. I knew even before that experience I would be working with him. Each individual is chosen to do this work on a case by case basis.

If anyone reading this book has an inclination toward healing, do not feel discouraged by my words. If you love God, love people, and have even a modicum of compassion, empathy and sympathy, then go for it. You may not do the work the same way I did, but that is not important. What is important *is* that you answer the call of your own soul. No matter how many people you heal in a lifetime, what is important is that you are used as a channel to heal; that you allow the love that you are to flow out, to fulfill *who* you are in this incarnation. I would always encourage you to try.

On earth today there are many Reiki healers doing great work for this planet. Most of them are not even known by the public. They are hidden vehicles that God and spirit are using, and their work is valuable. I am answering as I am, but again, I want to encourage everyone, if you are inclined in the direction of being a healer, do so.

Am I coming through very differently from how Saint Germain comes through? My using Philip directly like this actually began to happen some time ago, and we have said we would allow for this, because Philip's other guides and teachers have wanted to come through this way. We have been waiting for this, and it is very exciting for me!

Dr. D: *If people do not know they will do healing work before they come into a lifetime, can they still choose to do it after they come into the earth plane?*

KK: Dear, if someone is to be a healer, it cannot be stopped. I could not have stopped being a healer any more than the man in the moon, because it was my path. Some people have a different experience. Emmanuel Swedenborg from Sweden did not become a mystic and was unaware of his own clairvoyance or spiritual gifts until quite late in his life. When it happens, it happens, and that is when it's supposed to happen. It is in a person's spiritual DNA as to when that individual is born on earth. A child born to a large family is supposed to come as the ninth, seventh, or third child. Everything is in divine order, and what is to be will be in the life of an individual. If it is not to be, it will not be.

Does this mean that just anything crossing the mind is what a person should do? No, that would be foolish. We should pay attention to things that keep appearing in consciousness, the things that attract us and do not go away. Mere curiosity toward this work is not enough. There must be more than curiosity, desire for fame, or desire for spiritual phenomena. It must be deeper than that. If the thought of becoming a healer surfaces on the outer layer of consciousness and does not penetrate deep within the heart, probably that individual is not intended to be a healer. But who am I to say?

That is why Saint Germain and all of us would teach you to listen to the voice of God within. It cannot fail. You can know what that voice is saying. You can know how urgently it is telling you to do something by how unceasing it is in pushing you in a certain direction. We have heard you say you became a hypnotherapist because you were pushed in this direction. You felt you *had* to do what you are doing, so I am sure you recognize the truth of what I am saying. You listened to the voice within, and you felt compelled to act. The signs were there to go for it, and you went for it!

I am smiling because I so much enjoy this experience we are having, both personally and being in your energy, which is quite pure. I am also happy with the idea that people will be hearing my words. I so much want to be heard, not as a personality, but to bring truth.

Dr. D: *How did you come to choose Philip Burley as a channel?*

KK: Well, we threw the dice! *(Chuckle)* Not really. I have already answered this question indirectly, but I will explain more so that the reader can better understand the attributes necessary for this work.

It was Philip's destiny to do this, and he was born for this work. He has certain qualities of character and personality such as cooperativeness, openness, and sensitivity that are of primary importance. He did healing work by removing spirits from people at one time, but he backed away from that, and we did not disagree. He is still a healer, but his greater work involves healing people through words, including the words of Saint Germain and others channeling through him over the years. The energy that is in him, around him, and that comes out of him is healing energy. Anyone who sits with him for a period of time cannot help but feel a certain calming energy that brings peace to the heart. It is not just when we are there or when we come through him; it is who he is.

For all who would do a significant work, or even a small work, there must be a certain level of suffering. Suffering is not a bad thing, though anyone in emotional or physical pain may think so. If Philip had not gone through what he went through, he could not be who he is today. In the world, those who would judge others might say, "Oh, look what he or she did. Look what he or she went through." Such people do not know the heart of God, because no human being who is a target of God's use will be without suffering. Look at Jesus. Look at all the great ones. They are not great because they sought to be great. Through their suffering, their own God presence came forth. They discovered what worked and did not work, and their innate qualities were brought forward. A refined self was born out of the caldron of suffering.

That refinement, that sensitivity of energy, that beautiful aspect of all human beings at the soul level, is what attracted us to Philip first. His light was bright from birth. We did not just happen to notice him, like a flower to be plucked out of a garden of many, but we had discussions like you do on earth. We look deeply into any individual whom we are going to employ in doing this work. We look at potential and at the long range outcome, not just at today or tomorrow. What will this person be like and have to go through for us to use him or her? Philip qualified, because he had what we needed. There are not many, but some others like him. I do not say that in prejudice toward anyone, but it is not common for someone to do what he has done over the period of time he has done it. We are proud of him because he has endured.

I also had the quality of endurance, and this was one of the things that gave me rapport with Philip. To endure, one has to believe. One has to have faith, hope and trust, not just in the mind, but also in the heart. These are the qualities that drew me to Philip.

Dr. D: *You mentioned faith, though you did not conform entirely to the religious direction of your day. Could you comment on that?*

KK: I was a follower of Christianity and an ardent lover of Jesus, because I felt I understood him. Of course, my understanding of the Jesus I know now compared to my understanding of the Jesus I knew then is quite, quite expanded, but not essentially different. The Jesus I experienced was the Jesus of unconditional love. When he visited me, he brought such compassion and such love that when I communed with him I felt as if I were with a spiritual lover. In saying that, I am talking about heart to heart love or soul love. How do I put it into words? I was loved with such care and sensitivity, such knowingness of me, that I knew I was in the presence of divine energy.

The quality of the Christ Spirit, which is in everyone, is the quality of self-effacement. It is to think of others to such an extent that one forgets oneself. That is who Jesus was and still is. I knew Jesus loved all people, because he came from God, who loves all people. At that time, I did not find this within the rank and file of what we call fundamental Christianity. I found Jesus there, yes, but generally speaking, I did not find that all-pervasive universal spirit. It was as though they were saying, "Unless you become one of us, we cannot embrace you. You have to proclaim Jesus." What about those who never had the chance to know Jesus? Are they not *also* the children of God? I knew innately that all people are children of God. I saw that in my experiences.

What was most important in my work, and to Jesus, still brings tears to my eyes. It is the suffering of humanity *resulting from ignorance.* Not knowing the heart of God, not knowing what the Father's intent is for each individual's life, many look upon suffering as something to avoid. They see it as something that results from their stepping away from higher reality. Not so. All is God's work. How does the child learn to walk unless it also falls down? It is in the falling down and getting up that a child's thighs, hips, calves, feet, arms and legs become stronger. It is not the suffering itself that disturbs us, whether

I'm talking about Jesus, myself, or others who feel compassion. It is humanity's ignorance toward suffering that is saddest to us.

Jesus was crucified. Who could endure such suffering? Jesus knew why he was suffering, because he had communed with God. He was not ignorant. He *knew* his purpose, and that is why he did not run from the cross. Even though, in his humanity, Jesus wanted the cup of suffering taken from him, he went toward it with valor and dignity. When they persecuted him, stripping and beating him, he did not utter a word. He knew he needed no defense. He knew that in time he would be glorified, and his spiritual stature would cause individuals to have remorse for how they had treated him. He was a man of great dignity who knew his purpose. He is here now. You can feel him.

I tried my best to embrace the universal Christ. I did not conform out of fear to the way of some churches of that day, and so I was criticized. The proof in the rightness of what I did was in the outcome of my ministry. There is still today significant testimony to what God did through me. I take no credit for that. Anyone who knows me knows that. My work speaks for itself. In no way do I equate myself to Jesus. In no way do I think of myself as important. Self-effacement is an element of the Christ Spirit, through understanding that God is first, God is greatest, and God is the source of my life. Being humbled to that reality and bowing to it, not in subservience, but with the deepest of gratitude, is what *ultimately* heals and *ultimately* makes one whole. I come as a servant, not as a heroine.

I am quite emotionally affected by sharing all of this, but I have wanted to speak my heart for so long about some things I have held back. Today I have been able to speak some of it, and I am so grateful, because it liberates me from some of the pain of misunderstanding.

Dr. D: *What is the downside of being a healer, if any?*

KK: If any? Oh dear me! *(Laughter)* There are many downsides, not the least of which is that you never get a chance to sleep very much, because if you are truly in love with humanity, you cannot rest, knowing the suffering of so many. It is not always the overt suffering, but the suffering due to ignorance that is most painful for me, especially as I come from the spirit world where I have seen the bigger picture.

Being in the public limelight and doing my television show, public speaking engagements and healing work, I was on the go all the time. I did not eat regularly, I did not get to sleep in my own bed much of the time, and there was always a demand on me. That part of being a healer can be very taxing. I was exhausted at times. My physical energies began to wane as I got older, yet my zeal for healing continued. There was conflict between the youthfulness of my mind and the aging of my body, and eventually I died. My body gave out. I did not know in those times how to replenish myself. If I had followed a healthier diet, I would have lived longer.

To the person who is reading this, I would just say that the downside is an upside, really. That is, in order to do this work, one has to be totally dedicated and devoted, and one has to be humble.

That is not easy in daily life. If one is not wise and is too attached to the outcome of any healing experience, this can also be very taxing. Do not worry about "Is it going to work? Am I going to be used?" If you are in that frame of mind, you can still be used, but it will cause a certain amount of stress within your mind and your body. I would say this old saying to all who would make this effort, "Let go and let God." That is the true secret. It took me awhile to learn this, but once I learned it, I became a clear channel, and I was used in a significant way.

Dr. D: *Is there anything Philip can do to continue to be a good channel, while increasing his energy and health?*

KK: If I were to tell the truth, I would say to bring him out of trance and tell him to go home! *(Chuckle)* It can be tiring to do this work, but Philip came into this world to do it, and he balances his work with rest. There is not much more he can do than to make sure he gets plenty of fresh air, sunshine, and exercise. I didn't get enough of these three things, and they are absolutely necessary. The sun can revitalize you, and one needs to get out into it every day for a certain period of time. It replenishes energies in a way that nothing else can, neither artificial lamps nor pills. Otherwise he is doing just fine. His mind has never been in a better state, and thanks to you and others who have worked with him, this day has arrived.

Dr. D: *What are the benefits of being a healer?*

KK: Well dear, as you have experienced in your own work, the greatest benefit of being a healer is seeing the person you are working with being made whole. When you see the results of the input, the overshadowing of the energies, and the transforming power heal someone and make that person whole, and you see that soul rejoicing, there is no greater joy. Public acclaim and recognition pale greatly by comparison. I always marveled at how well the spirit worked and at how this force of energy came through me and all around me, through the cooperative ministry of the spirit world, angelic world, and human spirit. It was absolutely astounding, absolutely amazing, miracle after miracle.

I benefited so much from seeing all of this, and I *knew* God was real, spirit world was real, the Holy Spirit was real, and Jesus was real. Thus my life was not one of faith, but of direct experience. This gave me such an advantage that I could live most literally with God, night and day. How could I not? Even those who came one time to my healing services and saw the intercessory healing energy of God and spirit were transformed. They could never be the same. They might doubt it, but their doubt could not erase what they saw, heard, and experienced.

This is why spiritual experiences are important. One should not seek them for their own sake, but on the way to God, to ask for spiritual experiences is not wrong. Ask yourself *why* you seek them and how you will use them. For me, they were stepping stones on my path to God. They validated for me that my faith, hope, and belief were not wasted. They were investments in a substantial reality, an ultimate reality called God, divine energy, divine love, an ever-expanding invisible world of reality. There are many, many benefits, but these are among the most important that I can tell you about.

Dr. D: *Is there anything else you would like to see included in the book?*

KK: You are doing a significant work, and God is working through both you and Philip as channels. The various chapters in the book will heal many hearts through bringing understanding and removing ignorance, and God will use the book to touch the lives of those who are ready to be touched. Not everyone will approve of it, agree with it, or even be interested in it, but there are many who will benefit, and that is all that matters.

We see how you persevere, because we stand by you as you work, transcribing these tapes and checking the word or words as you do so. You are diligent. And just know your work is not in vain! If there is more to be said, then it will come, perhaps when Philip reads the transcription of my words. There may be things I prompt him to change or add.

We have covered a great amount of information today. Please forgive my indulgence in personalizing some of my words, but I would not be Kathryn Kuhlman if I did not do that. On earth it was known that I was sincere, and I still am. That part I have brought with me here, because it is the part of the essence of my character.

I am going to let you go now if you let me go. *(Chuckle)* It is just so dear to have this opportunity. God bless you. This is Kathryn Kuhlman.

Dr. D: *God bless you. Thank you so much for all the information.*

Saint Germain Speaks:

SG: *(Deep breath)* This is Saint Germain. I am so pleased with the work you and Philip did today. This dear sister, Kathryn Kuhlman, is a great soul, and she is unduly modest. This is her legacy, because here in spirit, while she glows with such a brilliant light, she does not see it. All she sees is God and people. She wants her God presence to meet the God presence of others so that together they may glorify God. This is hard for you to understand, but on our side, it is the hallmark of sainthood, and more than that.

We have used Philip enough today, and we would like you to bring him out. Thank you so much for being the facilitator for all this to happen. God bless you. This is Saint Germain.

End of session.

ELEANOR ROOSEVELT

Anna Eleanor Roosevelt (October 11, 1884—November 7, 1962) used her position as First Lady of the United States to promote human rights, civil rights, women's issues, and international cooperation. Her husband, Franklin Delano Roosevelt, served the United States as President from 1933 through 1945. Following his death, Eleanor Roosevelt became an author and speaker to support the causes she believed in, including human rights and the work of the United Nations. In honor of her extensive public service, President Harry Truman called Eleanor Roosevelt the First Lady of the World.

CONVERSATION EIGHTEEN

Eleanor Roosevelt

You suffer much because you do not realize the degree of your influence. In the darkness of the night, in a vast, vast area of darkness, one little candle can dispel that darkness. I tell you nothing new, but I rekindle that vision so that each one of you may burn brightly in prayer and in faithfulness for the sake of self, nation, and all people; for the sake of the world.

—Eleanor Roosevelt

ER: Yes, I am here. I was ready quite a bit before Philip was, but your putting him into the relaxed state made it easy for me to just slip in without causing any disruption in his nervous system.

I greet you and thank you for making it possible for me to step through the doorway from spirit into the earthly plane. I am so pleased to be here. If you could feel the current of electricity from spirit, you would know it is absolutely sweeping through Philip. I am imparting it and also receiving it, because when spirit meets flesh, a miracle happens. Life takes on the fullest expression. That is why we are drawn back to the earth plane. Sometimes we hunger for this environment because, if we have not completed our spiritual cycle from beginning to end, we must partake of the energies that I am now experiencing. Call this energy whatever you want to. Earlier today, in your conversations Philip referred to it as "chi."

I will not prolong my comments now because there is some rich, rich material relating to your questions that I want to address. I am just so very pleased I could come through today and be here with you.

Dr. D: *How are you doing in the spirit world?*

ER: Dear one, if you cannot tell from my voice how I am, you never will know. I come through as the personality I was on the earth plane, because that is who I am. Of course, I have learned many things that have made life in spirit a great joy, and I understand more clearly what life is all about. While on earth, you all struggle because you do not know the beginning or the end. You only know everything in between as you move through life. There is a great plan for each person. Not all plans are big, because that is determined by the individual's mission or role to play on earth. Still, each person has a story, and it must be played out, chapter by chapter.

While you are on earth, you can only follow directives that come through your consciousness. If there are things you think you should have done differently, and you look back at your life from the spirit world, you will understand that what happened was not *intended* to be different. This is because you had to learn spiritual or physical lessons in those situations. It is all about confronting self. You know that as well as I do, don't you? Life evolves to mirror back to us who we are exactly.

I am doing very well because I am a quick learner, as I was on earth. I do not get too much in my own way by thinking I already know everything. I know I don't know everything, and I still have many things to learn. I am just grateful, very grateful, that God Almighty has made it possible for us to have an existence that enables us to learn all that we are to learn. I am grateful first because it is thrilling, and second because it brings awareness about self in such a magnified way that one cannot help but be filled with light and joy. I am just so happy about that. I do not know if that helps you understand how I am *(chuckle)*, but that is how I am, and that *is* how I am doing.

Dr. D: *Are you and Franklin together?*

ER: No, as a matter of fact, we are not. Oh, we see each other because we were related on earth, both as distant cousins and through marriage; but I will not surprise the reader when I say that the kind of married love that exists among some couples did not exist between us. I understand now what happened and why that was so. I understand the roles that he and I each played in the unfolding of our lives on the public and personal level. It really does not matter as far as God is concerned. We come into the world to play both public and private roles, depending on our purpose in coming into life. Many personal things that people poke around in, and that the news is interested in, are really no one else's business. Because we were public figures, we were ripe for the picking, for pictures to be taken, for things to be written about us, and for our private lives to be invaded.

Franklin and I had an unwritten pact. We agreed we would honor and respect each other and carry out the public roles we were given. I stood by him for that purpose, for the sake of the nation. In that sense, it might be said that we were enlarged souls, not just centered on ourselves. That was our upbringing, too. When you grow up with privileges, you are taught to be responsible. You learn to use all the advantages you have for the greater good of humanity, or at least, at the very least, for the good of your nation. That was our idealism from our youth up, so we went ahead on that basis. We found ourselves together, and we continued to work together.

It is love that draws people to each other in the spirit world. We did not have the kind of love that some have in marriage, and so naturally the magnetism was not there to bring us together again in that way. We are very, very good friends, and we are pleased and happy with what we were able to accomplish together on earth. All of our experiences on earth are here for us to see. We are individually aware of them. When we reflect on situations where we may have stumbled, we are not pleased with what we did, and it is the same for everyone here. But we are also able to see things that were of a good nature that we did on earth, and that is part of our glory here, if you want to use that word. It might also be said that it is part of our legacy.

Dr. D: *You mentioned you and Franklin had a pact. Where and when was that pact made?*

ER: This was an understanding that came up early in our marriage, and it became especially important in the beginning of Franklin's presidency, as we knew we were headed for a life in the public view on all levels. I was disappointed that Franklin did not love me the way I wanted to be loved and that he could not find me the apple of his eye. Still, I understood human nature. I understood that life is not perfect and that you have to deal with it positively. Many give up, but I did not.

In today's world, would we have divorced? We might have, because it is a different time now. Because we were both stuck on the ideal of public service, we decided to stay together. I, especially, decided I was not going to hurt him or the nation, so I simply lived my own private life. I lived positively. The more I accepted my lot in life, the more goodness and opportunity came to me to use my personality and talents to help the world. That is my legacy and I am proud of it.

As time went on, I knew Franklin was not totally loyal to me. Of course I was deeply hurt, and he was extremely apologetic. Again, we were at a crossroads. We decided, not without fits and starts, that we would stay together and ride out the storms of our lives on the ship of our destiny together. We did that. After Franklin became ill, and his life declined, I stepped in. I was able to do that because we were one in our desire to do the highest and best good we could for the nation. We endured.

Dr. D: *Thank you. Are there some occasions when presidents and wives of presidents all assemble in the spirit world?*

ER: Yes, though it is case by case. When you play your roles on earth, it is like putting clothes on. There is some clothing you really like and wear often, a particular dress or shirt, and other clothing you wear just because you want a change in color or a change in the look, even if you don't particularly like it. In hindsight, the role of first lady is like that. Some of us are very much caught up in the role, while others are not. Some see the role of first lady as a passing experience. When they come here, they may have higher ideals that they relate to. They are more interested in the beauty of things and dealing with higher aspects of life.

I have met and spoken with Jacqueline Kennedy. In the spirit world, she is very much into the beauty of things and is very different from the person you knew when she was on earth. She was sometimes criticized by the world, as I was, but she has a noble mind. With a number of other first ladies and presidents, she and I are both still concerned about the nation. We had a role to play and a certain path to follow, and we continue on that path today by working through others on earth. It only stands to reason that whoever was a first lady would, in some way, shape, or form, come back from spirit to the earth plane to continue walking that path through other first ladies or "leading ladies." It would not have to be the wife of a president, but any lady in a leading position with whom we found rapport. In the same way, presidents come back to work with presidents or leaders on earth who have a significant role.

Since we have much in common, we do gather here, but it is not our all in all. If you were to come here you would be blown away, to use your modern vocabulary; you would simply be overwhelmed by the magnificence, freedom and beauty of it all, and the absolute awareness of the God presence. There are no words adequate to describe what I am telling you. God is always present, always available, in all forms, and on a personal level as well. Once you are here, you are not necessarily stuck in your former life or interested only in the career you had on earth. I am sure that to the reader this is obvious and logical.

How are we doing here? Can you tell it's me?

Dr. D: *I can tell it's you and that you are excited to be coming through.*

ER: Yes I am very excited, in more than a subtle sense.

Dr. D: *My next question is this: What do you think of the present world situation?*

ER: Oh, my, my. What a big question!

Dr. D: *Can you reduce it down? (Chuckle)*

ER: Yes, of course. Let me say to you and to the reader that our world is bigger than your world. Those who are advantaged to be close to the God presence can see the past, present and future. Most of us at the level to which I have come have some of that awareness. We can see trouble born, trouble worked out, and trouble ended; a war begun, a war fought, and a war ended. These realities have to do with individual souls who are participating. War is made less abstract by specifying the Vietnam War, War of 1812 or the Civil War, but we are really talking about the lives of human beings, aren't we?

They have come to earth to live out their lives and realize what they are intended to realize. The particular role each is playing for karmic purposes determines who is involved in wars and what that has to do with the purposes for which each one came to earth. Everyone, from the President on down, on a political, social, economic, religious, or educational level, is playing a different role in this particular chapter in human history and in the chapter of your nation.

There are future chapters to be written. This time shall pass away, and a new chapter will come. I am not allowed to talk about this in detail because you have to live it out. Otherwise, it will not bring the challenge that is needed to test your souls, to try your spirit, to enable you to see who you are, and to overcome. I would not like to paint the canvas of your nation with black paint, but with different colors. There are many good things ahead.

What will happen to individuals depends on each one and why that person came to earth. In all situations of human conflict, human difficulty, and human joy, there are those who participate, those who do not participate, and those who do not even know about the situation. Right now on the earth plane there is war, but there are millions of people quite removed from that war, having nothing to do with it. There are some in more remote areas of the world who don't even know about war. People are where they are according to why they came to earth, and they will realize what is to be realized according to what crosses their paths.

Whatever is indeed to happen in your life will happen, in spite of you, so it's better to accept it, whatever it is, and make the best of it. When you pass from this plane to the next plane, you will look back with the questions, "What did I do with my life in all circumstances?" Was I consistent? Did I love unconditionally? Did I continue to hold up hope and faith in a greater power through the darkest times as well as during the best of times? Was I steady in my service to others and myself? Did I use every situation to learn to love, and love sacrificially?" All of these questions, and more, will be stuck in your heart and mind. That is why we are on the earth, and that is what I have learned. I knew all of this on the earth, but I didn't know it as well as I do now. How could I? I, too, had to go through all of life's labors to derive what I was to get from my life. That is why I come back with great excitement and joy to be able to share in this way, to shed even one little shred of light, one little ray of light, to let you know all is well. All will come out well.

The degree to which each individual is aligned with goodness, ultimate goodness, is the degree to which that person is valuable to God and is used to carry out higher purposes and answer the higher callings of life. We would also ask those humble people of the world, those who seem to have no influence or power, to be the light of the world. We would ask them to be the ones to change things, to move the leaders, and to move the heart of God by the power of prayer. You suffer much because you do not realize the degree of your influence. In the darkness of the night, in a vast, vast area of darkness, one little candle can dispel that darkness. I tell you nothing new, but I rekindle that vision so that each one of you may burn brightly in prayer and in faithfulness for the sake of self, nation, and all people—for the sake of the world.

Dr. D: *I assume you are continuing your world service on the spirit side. Can you tell us about that?*

ER: Yes, I am, of course. I have alluded to that in what I have said thus far, so I don't think I need to say much more, other than to say that what I am doing *at this moment* is world service. I usually do not do world service by channeling through someone. This is really my first experience in doing such a thing at length. I work to help those who are helping others on earth; not a few, and not just those in high positions. I am drawn to those who are of a like nature, and I have that level of self-mastery where I am allowed to manifest in a number of places at one time.

Dr. D: *Previous speakers have shared information about what their life is like on the spirit side. Is there anything about your life in spirit that you would like to share?*

ER: I think I have shared enough about that. You can tell from my enthusiasm that it is a wonderful place to be. That is a great understatement, of course. It's a great place to be, not a place to dread. Just be mindful that death is not painful. It happens in the twinkling of an eye. What is painful is not to have lived correctly and then to come here and face the reality of what you have created in spirit. So I would say to readers, do not fear death. Don't even fear living. But check yourself to see whether or not you are doing the best for self by using your precious energies for your highest good and for the highest good of humanity.

Dr. D: *Is there anything else you would like to say about your life on earth?*

ER: I have gone through difficult, heavy times in my life, including the death of my husband and many of my friends. Some of my friends were still remaining, and I had acquaintances with people in the political and social fields, but still, I was lonely at times.

I would have to say that my greatest joy in my later life was working for the United Nations. From my perspective, that was my greatest public achievement.

Dr. D: *Is there anything else you would like to say to the readers?*

ER: Each one needs to deeply, deeply appreciate who you are, including the uniqueness of who you are. I would like to say to everyone, embrace your life completely so that the reality you live in can be changed to higher and higher levels. Love yourself, for God lives in you. Do not diminish or insult that presence within. Let it be born in you as you awaken to it. Seek it with all your heart and mind. Then, when you come here, you will feel completely at home.

Dr. D: *You spoke earlier of the roles we play. Were you aware of the role you were going to play prior to coming into the earth plane?*

ER: I was not consciously aware of the role I was going to play. This is no different from any other human being. Otherwise, I would not have been able to play my role correctly. There were down times, tests, and struggles in my life. If I had known about them ahead of time, I would have worked very hard to avoid them. You see, what happens to us is intended to happen, whatever it may be, because the soul is never touched or destroyed. The soul comes to earth in the encasement of the body, and the soul leaves.

It is for the edification, the glorification, the uplifting, and the amplification of the soul that you come to earth. All of this is for the supreme good, and that is the most important thing. I am by name, Eleanor, but in spirit I am light. I am divine intelligence. I am unconditional love come to earth. I partake of the fullness of the Creator of life, and I am co-creator, singled out in this expression, this ray of energy. I am from that source and connected to it at all times. I live in that awareness endlessly. The same is true for everyone who exists, whether they presently know it or not.

Dr. D: *Is there any more information you can give to the readers about your experience with God?*

ER: On balance, I think I have said what I wanted to say. Of course, as a human being, as a God presence manifested in this form, there are many things I could say, but for this time, in this place, it is enough. This is Eleanor Roosevelt. My love is with all on Mother Earth. God bless you.

Dr. D: *God bless you, and thank you so much for coming.*

End of session.

Comments:

PB: Of all the channeling, that was the most amazing experience. She was so present. The electricity running through my body was a constant current. I was deep in trance, but I could feel a constant current of love.

Dr. D: *I could feel her energy. She was giggling under her breath, and she was so excited.*

PB: Of all the times I've experienced spirit coming through, I have never doubted the others, but this was a unique experience that confirmed to me more completely than any other time that this was an absolutely authentic presence. It was so gratifying.

MOTHER TERESA

Mother Teresa (August 26, 1910—September 5, 1997) was born in Skopje, Macedonia. At the age of eighteen, she joined the Sisters of Loreto, and after teaching school in Calcutta for many years, she received permission to devote herself to working among Calcutta's poor.

Mother Teresa's work drew volunteers and financial support, and in 1950 she received permission to start her own religious order, The Missionaries of Charity. The order now has branches all over the world, serving people who face poverty, hunger, natural disaster, homelessness, and illnesses of all kinds. Mother Teresa received numerous awards for her humanitarian work, including the Nobel Peace Prize in 1979. Following her death in 1997, she was beatified by Pope John Paul II in October of 2003. In September 2016, she was canonized by Pope Francis and designated St. Teresa of Calcutta. Many continue to affectionately refer to her as "Mother Teresa."

CONVERSATION NINETEEN

Mother Teresa

It is difficult to walk among people who are broken, deeply broken. Yet, many of them have learned the lesson of humility, and when they come to the spirit world, they are some of the greatest souls here. Those who have taken their suffering in a positive way are grateful for the higher lessons learned through their suffering... They taught me. In my heart I did not see the squalor, disease, and poverty because I saw the light of Christ in each one.

—Mother Teresa

MT: I am here. This is Mother Teresa. Bless you, my child. It is more deeply meaningful for me to be here than those who adhere to my work might think. Anytime you want to engage me in questions, I welcome them.

Dr. D: *Thank you. You have now been made a saint by the Catholic Church. Does this make a difference in your status in the spirit world?*

MT: Not at all. I am just as I am. Receiving an honorific earthly title is flattering to those to whom it is flattering. I am grateful if people recognize the work of my Order, not by its name, but by its character. It would be good for more people to practice service, though not necessarily in poverty. As a way of removing ego attachment and giving all glory to God, the source of life, I embraced poverty, but there are other ways to serve.

To be beatified or to acquire the name of saint is thought of as a great honor in the church to which I belonged, but for me it changes nothing except that it causes more people to pray to me. I am honored to have been recognized as one through whom miracles manifested, but this does not affect me in the inner aspect of myself. Outwardly, I am more burdened than I was before with the calling of my name and with people's requests that I use my status to catch the attention of God. More people are asking me to plead their case or to bring the result they are praying for. This is even truer for Mary, Paul, and all those who are held up as saints. They are being called upon by all who believe in such a principle and system. Though we do intercessory work, it is not the highest of manifestations.

I feel an urgent need to teach you to call upon the blessedness or sainthood within yourself, the light within yourself. Attach the name of saint to your own name by your efforts to live a life of purity, centered on divine love. This will bring forth the God presence. By the way, you will find the term "God presence" repeated throughout this book, because we use it often in the spirit world. There is no better way to explain what we mean in simple terms.

Dr. D: *Church histories and biographies sometimes glorify individuals to the extent that we never learn about the full reality of their life experience. Do we have a true and accurate picture of your personality and life in what has been written about you in secular and religious literature?*

MT: In our soul of souls there are two aspects: faith and faithlessness, belief and non-belief. This is the path of all people, whether or not they call themselves religious or spiritual. On some days people feel good and believe in their lives, and on other days they do not feel good or have faith in their lives. It was not different for me. Though it is not written about in significant detail, I went through temptations that caused me to come close to giving up what I felt was my calling.

I am human. I had a physical body, so I had cycles of life like everyone. I had sexual feelings like everyone does. That is not what makes the difference between those who achieve high spiritual goals and those who do not. What makes the difference is how one looks upon things as they are happening. The human body is a gift, both for procreation and for glorifying God. If you use your body for an array of good things, then you are using your body correctly. The opposite is true if you misuse it. I had to learn these things, and I was sometimes naive about them because of narrowness and spiritual blindness. I would call a thing wrong only because I looked at it incorrectly, when in fact there was nothing wrong with it.

In the spirit world there are many celibates who did not partake of sexual love and therefore cannot look at it. They have an aversion to sexual love because they saw it as being outside of God's blessing. There are some who saw it within God's blessing, but those who did not thought it was a lesser use of the physical body. They aspired more and more to the subjugation of feelings and thoughts that were a part of what leads to the procreative act, even within a solid marriage reflecting deep affection and oneness. In the spirit world, such people cannot look upon marriage or couples without feeling a tinge of discomfort. On earth you have people manifesting with the same aversion.

I did not have such feelings, so this was not one of my problems. Because of delivering babies and taking care of people with all kinds of diseases in my everyday life, I was too close to the reality of nature not to see the truth of things. I did not choose marriage for myself; that is, marriage that would include sexual intercourse. I felt I should put that behind me because I observed that Jesus had put it behind him. He was my example.

I may surprise and even shock some people as they read this, but I cannot skirt the truth of things. In the spirit world you do not do that, because all truth is known. I am not going to fabricate some story to make people feel comfortable so they do not have to look at the truth of things, especially higher truths.

Everything is good when one looks at it from God's perspective and considers the purpose for which it was created. This is true even of suffering. Without it, people would not search for a way to alleviate pain. Even sickness is good from the standpoint that it causes you to ask questions and seek answers to resolve the problem. If you come down with an enduring sore throat, you go to a doctor to get medicine to cure it. When you feel lonely and separated from yourself and God, your loneliness is good if it causes you to read, pray, meditate, and talk to others in an effort to find peace and come closer to God. All is good from that perspective.

Dr. D: *You are known for your sacrificial service to the downtrodden in India and in other parts of the world. Sometimes what you did seemed almost impossible to bear in the presence of so much squalor, poverty and disease. I offer this question with the utmost respect: How did you do it? How could you bear up under such circumstances?*

MT: *(Voice shaking)* As you can see, I get choked up even to this day when I recall the suffering that I saw. It still touches me. It is difficult to walk among people who are broken, deeply broken. Yet, many of them have learned the lesson of humility, and when they come to the spirit world, they are some of the greatest souls here. Those who have taken their suffering in a positive way are grateful for the higher lessons learned through their suffering. I am tearful right at this moment, thinking of such people. They taught *me*. In my heart I did not see the squalor, disease and poverty because I saw the light of Christ in each one. I saw in each of them what was also in me. For me, this glorified God. I understood that God is closest to those who suffer the most and yet still seek him.

The people I served had a language and religion that were different from mine, but they still spoke of God and believed in a higher power. They demonstrated this in various ways, though differently than I did. They burned incense before images or idols. Still, what I saw within them was a desperate need to find peace through an experience with God. I sought to give them that, not by preaching, not by teaching, but by service. I sought to be a channel for the love of God and Christ, and that is why I was effective. That is why my work grew and became successful. It was and is a working model of how to truly bring God to earth.

We fed people first. If we had brought God to earth in any other form but food for people in such need, they would have turned away from us. We cared for their bodies and fed them first. Because they experienced something they could not experience elsewhere, they were touched. Some of them came before me and bowed with tears of gratitude streaming down their cheeks. I took none of the glory, and they knew that. I moved away from that as quickly as possible so they would not center on me.

Many Sisters joined us who were moved by God through my example. I say to anyone, if you have the love of God in your heart, and truly so, you can go anywhere and see God in everyone. You will not see the outer circumstances of a person as the prevailing factor. No. You know this when you have a sick child who is throwing up, a child who has the measles or any disease, even a runny nose. You just love that child more. This is because God's heart is such that he can feel with you, and he becomes you. When you are a container for God in the way that I aspired to be, then that is all you will feel. My work, as tiring as it was, as exhausting as it was, as endless as it was, became a thing of great joy.

I am tearful because I want to see more of this kind of love on earth. *(Crying)* Forgive me my human reality, but I am proud to be able to feel, even here, manifesting through this medium's body. It is the hallmark of having found God through serving him. *(Deep breath)*

Dr. D: *Is there anything you would change about your life on earth if you were to live it over again?*

MT: Only that I would like to have been a thousand people doing what I did. That's all! *(Chuckle)*

Dr. D: *Because you worked mostly in Calcutta, India, when you passed into the spirit world, did you find yourself in the spirit world of India or somewhere else?*

MT: Dear one, the first thing you find when you come over is yourself. You face yourself. Having tried my best, having tried in good measure to do good, I saw that I *had* done good. I saw that I *had* done my best. I saw that God was present in me to a great degree because I tried to live the life of Christ, the exemplary life of manifesting God on earth. Without any immodesty, I can say that to a certain degree I achieved this. My work reflects that, don't you think? *(Yes.)*

I do not give glory to myself. I give glory to Jesus and to God for what I was able to do. I was surrounded by my own angelic force, those in the angelic world who worked with me. I was also surrounded by my spirit guides and teachers, some of whom were former priests and nuns. There were more than a few, because my mission was expansive and many-faceted. It took many spiritual guides to help many people on earth, and my wisdom was drawn from their presence. They poured into me a mixture of their knowledge and love, and combined with my own, it poured out into the world through the Mother Teresa.

I helped many who passed on before me, and they greeted me when I came here. They were from Calcutta and other parts of India, and I immediately recognized them. A young girl whom I personally loved and cared for in the earlier part of my work was there to meet me, as were others. It was a great and joyful reunion, and there were many tears. Yes, we cry here, sometimes out of regret, but where I am, we cry mostly out of joy. As I moved beyond those I had known in India, I met leaders from the world community. I had been a world figure, and leaders from the highest levels of spirit manifestation came to greet me. I had met them on earth, and they had embraced my work, made deference to it, and contributed to it. There were more than a few who did that, and I am in debt to all of them.

In the spirit world we do not single out one person as higher or better than another. We see that it is through the cooperative efforts of a considerable number of people that God manifests on the earth plane, so who can claim the glory? Who can stand higher? All who are part of this cooperative effort should have the title of saint before their names.

Dr. D: *You lived your entire life as a Catholic. Are you still a Catholic, or have things changed for you since going into the realms of spirit?*

MT: As you know, the word "catholic" means universal. In that sense I can say yes, I still hold an allegiance. I have met some of those in the line of Popes, those whom I served and those who went before.

When you live in true love it makes you a universal person because you see everyone as yourself. Because you see God in every person, you do not differentiate among people based on religion. These are the characteristics of a universal soul. It is not that you have traveled the world or met people from various countries or that you speak many languages. No. It is that you have a universal heart to see all people as yourself. My spirit world is the whole spirit world, from top to bottom, side to side, inside to outside, and from outside to inside. *(Chuckle)*

There will be those who are surprised at my words. They may even say, "Hmmm, that doesn't sound like the Mother Teresa I knew." Well I am *not* the Mother Teresa you knew. I have graduated to a higher level of awareness. How could I be the same? Nor would *you* be the same if you had made the transition into the world in which I live, a world of unending light and love. When you pass through the process of death, your body is disposed of, and you move into the spirit world, so how could you be the same? Arriving in the world of spirit makes you a believer in a broader, deeper, higher way because of the many things you discover that you did not know before.

Dr. D: *How do you personally spend your days in the spirit world? Are you still single?*

MT: I am married to Jesus, and he has not asked for a divorce yet. *(Chuckle)* I am still single. Maybe in eons of time, I will take a mate, but right now my mind is still infused with a love for humanity and the desire to make a difference. I came here with that soul-centered reality, and it continues. You can well imagine that my work is broader, deeper, higher, and includes more knowledge and sensitivity than ever before. I am still working with my nuns, my beloved sisters on earth. I am working with them to expand the work to help more people and to work with others who are like-minded. I am teaching here as I did on earth, but it is my nature to teach mostly by example. That is what I do. Your imagination can fill in all the spaces.

Dr. D: *What do you think about the work we are doing in inviting well-known people from your world to share their thinking about various topics?*

MT: My child, keep doing it, because it goes hand in hand with my work. If you were not doing this, how could I be here? How could I bring to earth even the little truth about me that I have brought? How could this truth make an impact on the minds of those who read about us? If you did not do this, how would all of this information come to the earth plane? Keep doing it! It is a small flame now, but it is going to turn into a bonfire to help many.

I know the two of you are not looking for glory any more than I was. You are looking to help people help themselves. That is what I tried to do. I did not seek to make people well so they would follow me. I sought to make them well so that they might follow Christ and find God in their lives. That was my ultimate desire, and that is your ultimate desire. I see that. Believe me, I would not be drawn to this light if it were not great enough. I am too busy to take my time out for just any channeling. I thank you for doing this and for asking my opinion.

Dr. D: *One last question. Is there anything . . .*

MT: You promise? *(Chuckle)* Because on this side, they are waiting for me to get on with what I am doing here.

Dr. D: *Is there anything you would like to add to what you have already shared with us?*

MT: Yes. I would like the reader not to just believe everything you read in this book. Instead, go deep inside yourself and ask, does this ring of truth? Does this seem like truth? Does this taste like truth? Feel what you are feeling. Do you feel more elevated as you read these words? Do you feel greater peace? As individuals speak, and taking the book as a whole, what is it doing for your soul? If you ask yourself these questions, you will know through your own experience and not through my words, but through your own heart, whether or not we speak the truth and whether or not to place value in such a work as this book.

That's all! This is Mother Teresa, saint or not. God bless you.

Dr. D: *And God bless you. Thank you for coming.*

MT: You are very, very welcome. You know that.

End of session.

Comments:

PB: The energy was great.

Dr. D: *When Mother Teresa came forward, you became very quiet and soft spoken.*

PB: Apparently she was tearful.

Dr. D: *Yes, at one point I choked up, and it was hard for me to speak. Then I noticed you were also becoming tearful as she was speaking.*

JESUS

Jesus of Nazareth (born circa 4 BC) was a Jewish teacher of humble origins in Galilee, north of Israel. According to various accounts in the New Testament Gospels of Matthew, Mark, Luke, and John, he was born in Bethlehem, taught in the temple as a young boy, baptized by John the Baptist, and had a brief ministry of teaching and miraculous healings in ancient Israel. Jesus challenged religious traditions of his day and was ultimately charged with blasphemy and sedition against the Roman Empire (Luke 22: 70-71). He was condemned to crucifixion by a Roman official, Pontius Pilate. Though the exact date of his birth is unknown, Christians celebrate his birthday on December 25. The Bible indicates that he died at the time of Passover, and Christians commemorate his death at this time each year.

Orthodox Christian theology teaches that Jesus is the son of God who was born of a virgin (Mary) by a miracle of the Holy Spirit (Luke 1:26-38), and that he suffered crucifixion to bring about the forgiveness of sins and the reconciliation of humankind with God. It also teaches that Jesus rose from the dead, appearing to his disciples after the crucifixion (John 20:19), and that he will come again to bring the Kingdom of God on earth.

Jesus used parables, such as the story of the Pearl of Great Price, to illustrate his teachings. He encouraged forgiveness of one's enemies and sacrificial, unconditional love for others, especially those who are sick, poor, or vulnerable. While adherents of many religious and spiritual perspectives have varying views of Jesus, most hold him in great esteem.

CONVERSATION TWENTY

Jesus

This is my attempt to make a difference; to have another chance to awaken those who hear my words and the call of my heart to step forward and take up the cause of loving as God loves. I am speaking for the purpose of bringing heaven down to earth in your life and in every life that you touch.

—Jesus of Nazareth

I am the man Jesus. I am more than happy to be able to come in this way and share my mind and heart with you.[1] Given the opportu-

---

1   With the exception of Jesus, all of the individuals who delivered messages for this book did so by speaking directly through my vocal cords while I was in a deep trance state. Before I could channel Jesus, however, one of my vocal cords tore, and I had to restrict using my voice to the extent that I even considered omitting the final chapter so I could finish the book. But Jesus appeared at my bedside, as he has done many times in my life, to say he would dictate his message. I readily agreed because Saint Germain had dictated most of the material for my first book, *To Master Self is to Master Life*, and I trusted the process. Over a three-month period, Jesus came in the early morning on four occasions, and I went directly to my computer and simply typed what I heard him say. His words flowed so clearly each time that I could not doubt the validity of the communication. It was a joy and privilege to spend these special times with the Master.

nity to speak, I will not spend my time getting involved in a detailed personal history of my family life, except here and there.

As it is written in a number of contemporary books, the history about me is questioned or even thought to be mythological. The motivation behind some writings about my life played no little part in how my character was presented, including what I said and did and why. As with any history—especially oral history, which mine was for many years—the facts were altered, gradually in some cases and quickly in others, as the ends came to serve an individual's or group's purpose and not the purpose of passing on the pure, unembellished truth about my person. That aside, it is well known that when verbal information is passed from one person to another over many generations or even for a short span of time, what is spoken from the first to the last is different from the original spoken words.

There is no question that I and those who came after me in my name were out to awaken others to my person and teachings. And I sent out my followers to give witness to both. But as with any good salesman seeking to sell an idea or product, not only are the good points dutifully emphasized, but exaggeration can easily fall into the sales presentation. While some stories about me that grew out of those early beginnings were close to exact renderings, others became a mixture of fact and fiction.

You may ask how I know these things and why I would even comment on them. I have been here in the spirit world for over 2,000 years, so why would I not know these things and want to comment on them? I am simply trying to bring greater clarity and understanding of me and my work: *I taught of love and of God, and in this communication I shall remain, directly or indirectly, with these ideals.*

I Did Exist

One important truth is that I *did* exist. And yes, I have been working constantly behind the scenes to keep my name and work alive; but more urgently, to keep the love I sought to bring and its Author alive in that which evolved to be called Christianity. I and the force that surrounds this work that I do are most definitely focused upon the individual as the target of God's love, and it is the individual that matters most to me, whether leader or follower in my Church. I am concerned about all individuals on earth, but because of their allegiance to me, I feel a special responsibility for those who follow me within Christianity.

While there are a number of errors in the many interpretations and presentations of my life, including some of my teachings and various claims about me, I have been about the business of carrying on what I came to do. Because of this, my words may cause consternation for some who believe in me, but that is not my intention. Rather, *I want to share the truth about my life and about God and man's true relationship, in order to correct and clarify your understanding so you may be liberated to go even higher and further in your spiritual pursuits of God and eternal life.*

The Human Heart Where God Dwells

Why have I said that the individual is most important? It is the human heart—where God is and moves—that is the object of what

I did and still do. It is in the spiritual human heart that each human being knows and experiences the truth of what I taught; the most important being that each of us contains God. And it is in the focused energies of the human heart that such awareness is experienced. If and when the human heart can be moved—and the heart does not lie, as God *is* contained there—the individual commits his life to the highest of highest of causes: *love itself and loving as God loves.* That was who I was and what I was all about. It was out of this reality that I was moved to forgive, to heal, and to call upon and preach of the love of God. This love is still what the world needs, and my character and message in this area have not changed. They have been refined, yes, but essentially not changed.

My Beginnings

To truly understand me and my message, you must know more of my beginnings than has been previously presented in what has been written about me. When I say beginnings, I mean my awareness of the spirit world at the age of twelve and even younger. Because I was spiritually perceptive, I could and did communicate with spirit beings at a very young age, and they guided me throughout my life. However, many of my experiences were unknown to anyone and never recorded.

In addition to those helping me from the spirit side, there were those on earth prepared to guide me who appeared in my life with uncanny synchronicity, from my childhood through my adulthood.

Such individuals would often approach me when I was alone and impart messages from the spirit world, saying they knew about me and were guided from above to aid me with information from spirit to help me on my way. Why would I not have such experiences in light of what I was sent to earth to accomplish?

As it is written, both of my parents also had a number of encounters with the spirit world. As you can imagine, they had many that were never made public in any way; but I knew the details only of the ones that pertained to me. It was most important that I was born into a family not unfamiliar with the spirit world or spirit visitations in dreams and in visions, because I came to bring to humanity the realization that there is not only this physical world but also a spirit world. I came as an example of a spiritually evolved man standing between the physical and spiritual worlds, simultaneously aware of both and able to consciously communicate with both. As one who stood in this position, my heart was greatly expanded for both heaven and earth.

Holy Scripture is replete with spirit world breakthroughs, including many visitations from angels to inspire and guide those contacted. The appearance of angels at my birth is an outstanding example of the heavenly spirit world interceding to guide spiritually blind man on earth. In the context of the day, of course, the sharing of spiritual manifestations could be problematic, as superstition and fear often took away from both the reality and importance of such experiences. But our people had a long history of prophecy and contact with God and spirit. As they were led by Moses out of Egypt, across the desert, and eventually into the Promised Land, they consistently witnessed spiritual phenomena throughout their journey. And, as it is written, Moses experienced direct communication with God in the tabernacle and on Mt. Sinai. It was on the foundation of such spiritual experiences that Judaism was born. Yes, I was sent to advance man's spiritual understanding both by my message and by my example, but I did not step into an entirely ignorant culture when it came to my people and spirit world appearances and guidance.

As I said, quite early in life I began having experiences with spirit beings, most of whom stayed with me to the end. My personal encounters with the spirit world often came in the early morning hours when everyone else was asleep. It was in these times that spirit spoke to me both on a personal level and as to the reality of what I came to earth to do. I was guided by these precious spirit helpers, even as my parents were guided before I was born. My mother was visited by the Archangel Gabriel who came to tell her she would be with child; and an angel came to my father in a dream to say the child she carried was of the Holy Spirit. My father had been beside himself when he learned that my mother was pregnant, and it was because of the angel's words that he could accept her.

Because I was spiritually open and well attuned to the spirit world, I also knew things beyond the normal. My parents were aware of some of what I was experiencing, but in spite of their own spiritual awareness, they were not eager to have me too involved with spirit visitations. After all, Holy Scripture told us to avoid such contact! But it was the desire of Providence and the intended outcome of the nativity story that I would inherit openness to spirit and could eventually know and do things of a spiritual nature beyond the average. As I carried out my mission, I healed, discerned others' hearts and minds, foresaw the unfolding of things, sometimes far in advance, and prophesied about them. I communicated directly with spirit, including with Moses and Elijah, who were my lifelong guides. In fact, the night before my arrest, Moses and Elijah appeared from the spirit world and spoke with me at length. Peter, John, and James, three of my closest disciples, saw them as well, and this is recorded in plain sight within scripture.

Visiting the Temple

The Bible says that at age twelve I disappeared from my family for a number of days until my mother, in a most worried state of mind, came to find me in the temple in Jerusalem. During the Feast of the Passover, I had come there with my parents from Nazareth, many miles away, to offer sacrifice according to our religious teachings and tradition. I had spent the time in the temple away from my parents, five days to be exact, listening to teachers and asking questions.

I was more advanced than most my age because of the way I was brought up and because of my ongoing conversations with my spirit guides and teachers. I was also a very obedient student of the religious teachings of my people and attended religious services regularly, disciplining myself greatly to learn and know as much as I could of spiritual matters. Because of this, some of those I spoke with in the temple may have thought I was precocious and others were just curious, but the more open and sensitive among them readily understood that I was not a typical twelve-year-old. For various reasons they asked questions of me and listened closely to my answers.

Scripture tells the story of my time in the temple, but it does not relate what I was learning, what questions I asked, or what questions were asked of me. While I showed a maturity beyond my years that drew attention, I also broached the subject of life beyond. Open as I was, I readily perceived the other world. How else could I have been who I was and done what I did? I was prepared from that time on to expound on what I knew based on what I had experienced. I was seeking more advanced understanding, so I used my time in the temple to inquire more fully about my spiritual experiences, the spirit world, and especially how my experiences interfaced with the history of my people. Being in the temple was my initial and grand opportunity to gain as much insight as possible and to be as surefooted as I could be in receiving ongoing guidance from my spirit world hosts as I carried out my mission. I was led to such inquiry that I might know these things and understand them more clearly.

Discussions in temple circles were more about Mosaic Law than anything else, but during my five-day visit, I sought to steer the conversations to the subject matter of life beyond. I did this not only to increase others' awareness of my being, but also to solicit responses that I might share and learn more. This was in keeping with what I was born to do.

As I said earlier, I was continuously guided and taught by spirit beings and quietly aided by mystical types who were equivalent in their psychic ability to some of your modern-day mediums. Without these spiritual experiences and well-placed individuals, such as those near my home and those I met in the temple, I would have been hard pressed to comprehend what I was about or to fully know what my mission was or how to carry it out. How else could I have come to know myself and God's will for my life? Such knowledge does not just fall out of the sky, and at the age of twelve, one cannot reason these things out. Even if one could, the reasoning could not include the needed wisdom or depth of understanding that comes from many years of such experiences.

Some may ask why my parents were not most instrumental and central to helping me with my spiritual pursuits. While my father initially got through his concerns about my conception and birth, they caused him to distance himself from me; and my mother was not comfortable in showing deference to me over my siblings. Though they both did their best, the circumstances surrounding my birth prevented them from being my primary spiritual mentors.

The Mistaken Idea about Me

I must add that the mystical people I met throughout my life taught me not only about my mission and the spirit world, but of finding God within myself. As a young child, I already had inklings as to the existence of God and through what part of me God spoke and had his being. That is how I began to develop in my spiritual life. But my conversations over time with those sent to me from the spirit world and on earth gave greater credence and higher understanding to the truth of God's presence in me and in each individual. It was but a step from this understanding to a daily and continual awareness of the very existence of God within me. And by the time I began my public ministry, I could say without question or equivocation, "He who has seen me has seen the Father." I knew this to be the rule for all and not the exception, regardless of what others did or did not know about themselves and God within them.

The mistaken idea was that I was speaking exclusively about myself when I said, "I and the Father are one." No, my intended inference was that you, too, contain the living God. And though it is not written, I told some people directly what I meant—that they were no different from me in that way. Some of them took exception and thought I was too bold or even blasphemous, in temple terms, in saying God lived within me or within anyone else.

In light of the history of my people, it is understandable that there were those who took exception to my words when I said the Father and I were one. When my people were led by Moses in the wilderness, the tabernacle they carried with them was a tent-like structure where God descended, dwelled, and spoke to Moses. In my time, the temple had become the place where people came to find and worship God. Having been taught to meet God in the tabernacle or temple, many of our people had come to believe that God was in these places rather than within me or within each one of them. This was not so with the more advanced individuals in spirit and on earth sent to me to help with my mission. They knew firsthand the truth that had become self-evident to them: *We are all temples of the living God, and God has his highest dwelling place in the human heart.*

Meditation

Because God dwells within each of us, divinity is my core nature and also your own. The energy of that abiding presence rules your life whether you know it or not, and those who pursue this reality with maximum effort consistently practice *meditation* to uncover and discover God. My own practice of going within played the important role of attuning me to the higher frequencies or vibrations of the invisible world, including the experience of meeting God within myself.

Spiritual awareness came to me most naturally when I was in a passive or meditative state, as when I was waking up in the morning and my spirit guides and teachers appeared. So I practiced becoming very still and quiet, and this resulted in easier and finer attunement to receiving from spirit. I eventually learned, on my own and through those sent to help me, how to readily remove my mind and emotions from the world to access the world beyond.

At times I would sit and formally pray and meditate, but as I progressed, much of my meditating was done on my feet as I spent time alone in the countryside away from people. There I would walk for hours and think and think about my life and its unfolding. I spoke out loud to God and heard a distinct and growing voice within and sometimes outside of me. I grew in my experience and knowledge of God and spirit during these hours alone. Yes, I prayed as many pray today, but I later taught my followers to pray less and listen more and not to make public rituals of prayers that often are more about drawing attention to oneself than to God!

Without the art and practice of meditation, I could not have been who I was or attempted to do what I did. Ultimately, mastery of oneself is achieved through meditation, where we transcend earthly concerns to get in touch with the divine and with our eternal spirit.

Meditation Is Natural

Meditation is *natural*, not unnatural to human beings. Going within is a common practice, and we are all aware that our perception is both inner and outer. As we pause to consider or reflect on something—with or without closed eyes—each of us experiences that we perceive from some deeper inner aspect of ourselves. Even when we are not formally meditating, we all know the vast difference between noise and silence. Life teaches us these differences; and to the degree that we consider them and use them, we grow in our awareness of our various and higher states of mind.

Again and again, during my deepest meditations, I saw my universal Self and knew that all that was, was within me. I experienced directly that the Creator or divine energy, if you will, became me. I saw that this was true for each and every person because we all come from the same source. In other words, I saw that there was no difference between the energy that is you and me and the Energy that is God, since God is the reality behind *all* appearances. During these experiences, I realized that unless one could rise above the earthly to the spiritual plane, the physical world could appear as the only reality in existence, and humanity could remain blind to the awareness of the Supreme and the spirit world in and all around them.

I knew from my experiences and the teachings of a few other mystics the how and the why of communications between the world of spirit and human beings on earth. The spirit world and the physical world are to act as one—each supporting and benefiting the other for common purposes designed and supported by the Creator. Communication with those in spirit is an imperative because their advanced awareness makes it possible for them to guide us to know and do the right thing. It is the mission of higher spiritual beings to guide human beings during our time on earth, and the mission of human beings to discern this guidance and act on it. The two worlds must interface, and it is only natural that they do so.

As you can imagine, as my understanding deepened, it was all about surrendering, surrendering, and surrendering. In the end, through meditation, I was rewarded inwardly with greater spiritual awareness and ongoing experiences of the outpouring of the love and care of God. Being raised up into this love from within was the supreme arrival point.

Practice Is Required

Meditation, like any art form, must be consciously practiced to gain the greatest benefit. You cannot plumb your mind, your heart, your soul without spending quality time in silence; and you cannot go beyond your mind, which keeps you perpetually caught up in the material world, without transcending it through meditation. The consistent practice of meditation can lead you to encounter a silence so deep and so vast that there are no words to tell others what it is like; and a light suffused with a love so great that it is beyond measure or comprehension. By going deep within, you can discover the truth of your eternal being. And only in this elevated state of mind and being can you make sense of this world in which everything comes and goes and nothing lasts forever. In this transcendent state, you will see reality in the larger scheme of things and discern the real purpose of life.

By this time, your science has discovered that we are all multi-faceted and multi-dimensional. The study of brainwave frequencies, combined with modern medical probing of the brain during operation procedures, has revealed this to be true. The Ancients from civilizations such as India and China and some obscure lost civilizations knew the reality of the human being and our infinite, eternal, spiritual self. In such cultures, adepts at meditation, first by personal discovery and later in ancient schools set up for this purpose, knew well that they were divine and eternal, and they made all efforts to enlighten others as to this reality.

Until we consciously understand and practice meditation, the spiritual eternal self cannot be experienced except in small glimpses as we dip in randomly or intermittently to the inner dimensions of ourselves. Without mindfully attending to meditation, this most important human practice, it will not become central to our existence or way of life, and it will be relegated to a backseat endeavor attended to when everything else on earth has been completed at the end of the day. But this is putting things backwards. I had no other choice but to put my spiritual practices first, for I needed continuous contact with God and spirit; and to have that, I needed to go into the altered state made possible through meditation. I had to work at this, as it is with all of you, and I had to refine my practice to be most attuned to those from the other side who were aiding me to accomplish my mission.

The practice of meditation on earth today has to do mostly with gaining peace of mind and healing the body. And this is good. But deeper meditation makes it possible for us to fully and freely communicate with the eternal world of spirit. It provides what the heart must have in order to thrive—a deep communion between each person, God, and the heavenly spirit world.

I Have Returned at This Time . . .

I have returned at this time, for this writing, to say all I have said so far; but, above all else, I have come because of my abiding love of mankind for whose sake I came two thousand years ago. I was sent by my Heavenly Father then, and he has sent me again to speak my truth and to bear witness. I have lived this way from the beginning, and my desire and nature to aid, to guide, and to love has become even greater with the passage of time. Since my name and persona are still a deep part of human consciousness on earth, I am in great need of continuing to guide to proper ends those people who pray and do things in my name.

To speak of the *spirit world* and its involvement with you on earth and to speak of *God within* combined with the topic of *meditation as a means to both of these ends* has been my purpose in coming at this time. As you can imagine, there is much more I could say that I am holding back as not relevant to these topics and not timely. But, dear child of the living God from whom you and I descend, I have shared as I have that you may know me better and, in turn, know yourself better so that you may draw closer to both. I have shared from a heart filled with more love than I can hold because it is the infinite love of God.

Ultimately, I came on earth to bring peace, but my words and my name have been used to justify countless wars in which millions have perished. You know the earthly side of history, but if you could only see it from our side and see yourselves as we see you, you would change immediately. You must understand that I have stood back and watched humanity evolve with all of its good and bad points, and I have seen from this side the core realities that have brought both good and evil on earth. I have wept so often and so much because of the suffering, not only of those who professed to love and follow me, but also for all on earth, because none of you has truly understood the full reality of life. You grab at straws for nothing when your soul is dying for want of higher knowledge and true love—the unconditional love of God ever present within you.

I am making this appearance in these days of great earthly strife to awaken you from ignorance and to stem the tide of suffering. I want to end your inner fears and insecurities by driving home the point that what you are looking for cannot be found in any *ism* or anything external to you. All the answers you seek must be found within your very self. What is the purpose of a church, a temple, or a mosque? They are thought to be places where worshippers can assemble to meet God who comes from heaven to earth in the midst of the believers. But I tell you, greater than this is the temple of your heart where God is always present. And until you come to approach this reality within, you will not awaken to just who and what you are.

The greatest gift you have is being human; and with it, the blessing of being born on earth. Why? Because, as I have said in different words, you are the manifestation of God come to earth in your form, even as I came as God to earth in this form called Jesus. You came with a purpose written in your soul, and your life is about finding that purpose and unfolding it in a lifetime. Your body is your greatest asset because it furnishes you with the energy to develop maturity of spirit through your actions.

My Closing Words

I am the same Jesus I was the day I was born, though I have become the person on whom great praise and adoration have been heaped for generations. Until you come here where I am, you will never completely understand my heart or what I am about. I still carry the great burden of watching humanity suffer because of your lack of awareness of the presence of God and spirit within and all around you. From this side, I cannot do what I could have done when I was on earth; but I come to speak in this way for the purpose of awakening you to yourself and to ultimate reality.

There are billions of us here in the world of spirit armed to the maximum degree with love unending. We are ever present with you, rejoicing over the goodness of your lives but also hovering and brooding over Mother Earth because of our deep desire to stop human suffering. We intercede, we protect, we warn; but we cannot think and act for you. That is up to you. When you do fully awaken, as I did spiritually, you can know our presence and cooperate with our coming to lend our message to those on earth, even as this instrument I am speaking through is doing this moment.

This is my attempt to make a difference; to have another chance to awaken those who hear my words and the call of my heart to step forward and take up the cause of loving as God loves. I am speaking for the purpose of bringing heaven down to earth in your life and in every life you touch.

Those who have spoken in this book have spoken the greatest truth of all: that God lives in you and you live in God. There is no separation between God and man; only ignorance and a lack of awareness that keeps man from knowing his limitless capacity and eternal worth. When it is said that you are the temple of God, it means *literally*, not figuratively. I realized this fact at a very young age. Spirits guiding me told me this was so and taught me how to access this Reality within me. I simply followed what they said, not totally comprehending but obedient. As you allow yourself, especially while in meditation, to experience that you are an eternal spirit living in a physical body, you can have a profound spiritual awakening; an epiphany intended for you to have while you are still on Mother Earth.

With all those whose words are recorded in this book, I have come for this purpose: to speak the truth that God always has been and always will be within, and to share all that this means to you as an individual and to humanity everywhere. Trust my words enough to go within knowledgeably, with the world put temporarily aside, and focus your heart upon what is within. To the extent that you do this, you will find through your own direct experience that I am telling you the truth, the very same truth I sought to teach two thousand years ago.

This is the Master Jesus.

ACKNOWLEDGMENTS

—Philip Burley

Because it contains content channeled directly through me by twenty spiritual and secular masters while I was under hypnosis, I consider this the most important book I've produced. All credit goes to those who came very close to speak directly, simply, and straight from the heart. I'm grateful to all those who came through, but especially to Edgar Cayce, a gifted medium who used his own gift of mediumship under hypnosis to receive volumes of information from the spirit world. His work contributed greatly to my decision to bring through the words of the masters in a similar way.

The skill and sensitivity of Dr. Dolores Proiette, professional hypnotist, were critical to my success in channeling the material for this book. Her ability to guide me into a deep trance state and her objective observations about my changing demeanor as distinct

personalities spoke through me increased my confidence in everything that transpired while I was under hypnosis. Readers of the book
will also benefit from knowing that an experienced hypnotist with
two doctorate degrees was consistently present to guide, observe,
and record each session. Thank you, Dolores, for your unwavering
commitment to finding the truth about channeling under hypnosis,
your consistent dedication to this project, your objective but open
mind, and your generous heart. Most of all, thank you for your sustaining friendship.

I have worked with my editor, Anne Edwards, for more than a
decade, and I have never called on her without getting a quick and
competent response. With her skillful editing of the channeling transcripts, Anne maintained the integrity of each master's message and
personal style while making the content easier to read. This book is
only one example of her ability to bring greater clarity to a sentence
without changing the meaning, vocabulary, and voice of its author.
As a spiritual medium, I can say that Anne's editing gives a whole new
meaning to the term *ghost writer*! Thank you, Anne, for your great
help on this and countless other projects, large and small!

As always, my assistant, Lynn Mathers, filled in the gaps, took up
the slack, and anticipated next steps to keep me moving forward on
this book. She handled much of the communication with our design
company to get this book to press; and she has been matchless in her
work on technical aspects of digitizing all of my books and getting
the word out about them through email and the Internet. Lynn, you

have my great thanks for your dedication to this work and for being such a good friend over many, many years.

I am indebted to those contemporary teachers who have inspired me on my personal spiritual path through their writings: the Dalai Lama for his enduring example of humility, kindness, and unconditional forgiveness; Ekhart Tolle for deepening my understanding of the objective observer within; Deepak Chopra for his emphasis on meditation as a spiritual path; and Wayne Dyer for his prolific writings on our indestructible connection to the Source of All. Talented spiritual mediums such as James Van Praagh and John Edward have done much to raise public awareness of the fact that we live on after the death of our physical bodies, and this is a vitally important gift to all of us.

I owe great thanks to Joan Donnelly Brooks, an extraordinary medium who taught me much by example during three years when I attended weekly classes with her before beginning my public work in this field.

I cannot name all the people who have contributed to this book, but they include those who encouraged me to broaden my channeling work, those who read and commented on the manuscript, and those who have quietly and consistently supported my work for many years. My heartfelt appreciation goes out to each one of you.

I thank my family for their constant love and care. My children are especially kind and capable people whom I love and admire greatly. My dear wife, Vivien, has been a tremendous source of strength in my life, and I'm indebted to her for her love and support throughout the years. She is at the heart of our family, giving her time, attention, and loving care to all of us unstintingly. She is smart, competent, hardworking, funny, and beautiful; and being with her lifts my spirits. But among the many gifts she brings to my life, the one I value the most is that she always tells me the truth. Above anyone else on earth, I trust her. For this and so many more reasons, she has my eternal love and gratitude. Thank you, Vivien!

ACKNOWLEDGMENTS

—Dolores Proiette

My first thanks goes to my wonderful daughters, Kelly, Kari, and Kristi, for their unconditional love, caring, and support. No matter how busy their lives, they have always been there for me.

I am sincerely grateful to Philip Burley for the opportunity to be part of the project that resulted in this book. He first approached me stating that his master teacher, Saint Germain, had brought us together for an important task: a collaboration where I would serve as the hypnotist to help Philip bring through information from masters in the spirit world. At the time, I don't think either of us comprehended the magnitude or significance of the work we would be doing together. It was no small undertaking, and I deeply appreciate Philip's patience and fortitude, as well as the countless hours he spent in the completion of this book. I am truly honored to have played my part in bringing through such valuable information. Philip, you are my dearest friend and colleague.

I am grateful to each master who spoke through Philip while he was in a deep state of hypnosis, and there are several to whom I want to give my special thanks: Saint Germain took the lead in inspiring and guiding Philip throughout the channeling process and in coordinating the effort that took place on the spiritual plane. Buddha's presence during our session with him left me with a tangible peace that I still sense whenever I reflect on it. Albert Einstein's words were of special interest in providing an understanding of how spirit literally interfaces with this world; and Milton Erickson provided important information about how the field of hypnosis relates to the world of spirit. Since I began working on this book, Erickson's ongoing spiritual guidance has given me a greater understanding of how energy fields work within each individual.

Anne Edwards provided her expertise without reserve in flawlessly editing each page of this book. Thank you, Anne, for helping each sentence and paragraph flow easily, without losing the meaning of the content or the style of the person speaking.

Finally, I want to thank each reader for investing your valuable time to search for truth within these pages. May your efforts be rewarded with lasting spiritual blessings.

ABOUT
PHILIP BURLEY AND
DOLORES PROIETTE

Philip Burley

Philip Burley is a medium, author, and teacher who is widely known as a trance channel for spiritual master Saint Germain. Philip has had clairvoyant and clairaudient experiences since childhood, and he credits his spiritual gifts to his lifelong pursuit of God. Many consider him as much mystic as medium; he is a master teacher in the art of meditation whose students learn to connect with their own inner wisdom, loving spirit guides, and God. Philip is the author of numerous books on the spirit world, including some that include directly channeled information. He has given thousands of spiritual readings and presented hundreds of classes on meditation and the path to finding God Within. His popular radio show, *The Inner View,* reached international listeners. Philip and his wife Vivien are the parents of three children and the grandparents of seven grandchildren. They make their home in Lake Forest, California.

Email: PB@PhilipBurley.com

Website: www.PhilipBurley.com

Dolores Proiette

Dolores Small Proiette, DCH, PhD, has been practicing hypno-therapy, hypnosis, and past life regression therapy since 1993. She has doctorates in Clinical Hypnotherapy and Philosophy, a master's degree in Education, and a bachelor's degree in Psychology. She has completed advanced graduate studies in Professional Counseling and is a Reiki Master Third Degree therapist. Dolores is author of the book, *Unveil the Past, Heal the Future through Hypnotherapy.* She is a member of the American Board of Hypnotherapy, the National Guild of Hypnotists, and the Arizona Society for Professional Hypnosis. Dolores also serves as a board member for The Little Light Project (www.littlelightproject. org) and as secretary for Over the Rainbow Butterfly Garden, www. overtherainbowbutterflygarden.com. Dolores is the parent of three daughters and the grandparent of five grandchildren. She has her home and office in Flagstaff, Arizona.

Email: DoloresProiette@Hotmail.com
Website: www.HypnosisHealingsCenter.com

24848482R00244

Made in the USA
San Bernardino, CA
07 February 2019